The
EVERYTHING
Prayer Book

Dear Reader:

If you are reading these words, chances are that you are either curious about prayer, perplexed by prayer, or you know something about prayer but you would like to learn more. If so, you have come to the right place.

We wrote this book because we are both firm believers in prayer. It has done wonderful things in our lives, and in the lives of many of our friends and loved ones. We hope that it can mean as much to you, and we hope that this book will help you experience all that prayer can be.

We don't believe that anyone has to be taught how to pray. It is something so basic to life that we are literally born to be pray-ers. On the other hand, learning more about prayer—its different forms, its traditions, the people who pray and how they do it—can not only make you a better pray-er, it can enrich your prayer practice and make it even more enjoyable.

We wish you a lifetime of prayer!

The EVERYTHING® Series

Editorial

Publishing Director	Gary M. Krebs
Managing Editor	Kate McBride
Copy Chief	Laura MacLaughlin
Acquisitions Editor	Bethany Brown
Development Editor	Michael Paydos
Production Editor	Khrysti Nazzaro

Production

Production Director	Susan Beale
Production Manager	Michelle Roy Kelly
Series Designers	Daria Perreault
	Colleen Cunningham
Cover Design	Paul Beatrice
	Frank Rivera
Layout and Graphics	Colleen Cunningham
	Rachael Eiben
	Michelle Roy Kelly
	Daria Perreault
	Erin Ring
Series Cover Artist	Barry Littmann

Visit the entire Everything® Series at everything.com

THE
EVERYTHING
PRAYER
BOOK

Learn how to open your heart and soul
to find comfort, healing, and hope

Ronald Hennies & Sonia Weiss

Adams Media
Avon, Massachusetts

*To the special friends and acquaintances
who have guided us on our spiritual walks through the years,
and especially to our families.*

An *Everything*® Series Book.
Everything® and everything.com® are registered trademarks of F+W Publications, Inc.

Published by Adams Media, an F+W Publications Company
57 Littlefield Street, Avon, MA 02322 U.S.A.
www.adamsmedia.com

ISBN: 1-58062-957-1
Printed in the United States of America.

J I H G F E D C B A

Library of Congress Cataloging-in-Publication Data
Hennies, Ronald.
The everything prayer book / Ronald Hennies & Sonia Weiss.
p.   cm.
(An everything series book)
ISBN 1-58062-957-1
1. Prayer. I. Weiss, Sonia. II. Title. III. Series: Everything series.
BL560.H46 2003
291.4'3—dc21
2003008267

*This book is available at quantity discounts for bulk purchases.
For information, call 1-800-872-5627.*

Contents

Acknowledgments

No book is ever a solo act, and this one is no exception. The authors jointly would like to thank the many individuals who made our work possible, including Jessica Faust and Jacky Sach at Bookends, LLC; and the editorial team at Adams Media, who had the original vision for this book and entrusted us with its execution. Particular thanks goes to Bethany Brown for her patience and encouragement, to Michael Paydos for his expert editing, and to Laura MacLaughlin, the Copy Chief.

Much has been written about the need to come to know God and on how His grace transforms us as we do so. We would be amiss if we didn't acknowledge God, the source of all strength and wisdom, and the transformation He has worked in both of our lives. Fr. Hennies would particularly like to acknowledge the changes in his life brought about by the 11th Step of Alcoholics Anonymous, which calls for us to improve our conscious contact with God, as we know Him, through prayer and meditation.

Top Ten Things You Need to Know
About Prayer

1. Without prayer, we never fully understand what it means to be human, nor do we gain a full understanding of life's big issues—the big picture.

2. We can be good people without prayer. We can be strong and courageous and compassionate. But with prayer, we're even better—we know where our source of strength is.

3. Prayer helps us better understand and yield to God's commands.

4. Going to God in prayer can help us see beyond our immediate situation and start sorting out the details.

5. Prayer can reveal things that play a bigger role in our lives than we'd like them to.

6. It can be hard to know which direction we should take in life when we only rely on our own thoughts and feelings. Asking God for His opinion can help us get a better idea of the road we should travel.

7. It is important to seek God's wisdom through prayer so that we can better align our decisions with what He has in mind for us.

8. We don't know what the future holds for us from God's point of view unless we seek Him through prayer.

9. Prayer makes sense. If it didn't, we wouldn't feel called to do it. Nor would the billions of other people who make a conscious effort to connect with God on a regular—if not daily—basis.

10. Praying is the only way to learn how to pray.

Introduction

▶HUMAN BEINGS have searched for understanding since the earliest of times. We were born with inquiring minds and an innate need to understand the "big picture"—how the world around us came to be, and where we fit into the scheme of things. From those earliest of times, we have sensed that the answers lie not in what we can see, but in that which we cannot see. Prayer has been our means of communicating with the greater being or spirit that lies beyond human understanding.

Although we were born with the desire to pray—some call it "being wired for prayer"—prayer frustrates many people. They find it difficult to make time for it. They wonder if they are doing it right, and if they could do it better. Is it better to pray alone or with others? Silently or out loud? Should they kneel, sit, or stand? Should they call that which they pray to "God," "Goddess," "Father," or "Mother"? Does any one prayer style or any specific posture ensure that they'll be heard? Does prayer really get them anywhere?

The truth is, there is no one perfect prayer, no perfect way to pray, and no perfect pray-er. In this particular arena, there are no yes or no answers, no scales of comparison. There is simply the practice of prayer, in whatever form it takes. And that is what this book is all about.

Prayer is often written about in a fairly lofty manner, which can make it seem like we need to be experts at it before we can do it, and that we have to be on our best behavior when we do it. In the pages ahead, you'll find a great deal of evidence to the contrary. Everyone has to begin somewhere in prayer. In this particular practice, not only are we all beginners, we remain beginners.

Prayer is meant to be a lifelong experience. There is always something new to learn, another path to explore, another door to open. This is what makes prayer both challenging and exciting . . . even fun.

There is no need to be perfect angels when we pray. We can be angry, happy, sad, or elated. Throughout time, the people who pray have been all these things, and more. You'll see many examples in this book of people praying just as they were, without any pretense or artifice. They prayed, as is often said, with their warts on. They simply had a chat with God.

The "G" word—God—may be how you experience your creator. Then again, it might not. He goes by many names—Allah, Father, Jehovah, and of course God—which makes it difficult to choose one name when writing about Him. To keep things simple here, we refer to our creator as God, and sometimes the Almighty. This choice reflects the name that many people are familiar and comfortable with. But, it may not work well for some. If you are one of them, feel free to substitute the word or words that resonate with you whenever you see the word God.

Referring to God as "He" or "Him" may also be a problem for some. It's definitely a problem for anyone who writes about God. Truthfully, there's no pronoun that accurately reflects what God is. God isn't male, female, or "it." He transcends all genders. Here again, the pronoun Him used throughout this book to refer to God was chosen as it works well for many people. Feel free to substitute any word that you find more acceptable.

If you are new to prayer, you may be wondering what it takes to pray. Not much, really. The desire to pray, of course, is a big part of it. The fact that you're curious about prayer shows that you've got this one covered. Prayer also requires having some sort of a relationship with the Divine, which being curious about prayer also speaks to. The rest of prayer is all about details.

You may also be wondering what you'll get from prayer. Maybe the better question is, what don't you get? Without prayer, we never fully understand what it means to be human, nor do we gain a full understanding of life's big issues—the big picture. We can be good people without prayer. We can be strong and courageous and compassionate. With prayer, we're even better. With prayer, we know where our source of strength is. With prayer, we know God.

Chapter 1

The World of Prayer

Mother Teresa often said that everything starts from prayer. This was her take on the importance of prayer, and, frankly, she hit the nail on the head. History shows us that prayer has played a central role in the human experience from the very beginning of recorded time. And it continues to do so to this day.

Prayer All Around

The word *prayer* comes from the Latin word *precari*, which means to entreat. Interestingly, the word *precarious*, which means "dependent upon the will or favor of another person," is based on the same Latin word.

Even if you're not much of a pray-er, it's hard to find an aspect of life where prayer—either the act itself or some sort of reference to it—doesn't play a part. It appears in song lyrics and movie titles. Walk into any bookstore, or browse any online bookseller, and you'll find hundreds of books on every conceivable aspect of prayer—walking prayer, listening prayer, prayers for babies, prayers for parents, prayers for celebrating life, prayers for the dying.

We have prayer breakfasts and national days of prayer. There are prayer circles, prayer warriors, and prayer partners. Sometimes we ask people to pray for us. Sometimes we are called upon to pray for others. Sometimes we think certain people haven't got a prayer. And, sometimes, it seems like we're the ones who are lacking in this particular arena.

FACT

In a 1997 *Newsweek* poll, 52 percent of American adults said they prayed on a daily basis; 29 percent reported praying more than once a day. An overwhelming majority of those—87 percent—said they believe that God answers their prayers at least some of the time.

Yet, we live—well, at least most of us do—in a secular society, one that isn't governed by a religious body or bodies or controlled by religious or spiritual matters. In general, the world around us is defined more by ideas and concepts that can be scientifically proven than things that lie beyond the realm of human knowledge, which prayer, being the key thing that connects us to God, definitely is.

As the lines of scientific discovery continue to extend, more and more of the world's mysteries are being uncloaked. Thanks to such endeavors as space and deep-sea exploration, we now have a better understanding of the various physical forces that created our universe.

We now know the secrets behind how we're genetically programmed, which has allowed researchers to start knocking at the doors of cures for cancer and other chronic diseases. But such knowledge can only take us so far. As human beings, we also need to know how and where we fit into the bigger picture. We still seek the presence of God to help us find the answers to such questions, and, as we have done since the earliest of times, we do so through prayer.

Your brain is hardwired to find God. Until you do, you will not know who you are.

—Deepak Chopra, in *How to Know God: The Soul's Journey into the Mystery of Mysteries*

Why We Pray

Scientific inquiry has even extended into prayer, resulting in our being given lots of reasons why we shouldn't pray, and, on the other hand, why we should. Some of the strongest affirmations of what prayer can do, interestingly enough, have come from the medical and scientific communities, which had previously discounted its effectiveness in matters of health and healing.

The first scientific study of healing prayer, conducted in the early 1980s, showed that hospital patients who were being prayed for fared considerably better than those who weren't. Prayer was also put to the test in the field—literally—by researchers probing its effect on corn seeds. The kernels that were prayed for did better than the seeds that received no spiritual boost.

What science can't tell us, however, is why we pray. While prayer is considered by many to be an essential component of a rich and full religious life, and it plays a key role in formal religious ceremonies, the call to prayer clearly goes beyond any sense of obligation. Many people who claim no adherence to any one faith, or who don't even define themselves as particularly religious, do identify themselves as pray-ers. There is no need to be in a house of worship to pray.

Regardless of who you are, how you were raised, or what your spiritual beliefs are, prayer can be a part of your life. You don't have to go through a fancy initiation ceremony, join a specific church or worship group, or follow a prescribed set of prayers in order to lift up your heart in prayer before the Almighty.

QUESTION?

Do you have to be a "religious" person to derive the full benefits of prayer?
While having a relationship of one sort or another with the Almighty is an essential component of prayer, an allegiance to a specific religion or church is not a prerequisite for experiencing a rich and fulfilling life of prayer.

Some people believe that the urge or desire to pray is an indelible part of the human psyche. In other words, we're programmed to pray. Herbert Benson, the physician who founded the Mind/Body Medical Institute at Harvard Medical School, believes that people are, in his words, "wired for God," and that our desire to worship and believe in the Almighty is a deep and intrinsic part of our genetic programming. As the psychologist and philosopher William James wrote, ". . . we cannot help praying. It seems probable that, in spite of all that 'science' may do to the contrary, men will continue to pray to the end of time, unless their mental nature changes in a manner which nothing we know should lead us to expect."

Beyond any desire or programming, however, lies our simple need to be fed. We can handle the physical aspects of nourishment (many would argue all too well), but when it comes to providing for the mind and spirit, our attention must turn to God. As the following Psalm illustrates, the benefits of doing so are great indeed.

God is our refuge and our strength,
A very present help in trouble.
Therefore we will not fear,
Even though the earth be removed,
And though the mountains be carried into the midst of the sea;
Though its waters roar and be troubled,
Though the mountains shake with its swelling.

There is a river whose streams shall make glad the city of God,
The holy place of the tabernacle of the Most High.
God is in the midst of her, she shall not be moved;
God shall help her, just at the break of dawn.
The nations raged, the kingdoms were moved;
He uttered His voice, the earth melted.

The Lord of hosts is with us;
The God of Jacob is our refuge.

Come, behold the works of the Lord,
Who has made desolations in the earth.
He makes wars cease to the end of the earth;
He breaks the bow and cuts the spear in two;
He burns the chariot in the fire.

Be still, and know that I am God;
I will be exalted among the nations,
I will be exalted in the earth!

The Lord of hosts is with us;
The Lord of Jacob is our refuge.

—Psalm 46

I get so busy doing the things I want to do . . . that I forget to ask myself the why of it all; and I forget to ask myself what might be, what ought be, because I'm in the midst of doing, doing. Thank God for this wonderful secular life—but thank God for giving us a mind that can turn to Him, to ask "why" and "wherefore" as well as spend itself to exhaustion getting things done!
—Dorothy Day, quoted in Robert Coles's *The Secular Mind*

The Changing Face of Prayer

What has changed somewhat over time is how we choose to come before the Almighty. Like our perceptions of God, prayer doesn't stand still. It is instead an evolutionary process, and it changes when and as necessary. The English theologian Karen Armstrong notes that humans have always created gods, and that when one worship form or religion has ceased to work or has lost its relevance, it's simply been replaced with another.

The same appears to be true about prayer. It has taken various forms and styles throughout history and continues to do so. At times, communal or corporate prayer has been emphasized over other forms. It was believed that it was best to come to God in a set place of worship, and through a set liturgy. At other times, people went to God through an intermediary, someone who could act as a "go-between" and petition the Almighty on behalf of people because it wasn't believed appropriate to approach God directly.

FACT

Another term for liturgy is order of service. The word *liturgy* stems from a Latin term meaning "public servant." It refers to both the sacrament of the Eucharist as well as the overall set form for public worship.

God Is Dead

In the 1960s, "God is dead" was a popular proclamation of the hippie subculture. Their words echoed the beliefs of many intellectual pioneers of the last century or so. The work of such brilliant thinkers as Karl Marx, Charles Darwin, Friedrich Nietzsche, and Sigmund Freud had presented new ways of looking at the human condition, and God didn't factor much at all into the brave new world that they envisioned. The world had become more based in the secular and, in turn, increasingly less devoted to the sacred, or convinced that the sacred even existed.

Perhaps some people had indeed lost their belief in God. As history has shown us, however, it wasn't that people believed that God had gone away as much as they had once again changed the way in which they perceived Him. The increasingly dominant focus on the physical and material aspects of life lessened the emphasis on matters of a more spiritual nature. This made God seem extremely far away, and perhaps nonexistent.

What was definitely clear was that many people had lost their commitment to worshipping in the same ways that their parents did. Traditional religious practices—regular attendance at church, heads bowed in supplication at prescribed times during set-in-stone liturgies—didn't cut it for the "Me" generation, which was more interested in personal enlightenment than formal worship services. Institutional religion and religious doctrine became irrelevant for many people.

In Search of Spirit

For some, the answers seemed to lie beyond many of the better-known traditions of Western religion. Eastern spirituality, including Zen practice, became one of many alternative paths to a deeper spiritual experience. Others moved beyond the religion of their childhood and explored different pathways to spirituality, including yoga, transcendental meditation, and the more contemplative and mystical forms of prayer that had played a significant role in ancient worship dating back to the early days of Christianity. In so doing, they blurred the lines between the prayer forms that had come to define traditional religion and those that were perhaps less familiar but in no way any less valid or effective.

As more people embarked on their journeys to self-enlightenment, those trips often took them far beyond their previous spiritual experiences. Some integrated what they learned into their own religious traditions, whereas others found it difficult to do so. They left behind the religious traditions they had been raised with, and created their own personal brand of spirituality.

While many use the terms religion and spirituality interchangeably, they do mean different things. In his book *The Best Alternative Medicine*, Kenneth R. Pelletier, director of the Complementary and Alternative Medicine Program at Stanford University School of Medicine, defines spirituality as "an inner sense of something greater than oneself, a recognition of a meaning to existence," and religion as "the outward expression of spiritual impulses, in the form of a specific religion or practice."

The "Define-It-Yourself" Age

Today, the manner in which we approach the Almighty can best be described as eclectic. In general, there is less emphasis on institutional religion or doctrine, although they continue to play an important role. More and more, however, spirituality—or the quality or condition of being spiritual—is the focus. In fact, a 2000 poll by the magazine *Spirituality & Health* reported that one in five Americans considers himself spiritual rather than religious.

As Robert Owens Scott noted in the Spring 2001 issue, ". . . our spiritual journeys are now taking us down paths that were not available to previous generations. Not only are we exposed to a wider variety of religious practices, but the word spirituality has stepped out on its own. It now signifies a multitude of indispensable indefinables that give our lives meaning."

Many people seeking spiritual enlightenment are exploring a variety of points of view from many different faiths. Instead of asking their ministers to advise them, they're increasingly going it alone or employing the help of spiritual directors or guides. Prayer is often one of a number of practices—including such things as meditation, visualization, drumming, and so forth—that are done to keep body, mind, and spirit in touch with God. As such, it also takes various forms, with a decided shift being seen in more meditative or contemplative methods that emphasize being able to experience God in a very personal manner. Some people decry this "define-it-yourself" spirituality, but there's no question that it is the approach that works for many today.

FACT

Spirituality & Health's poll reported on many aspects of the "new American spirituality." Among its other findings: 59 percent of Americans think of themselves as both religious and spiritual; 23 percent view spirituality as the broader concept that embraces religion. An overwhelming majority—91 percent—see praying as a spiritual activity; 81 percent described attending worship services as spiritual.

Types of Prayer

Prayer has traditionally been defined as "asking, pleading, or petitioning." You'll find versions of this definition in virtually any dictionary, and examples of these prayer forms in all of the world's religions, as well as in the Bible.

Pleading or petitioning prayers could also be the kinds of prayers that you are most familiar with, and, perhaps, were raised to believe are most acceptable. That's fine, but to think of prayer in this manner barely scratches the surface. Ask anyone who has made prayer a part of his spiritual journey, and he'll tell you that his understanding—and experience—of prayer goes far beyond this.

Prayer can—and does—take innumerable forms. There are short prayers of less than a sentence, and prayers that go on for pages. Prayers can follow a specific form, or they can be simply prayers of the heart, offered directly and simply in no specific form at all. They can be vocal or silent, spoken or sung. Prayers can make requests of God—the Bible, in fact, is full of examples of petitionary prayer, with the ones attributed to the authors of the Psalms leading the list as being some of the most passionate and heartfelt. They can glorify and praise Him, they can simply thank Him, and they can ask Him for His forgiveness.

We can pray indoors and out, in places of worship or in our cars in the middle of rush hour. We can pray collectively or individually, with our loved ones, with congregations, or with total strangers.

Communicating with God

Central to all types of prayer, however, is a sense of communicating with God. Sometimes you'll see this communication described as talking or listening to God. These two-way dialogues are meant to take place at any time, day or night, just like you would chat with a friend. Through them, God comes to us and works with us, no matter where we are or the manner in which we've addressed Him. As we continue our conversations, we grow in our relationship with the Almighty. We draw closer to Him, and we allow Him to draw closer to us.

I like to speak of prayer as listening. We live in a culture that is terribly afraid to listen. We'd prefer to remain deaf. The Latin root word of the word *deaf* is "absurd". Prayer means moving from absurdity to obedience. Let the words descend from your head to your heart so you can begin to know God. In prayer, you become who you are meant to be.

—Henri Nouwen, Jesuit priest

Saint Ignatius called the prayer conversations that people have with God colloquies, and believed they should be no different in tone or content than two friends talking to each other, or a parent talking to a child. Many of the world's great spiritual leaders, both past and present, have described or defined prayer in similar fashion.

However, not everyone is comfortable with the concept of talking to God "one on one," such as it were. Some even find the notion of treating the Almighty with such familiarity somehow irreverent. If you do, it might take you some time to break through your current beliefs. But, as you'll see in the chapters that follow, developing an intimate relationship with God is a cornerstone of a fulfilling prayer life. As many people believe, it's what He wants us to do.

Getting Down and Dirty

God literally asks us to get "down and dirty" with Him. While there is nothing wrong in coming before the Almighty in a formal way, such as through liturgical services and proscribed prayers, the truth is that there is no need for formality in this particular relationship. We don't have to be washed clean and dressed in our Sunday best. It is perfectly all right to let our guard down and be ourselves in God's presence throughout the course of everyday life.

In *Open Mind, Open Heart*, Thomas Keating wrote: "When we say 'Let us pray,' we mean 'Let us enter into a relationship with God,' or 'Let us deepen the relationship we have,' or 'Let us exercise our relationship with God.'"

Going Formal

There are certainly times when it is appropriate to pray in a more formal fashion. Worshipping during a formal liturgical service in a church, synagogue, or mosque calls for following the order of service as it's set down in the prayer book. If you were at a wedding or a funeral, a casual colloquy with God would most likely not be in order.

At these times, following the prayers that others have written and allowing their words to substitute for ours is necessary, and it's the right thing to do, even if we feel like we're talking more at God than with God. But on an everyday basis, there is less need for such formality. We can just let the words flow.

Coming Clean

It is also not necessary to be squeaky clean and free of problems before going to God in prayer. Many people are reluctant or even afraid to pray because they feel they're not worthy of having a relationship with God for some reason. Some people feel they've "been too bad" and would in some way offend the Almighty. They're ashamed to turn to God because they're afraid of what He might say. Or they'd like to believe that such a relationship is possible, but they have a hard time getting one started because they've been disappointed in prayer in the past. Others are simply afraid to go where they haven't gone before, and fear that opening themselves to God will force them into examining behaviors and beliefs that they'd rather leave untouched.

It's easy to understand these fears, and even easier to put them to rest. Here's why: God knows us better than we know ourselves, and He understands better than we ever could. Nothing is going to come as a surprise to Him, nor is it necessary to try to explain it all to Him. All that is necessary is to come to Him and tell Him what's going on.

Where can I go from Your Spirit? Or where can I flee from your presence? If I ascend into heaven, You are there; If I make my bed in hell, behold, You are there. If I take the wings of the morning, And dwell in the uttermost parts of the sea, Even there Your hand shall lead me, And Your right hand shall hold me.

—Psalm 139:7–10

As hard as it might be, the times when we're feeling "less than," for any reason, are exactly when it is most important to talk to the Almighty. We might not always get the answers we want, or answers that we understand, but it is essential to keep the conversation going. Doing so not only deepens our relationship with God, it helps us remain open to the changes in ourselves that come about through that relationship.

Getting the Conversation Going

If prayer is as simple as talking to God, it should be easy to do, right? Perhaps so, but many people find that it isn't easy, at least not at first. They are concerned over doing it "right," although there isn't one right way to pray, or one way that's any better than any other. The way that works best for you is simply the "right" way. And, as you'll see in this book, there are many ways to go about it.

As human beings, we tend to make things more difficult than they need to be, and our tendency to complicate things can stand in the way. When it comes to prayer, we sometimes get tied up in knots worrying about how we're doing it. When we don't immediately see the benefits of our prayers, we think we're doing it wrong.

The answer to these concerns should be pretty obvious by now. Just pray. Put aside any fears or concerns that you have, and start talking to God. And don't forget to listen.

Chapter 2

The Power of Prayer

Prayer, purely and simply, is about being in union with God. When we make the commitment to experience that union on a regular basis, all sorts of things can happen, and do happen, both to us and to the people we pray for.

Changing Things Through Prayer

It's often been said—you've probably heard it more than once—that prayer changes things. In fact, you might have experienced firsthand some of the changes that prayer can bring about. You might have prayed for something and had your prayer answered. Maybe someone you know joined a prayer group and seems to be happier and more at peace because of it. Or you know someone who made a pretty miraculous recovery from a serious illness and gives prayer the credit for being able to return to wellness.

What you may not know, however, is exactly how these changes come about. But here's the inside story on that: No one really knows. Not for sure, anyway. Even the world's greatest theologians—men and women who have spent years getting to know the face of God, synthesizing their experiences and those of others, and writing about them—can't come up with a definitive explanation of the exact way in which God works. It remains a mystery of faith.

QUESTION?

What is it about our relationship with God that can change life's circumstances?
There's not an easy answer to this question, but it begins with the changes in ourselves that come about through that relationship. When we say that God changes things, the most important things He changes are the people who walk with Him in prayer.

What we do know for sure is that God promises to answer our prayers. In the Book of Matthew, Jesus tells his disciples that, "Everyone who asks receives," which is about the best testimony to the power of prayer that anyone could ask for. On the other hand, the Bible also tells us that if we don't ask, we don't get, which is pretty good justification for getting close to God in prayer. He might be all-knowing and all-seeing, but He's not going to answer our prayers unless we offer them to Him.

But what does "answering our prayers" really mean? If we ask God to help us become prosperous, will He help? If we pray for healing, will He heal? If we ask for His guidance, will He guide us? Yes, in all these things

God will answer us. But the changes in circumstances that we're seeking will often manifest themselves differently than how we think they will. Sometimes, in fact, they won't happen at all because His answer to our prayer was "No."

Personal Transformations

Another word for the changes that take place through prayer is *transformation.* Every relationship you enter into alters you in some way. So, too, does the relationship you have with God. In fact, the changes that God makes in the people who love Him are some of the most compelling examples of the power of prayer.

Through prayer, as we get to know God better, we also get to know ourselves better. We gain a greater understanding of what makes us tick, and what motivates us to do the things we do. We get smarter about how we handle the challenges of life. As we get to know ourselves better, we also are better able to understand others, and we become more compassionate and caring. In short, we learn how to be better people. It's a relationship, in biblical terms, that bears a lot of fruit, as the apostle Paul puts it in his letter to the Galatians: "But the fruit of the Spirit is love, joy, peace, longsuffering, kindness, goodness, faithfulness, gentleness, self control" (Galatians 5:22–23).

What God refrains from doing is telling us exactly how we should live our lives—He leaves the freedom of will up to each one of us. Instead, by talking to Him—that is, praying to Him—we gain a greater understanding of our actions and the motivations behind them, and, for that matter, the actions and motivations of others.

As we grow in our relationship with God, we also get better at knowing how to keep our dialogue with Him flowing smoothly. In other words, we understand what it takes to pray. In a nutshell, it boils down to five basic principles:

1. **Having faith.** As mentioned in Chapter 1, belief in God is a prerequisite for prayer. But having faith in prayer goes beyond this; it takes our believing that God is capable of doing anything and

everything—including answering our prayers. It also means that we have to believe that God works for good in all things, even during times when it doesn't seem like He is doing so at all.

2. **Being humble.** Humility before God means understanding where we are in relation to Him. Simply put, He is God, and we're not. It means accepting the fact that we're pretty puny when compared to Him, and that we very much need His help. And, it means being willing to allow Him to work within or through us, and to accept His will. His will, not ours.

3. **Being honest.** God has a great sense of humor, but He doesn't like being fooled with. While it's not even possible to do it, you'd be surprised at how many people do try. Being honest with God means coming before Him as we are, with all our earthly foibles. It also means asking God for His forgiveness if we've not been obedient to His word in some way.

You who believe, seek help through patience and prayer; God stands alongside the patient! We will test you with a bit of fear and hunger, and a shortage of wealth and souls and produce. Proclaim such to patient people who say, whenever disaster strikes them, "We are God's, and are returning to Him!" Such will be granted their prayers by their Lord as well as mercy. Those are guided!

—Quran 2:153–57

4. **Being patient.** We are, by nature, a pretty impatient people. We don't like waiting any longer than we think we need to, whether it's when we're stopped at a red light or when we're trying to access a Web site that's loading more slowly than we'd like it to. We want what we want, and we want it now. Well, there isn't much "now" when it comes to God. If there's one lesson that God teaches us more than any other, it's learning how to wait on Him. We have to wait, as the prophet Elijah had to do, for God's "still, small voice."

5. **Being thankful.** Giving thanks to God is also part of coming before Him with a humble heart. When we thank God, we're acknowledging the importance of our relationship with Him.

If there were such a thing as a magic formula for effective prayer, it would consist of something like these five principles. Come before God with these precepts firmly in place and you'll be able to offer up the kinds of prayers that He can do something about. Not only that, you'll better understand the reasons why you don't always get what you pray for.

When Prayer Fails

One of the things that keeps people from experiencing the power of prayer is that they've been disappointed in it. They've asked God for certain things, and they haven't received what they asked for. In other words, prayer failed them. Or did it?

Sometimes, yes, prayer can feel like failure. If we've prayed for healing, and it doesn't happen, it can be hard to believe that prayer can be effective. If we ask God for a new house, a new job, or a new car, and we don't get them, it's pretty hard not to be disappointed.

ESSENTIAL

Even the prayers that we think have failed are powerful prayers. While they may not deliver the results we had hoped for, their power can be seen, and felt, in other ways.

What is behind failed prayers? Some will tell you that prayers fail because the people who pray them are lacking in faith. In other words, they didn't believe strongly enough in what they were praying about, and they didn't truly believe that God could answer their prayers. There's some truth to this, but it's only part of the answer.

The Flip Side of Failed Prayers

As hard as it can be to deal with the disappointment and frustration that failed prayers can create, it is important to realize that they don't work against us. Instead, they work for us. To understand how this can be, you have to look at things from a different perspective. Instead of pointing a finger at God and accusing Him of not helping out, we have to take a closer look at why our prayers are ineffective. Maybe we're not asking for things in the right way. Or we're asking for things that may not be in our best interest. Maybe, in fact, we're the problem, not God.

In *Be Careful What You Pray For . . . You Just Might Get It: What We Can Do About the Unintentional Effects of Our Thoughts, Prayers, and Wishes*, author Larry Dossey notes that one of the key issues behind failed prayers is our inappropriate involvement in what he calls a "tightly coupled system." For the most part, that system performs pretty well, but when it doesn't, we try to fix things through prayer. But, instead of making things better, our involvement often makes them worse.

As Dossey puts it, "The issue is not that we pray, but how we pray. When something goes wrong in our life, we tend to invoke prayers involving highly specific, designated outcomes. We're certain that we have the knowledge to set things right, and we waste no time telling the Absolute what to do. We do not realize that we are interfering in a highly complex, tightly coupled system that, when tweaked, often responds in unpredictable ways."

The Problem of Playing God

What Dossey is getting at is that we tend to play God a bit when we pray for certain things. We let our egos get in the way of prayer. Instead of praying, "Thy will be done," we're saying to God, "My will be done." This isn't prayer, but rather it's our thinking that we can manipulate God into giving us what we want. But we can't manipulate God. Things just don't work this way in prayer.

To justify this sort of "naming and claiming" prayer, many people single out the biblical verses that seem to support it. In Jesus' "Sermon on the Mount," he tells his listeners to "Ask and it will be given to you;

seek, and you will find; knock, and it will be opened for you. For everyone who asks receives, and he who seeks finds, and to him who knocks it will be opened" (Matthew 7:7–8).

These are pretty powerful words. Taken literally, they tell us that God will answer our prayers, no matter what, and give us whatever we want. But Jesus, who was a master at allegory and metaphor, and used them extensively in his teachings, was, in fact, speaking metaphorically here. The lesson he's teaching is on the importance of having faith in God, and the results of our putting our faith in Him. Everyone who asks does receive, but the gift we get is God's perfect love for us, not a shiny new BMW.

> If God had granted all the silly prayers I've made in my life, where should I be now? The best antidote for our folly may be, as we've seen, not in praying for anything at all, but in adopting an approach in prayer such as "Thy will be done" or "May the best outcome prevail." This approach might offer fabulous protection from the most serious threat we face: ourselves.
> —C. S. Lewis, in *Letters to Malcolm*

The Real Meaning of Unanswered Prayers

The bottom line is this: We're not God. His words in the Book of Isaiah make this very clear:

"For My thoughts are not your thoughts, nor are your ways My ways," says the Lord. "For as the heavens are higher than the earth, So are My ways higher than your ways, And My thoughts than your thoughts" (Isaiah 55:8–9).

Because we don't have God's insight and wisdom, we have no way of knowing about factors that might be working against our immediately having our prayers answered. Or having them answered at all. Maybe it's not the right time. Maybe God has something better in store for us. Maybe we need to learn how to be more faithful or more patient. Maybe, simply, the answer is "no" because what we're asking for may actually make things worse.

In not answering our prayers, God teaches us one of the most powerful lessons of all: to trust Him, and trust in Him, no matter what. When we get that lesson down, well, miracles can happen, and often do.

Healing by Faith

Some of the greatest miracles brought about by prayer, interestingly enough, have taken place in the realm of health and healing. In biblical times, people routinely asked God to heal them. The Second Book of Kings, in the Old Testament, describes how King Hezekiah prayed for healing from a terminal disease:

Then he turned his face toward the wall, and prayed to the Lord, saying, "Remember now, O Lord, I pray, how I have walked before you in truth and with a loyal heart, and have done what was good in your sight . . . Then it happened, before Isaiah had gone out into the middle court, that the word of the Lord came to him, saying, "Return and tell Hezekiah the leader of My people, Thus says the Lord, the God of David your father: I have heard your prayer, I have seen your tears; surely I will heal you. On the third day you shall go up to the house of the Lord. And I will add to your days fifteen years. I will deliver you and this city from the hand of the King of Assyria; and I will defend this city for My own sake, and for the sake of My servant David."

—2 Kings 21:2–6

The New Testament contains a number of examples of how Jesus healed various ailments of the faithful. In fact, he even told his disciples the secret to it: ". . . if you have faith as a mustard seed, you will say to this mountain, 'Move from here to there,' and it will move; and nothing will be impossible for you" (Matthew 18:20).

In this era of modern medicine, we've tended to put our faith more in the healing power of physicians and less in the healing power of God. Recent studies, however, suggest that each has a place in the continuum of healing. Not only that, most of us prefer to have God be an active part of the equation.

FACT

A survey conducted in 1995 to assess the relevancy of religion and spirituality in medicine found overwhelming support for the intermingling of the practical with the spiritual. Fifty percent of hospitalized patients told surveyers they believed that their physicians should not just pray with them, but for them as well.

One of the most intriguing areas in which the power of prayer has been put to the test is in remote healing. In several experiments, people from many different spiritual backgrounds have been asked to pray on behalf of certain individuals in need of healing. Their long-distance prayers were shown to be pretty effective. In one study, about 1,000 heart patients who were admitted to a hospital's critical care unit were divided into two groups. For a year, a group of volunteers and the hospital's chaplain prayed for one half of the group. The result: The patients in the prayer group had 11 percent fewer heart attacks, strokes, and life-threatening complications. One of the cardiologists who participated in the study commented that it offered some interesting insights into the possibility that God influenced lives on earth. As a scientist, he added, he had no way of explaining how He did so.

The question of prayer's effectiveness when patients prayed for themselves was also put to test. Here, the focus was on how prayer could affect the mental status of critically ill heart patients. Again, prayer proved helpful—almost 100 percent of the individuals who prayed for themselves before undergoing major surgery reported that praying had been extremely helpful in helping them manage the stress and anxiety that so often arise when serious illness strikes.

Another study tested the power of remote prayer on critically ill AIDS patients. The twenty patients in the study received basically the same medical treatment. Half were prayed for by spiritual healers representing a number of religious traditions—Christianity, Buddhism, and the traditional practices of Native Americans among them. The others received no prayer support. All ten of the prayed-for patients remained alive throughout the course of the six-month study. Four of the others died, reflecting a standard mortality rate for AIDS patients as critically ill as these individuals were. A follow-up study conducted by the same researcher found that people who received prayer and remote healing spent far less time in the hospital, both in terms of frequency of admission and length of stay.

Clearly, the final verdict on prayer isn't in. But it sure looks like it couldn't hurt. Or could it?

Prayer was even proven to be effective in helping women get pregnant. According to a research team from Columbia University, prayer appeared to double the chances of pregnancy in women undergoing in-vitro fertilization treatments.

The Negative Power of Prayer

It's clear that prayer can definitely be good medicine. But it can be bad medicine as well. As it turns out, prayer has a dark side, too.

For many, this is an unspeakable subject. The fact that it is has a lot to do with our having whitewashed God's personage over the years. Most people won't even admit that prayer can be anything else but good. There is some pretty strong evidence, however, to the contrary.

If you know your Old Testament at all, you know that the Almighty could be pretty vengeful when He needed to be. The Israelites felt the hand of God on a fairly regular basis. Remember the story of Sodom and Gomorrah? God destroyed these two cities because the people who lived in them were so wicked and depraved. David, the beloved Jewish king, often called upon God to wreak vengeance on his enemies. David wouldn't have done so if he didn't get some results.

> O Lord God, to whom vengeance belongs—
> O God, to whom vengeance belongs,
> shine forth.
> Rise up, O Judge of the earth;
> Render punishment to the proud.
>
> —Psalm 94:1–3

The New Testament also contains examples of negative prayer. In the Book of Acts, Paul calls upon God to blind a false prophet who was trying to turn a righteous man away from God (Acts 13:6–12). Say what you will about the righteousness of his intentions, the outcome was a negative one.

Even Jesus prayed a negative prayer when he called on God to wither away a barren fig tree (Matthew 21:19). Admittedly, his actions were part of a lesson in faith to his disciples, but let's not whitewash what really happened here. The fig tree was alive, it just wasn't bearing fruit for some reason. Jesus said "Let no fruit grow on you ever again," and it died.

It isn't important to dwell on this topic to excess. However, to fully understand the power of prayer, you also need to accept the fact that there are negative prayers, and negative pray-ers. As much as we might like to think that these individuals are not aware of what they're doing, we know otherwise. In 1994, *Life* magazine reported the results of a Gallup poll that contained some pretty startling data: Five percent of the Americans polled admitted to having prayed for something bad to happen to others. Five percent may not sound all that bad, but keep in mind that this figure represents only the people who were honest enough to admit praying in this manner. The actual numbers are probably quite a bit higher.

The Nature of Negative Prayer

When we think about negative prayers we often put them in the context of intentional hexes and curses such as those cast by witches in children's fairy tales. More often, however, they're much more casual than this, and we're often not aware of them when we launch them. We can be praying negatively simply by thinking negatively about another person. All those little "damn you's" and "God damn its"—they're negative prayers, too.

Negative prayers can be as innocent as asking God to put us ahead of someone else as equally deserving of His favor. In *Be Careful What You Pray For . . . You Just Might Get It*, Larry Dossey calls these random and seemingly innocent prayers "prayer muggings," and issues a strong caution about making them, as they're usually made without any consideration for the effect they might have on the other party.

Even praying for someone without his or her consent may be seen as a negative prayer. Mary Baker Eddy, the founder of Christian Science, made this point clear when she wrote, "Who of us would have our houses broken open or our locks picked? And much less would have our minds tampered with? . . . Our Master said, 'when we enter a house, salute it.' . . . I say, When you enter mentally the personal precincts of human thought, you should know the person with whom you hold communion desires it."

QUESTION?

Should I pray for someone who hasn't asked for it?
Some people believe that it can be risky to pray for someone who hasn't specifically requested it, as doing so may not be aligned with that person's desires or religious beliefs. If you know a person who has asked someone else to pray for him or her, it's probably okay for you to join in. But it's a good idea to ask before you do so.

If you take anything away from this discussion of negative prayer, it should be this: Know that prayer can be very powerful, and be careful how you use it.

Avoiding Negative Prayer

One of the simplest ways we can keep from uttering negative prayers is to always remember that our prayers never exist in a vacuum. In some way or another, they will have an effect on something or somebody. What might seem like a positive prayer in your eyes may be very much the opposite to someone else. When you're praying to God, be mindful of your prayers. Ask Him for His guidance on them as well. He'll direct you to the positive side if you ask Him to.

What can you do if you feel like you're the target of negative prayers? Well, you can pray for yourself. Doing so may very well be your best defense. There are a number of different prayers that you can use if you feel like you want to harness the power of someone's words. "The Lord's

Prayer"—the prayer that Jesus taught his disciples when they asked him how they should pray—is one of the best prayer covers you could ask for. In fact, it even asks God to protect us from those who wish to harm us.

Our Father, who art in heaven, hallowed be thy name.
Thy kingdom come, thy will be done
on earth as it is in heaven.
Give us this day our daily bread,
And forgive us our trespasses
as we forgive those who trespass against us.
And lead us not into temptation,
but deliver us from evil.
For thine is the kingdom,
and the power, and the glory,
forever and ever.
Amen.

Chapter 3

How the Faiths Pray

One of the basic things to know about prayer is that it doesn't belong to any one religion or spiritual tradition. Prayer is universal, and it plays a key role in all of the world's leading religions. To understand how your prayer practice fits into the grand scheme of things, it can help to know something about the prayer traditions of the different faiths. We'll look at some of them in this chapter.

The History of Prayer

While there isn't an exact history of prayer in and of itself, we do know quite a bit about how people have sought to understand the world around them, both seen and unseen, and the religions that developed as a result of their efforts. It is in the history of these religions where we find the rituals and traditions that shape how people communicate with God.

What a strange fellowship this is, the God-seekers in every land, lifting their voices in the most disparate ways imaginable to the God of all life.

—Huston Smith, in *The World's Religions*

From the earliest of times, we have realized that there is something greater than we are out there. We have sought ways to understand what it is as well as ways to develop some sort of a connection with it. What's interesting about our efforts is that they're very similar to those around us. No matter how we come at it, we all end up in the same place. There is one spirit—a Divine spirit—that unites us all, regardless of how we perceive it or how we choose to experience it.

When you pray, you're both honoring that shared history and extending it to the generations that will come after you. As you pray, whether you choose to honor the traditions of a specific religion, prefer to pull from many in an eclectic mix, or you wing it on your own, you're tapping into a rich spiritual pool that goes all the way back to prehistory.

Prehistory describes the time before civilization, when humans existed and had cultures but had not yet developed a complete written language. During the times of prehistory, most of the handing down of information was done orally, by telling stories from one generation to the next.

Of the world's religious traditions, the three that share a common theology—Judaism, Christianity, and Islam—also claim the largest number of followers. These faiths are linked by a belief in one God, known as monotheism, as well as their shared history. In all of them, prayer takes the form of a personal relationship with God.

But prayer is not the only way in which people connect to that which is greater than themselves. There are a number of religions and beliefs throughout the world, primarily outside of the Western hemisphere, that acknowledge a greater being or spirit, but not God as we understand Him to be. They also experience the Holy in ways that are similar to, yet different from, the prayer forms that we are most familiar with. Buddhists, for example, don't pray to a God-like figure as most of us would understand one. However, Buddhists do pray. In Buddhist practice, prayers often take the form of meditation, and are directed toward acquiring spiritual enlightenment or illumination. Similar meditative practices are also performed by members of other religious faiths. What this illustrates is that there are many ways in which we can connect with the Absolute. Our spiritual beliefs will influence how we perceive this entity. It can be God or Allah. It can also be Brahma, the Universal Mind, the Tao, or the Void. It can even be the Great Goddess.

FACT

Buddhists sometimes pay their respects to images of Buddha, but not as a form of religious veneration. Buddha is not a deity, but the title of the being who achieved supreme enlightenment in accordance with the teachings of Buddhism.

Other religions pray to or commune with the energy, spirit, or power within and its connections to the universe. We know less about some of these religions—such as the ones practiced by indigenous peoples in Africa and Australia—because their histories are oral instead of written. Yet, they too are part of the mix.

The Search for Meaning

As previously mentioned, people have sought a connection to that which is greater than they are from the beginning of civilization. They have sought this link for a variety of reasons—for guidance, direction, or simply to ask "why?" In the earliest times, our ancestors experienced the world in a far more intuitive and organic manner than we do today. Their lives revolved around food and the pursuit of food (although some would argue that today ours do as well). They were astute observers of nature—and especially the weather—as they understood that the forces of nature governed their food supply.

For this reason, the gods they worshipped were also a part of nature. They worshipped the god of the storm and the god of the sun. There were gods in mountains, and in animals.

To ancient peoples, gods didn't create the flora and the fauna; their gods were the flora and the fauna. When a lightning bolt split the sky during a storm, it wasn't a god who sent that bolt— the bolt itself was a god making his presence known. Rain wasn't controlled by a water god; rather, it was part of a water god.

During this period, the family structure as we know it today had not yet developed. Instead, people gathered together in tribes, and the tribes worked together as a unit. Each tribe had its own gods.

The Sumerians and Their Gods

The beliefs of the earliest people carried forward to the first great civilization—the Sumerians. They too worshipped gods that were tied closely to nature and natural phenomena. The Sumerians, however, made their gods in the image of themselves—in other words, their gods had human form. They couldn't be seen, however, because they lived in the heavens.

The Sumerians believed that they had been created to work for their gods, and that everything belonged to them. Originally, each Sumerian city had its own god. Over time, the many gods were consolidated and organized into a hierarchy where some gods were more important than others. There were four main deities, each with a specific activity or role:

1. Anu, the father of the gods
2. Enlil, the god of the sky (the most important, because without him nothing was possible)
3. Ninmakh, or Ninkhursag, the great mother (who personified the fertility of the earth)
4. Enki, the god of the underground waters (who personified the masculine powers of creativity and life in the earth)

FACT

The collection of gods that personified the elements and natural forces developed by the Sumerians is said to be the beginning of theology. The Sumerians established one of the first historical civilizations in the fourth millennium B.C.E.

In addition to these deities, there was also a collection of minor gods, including Nanna, the moon god; Utu, the sun god; and Inanna, the god of the morning star.

The gods demanded a lot of the Sumerians. Elaborate rituals assured prosperity and a long life, but little more. But the Sumerians also felt a sense of protection from their gods. They understood that their gods controlled the environment and sustained life.

The Gods of Other Civilizations

The tradition of worshipping many gods also continued with the Egyptian civilization, which had gods in many forms, both human and animal, and also in the abstract and the inanimate. Like the early Sumerians, each Egyptian town had its patron deity or deities and its own religious community. The Egyptian pantheon, or collection of gods, was huge, numbering at least 2,000. Worship was in the form of cults led by pharaohs and priests. The gods they worshipped controlled the heavens and the earth as well as the world of the dead. Some of the basic myths of creation, divine kingship, and cosmic order can be found in the earliest Egyptian civilization.

Polytheism, or a belief in many gods, was the norm in most of the ancient world. In India, the Aryans worshipped nature gods, including

Indra, the god of the air and of the storm; and Agni, the sacrificial fire. The intoxicant they drank during worship was the god Soma. Varuna was worshipped as the guardian of cosmic regularity. Hinduism had its gods, too. Siva personified the cosmic forces of destruction and reproduction; Vishnu was the god of sacrifice who took two forms—Krishna and Rama. There was also Brahma, the great Creator.

The tradition of worshipping many gods is called polytheism, as opposed to monotheism, which is the belief or worship of a single god. Deism is the belief that a single god created the universe and then left it to its own devices without any influence at all.

The Romans had a simpler hierarchy, mostly based on the worship of Mars, who was an agricultural deity first, a god of war later. Religious ceremonies were simple but had to be orchestrated in a specific way in order to please the gods. Only then would they act. Failure to get the desired results was blamed on faulty ceremonies, not on the gods.

The Babylonians held close to the Sumerian tradition and had a system of gods. Each controlled a specific cosmic force—the heavens, air, ocean, sun, moon, and so on—and had a main temple in a particular city. Over time, however, one god—Marduk—elbowed out the others and took the lead as the primary Babylonian god.

From Many Gods, One

The Babylonians weren't the only ones who were beginning to place their faith in one deity instead of many. A small nomadic tribe that had wandered the Fertile Crescent of the Middle East for some time had entered into a covenant with the god Yahweh. Yahweh, the god of the Hebrews, was a mighty leader, creator, and judge. He was just as powerful as other ancient gods, but He stood apart from the others because He had no pantheon of lesser gods to accompany Him.

"I Am the Lord Your God"

Like the other civilizations of the ancient world, the Hebrews had a polytheistic heritage. The tribes who were their forerunners believed that there were many gods. However, they worshipped only their own god. When they strengthened that agreement by entering into a covenant with Him, whereby Yahweh agreed to return them to their promised land, they also agreed to dispense with their beliefs that there were other gods. In other words, there were no other gods before God. Nor was there ever to be, as long as the covenant between the two parties remained in place. God made this abundantly clear when He laid down the law to Moses, and Moses made it very clear to the Hebrews in turn:

I stood between the Lord and you at that time, to declare to you the word of the Lord; for you were afraid because of the fire, and you did not go up the mountain. He said: I am the Lord your God who brought you out of the land of Egypt, out of the house of bondage. You shall have no other gods before me . . . For I, the Lord your God, am a jealous God . . .

—Deuteronomy 5:5–9

The religious belief in one god set the Hebrews apart from all other ancient civilizations. The way in which they perceived their god did as well. Unlike the others, the god of the Hebrews took no human form. He was a transcendent deity, the creator of everything, who existed independently of His own creation. As Huston Smith describes it in *The World's Religions*:

Where the Jews differed from their neighbors was not in envisioning the Other as personal but in focusing its personalism in a single, supreme, nature-transcending will. For the Egyptians, Babylonians, Syrians, and lesser Mediterranean peoples of the day, each major power of nature was a distinct deity . . . When we turn to the Hebrew Bible we find ourselves in a completely different atmosphere. Nature here is an expression of a single Lord of all being.

The Hebrew word for prayer is *tefilah*, which, loosely translated, means "to judge oneself." This meaning sheds light on the introspective nature of prayer and its importance to people of the Jewish faith.

The Lord God All Around

The belief that the entire world belongs to God and reflects God's glory continues to shape how Jews pray to God to this day. No matter where they are, no matter how they're praying—in formal worship services or on their own—Jews find a way to praise God and His work in virtually everything. In doing so, they constantly remind themselves of God's presence and their relationship to Him.

Jews pray both formally and informally, publicly and privately, as has been done since the earliest times of the faith. Some observant Jews (especially the Orthodox, the most stringent adherents to the traditional aspects of the faith) pray three times daily—in the morning, the afternoon, and the evening—and follow a specific pattern of prayer. Praying in the morning and the evening is a directive from the Shema, the oldest daily prayer in Judaism, which commands the faithful to pray "when you retire and when you arise." Saying the Shema, which consists of verses from the Old Testament books of Deuteronomy and Numbers, fulfills the prayer commitment at morning and night. The afternoon prayer was added later.

The tradition of praying three times a day dates back to the sixth century B.C.E. At that time, the Jews were in exile in Babylon, and weren't able to offer their sacrifices in the temple, which was the central place of worship in ancient Jerusalem. Prayer was substituted for that practice. Since sacrifices had been held three times daily, a third prayer time was added to the two called for by the Shema.

In addition to the three formal prayer services, Jews also say blessings over just about every daily activity. These prayers fall into three general categories:

1. Blessings recited before eating, drinking, or smelling something pleasant
2. Blessings recited before fulfilling a commandment of the Lord or performing a good deed
3. Blessings that praise and thank God for His wonderful works, or that ask God for His help

As they have from ancient times, every Jewish prayer begins by praising God before it moves on to the specific subject at hand. The exact words that open all Jewish prayers are, "Blessed art thou, Lord our God, King of the Universe."

In the Shema can also be found the basis for two of the key visual symbols of the Jewish faith: the tefillin, or phylacteries; and the mezuzah. Tefillin, the symbols of faith that Jewish men wear on the head (above the eyes) and on the arm during prayer are symbolic of God's urging the Jews to bind His word "as a sign upon your hand, and . . . a reminder before your eyes." God's instructions to write His word "on the doorposts of your house and upon your gates" is symbolized by the mezuzah, which observant Jews (and even many Jews who aren't as observant) place inside the frame of the front doors of their homes to serve as a constant reminder of God's presence in their lives.

God Made Man

Christianity is a historical religion that is based on concrete events and historic facts that center on the life of Jesus Christ—or, to be more exact, on his brief ministry of teaching and healing. During his short career, Jesus went from being the son of a poor carpenter to being a prophet and a healer. He preached the need for repentance in the face of the end of time and Judgment Day, and both told and showed people what they needed to do to reach the kingdom of heaven.

FACT

The first four books of the New Testament—the gospels of Matthew, Mark, Luke, and John—tell the story of Jesus' ministry from different yet similar points of view. The remaining New Testament books document the early formation of a new religion—Christianity—based on Jesus' teachings and works.

Jesus had a firm education in Jewish scripture, and he was devoutly Jewish. During his life, he both upheld his Jewish heritage and was deeply critical of it. He was a strong opponent of many of its precepts as they had come to be practiced, and believed that they erected barriers between people instead of bringing them together. This, in Jesus' eyes, was not what God was all about. He saw God as compassion and love, and his visions of God formed the basis for his teachings.

To this day, prayers made in the Christian tradition follow the prayer pattern that Jesus taught to his followers when they asked him how to pray—to adore God, confess to Him, offer thanksgiving, and to petition Him. "The Lord's Prayer" is considered by Christians to be the perfect prayer, and is valued for its simplicity, its beautiful imagery, and its timeless instruction.

The prayer's opening words, "Our Father, who art in heaven, hallowed be thy name," describe how to approach God—with reverence and adoration. "Thy kingdom come, thy will be done, on earth as it is in heaven," reflects the desire to experience God's perfect kingdom and speaks to the necessity of living under His authority. "Give us this day our daily bread" again illustrates the need to rely on Him for all things.

The next line, "And forgive us our trespasses as we forgive those who trespass against us," asks God to pardon us as well as to give us the wisdom to pardon others. "Lead us not into temptation, but deliver us from evil," again asks for God's protection. The final lines of "The Lord's Prayer," "for thine is the kingdom, and the power, and the glory, forever and ever. Amen," takes us back to where we began as they adore Him and speak to His dominion over all.

In the Beginning . . . Allah

Islam, like Christianity, is a history-based religion. Chronologically, it came about after Judaism and Christianity, and it shares many theological concepts with its forerunners: There is just one God, and He is incorporeal and invisible. It also has a shared history with the other great monotheistic religions. As you may remember from the Old Testament, Abraham had a wife named Sarah. She couldn't bear children, so Abraham took another wife in order to fulfill God's commandments to "be fruitful and multiply." Hagar, Abraham's second wife, bore him a son whose name was Ishmael. Miraculously, Sarah also conceived and had a son, named Isaac. But Sarah was jealous of Hagar and Ishmael, and she demanded that Abraham banish them both from the tribe. According to the Quran, they traveled to Arabia. Muhammad, the founder of Islam, was a descendant of Ishmael.

"God Is Great"

Islamic worship is based on the five Pillars of Islam as they were set down by Muhammad. They include:

1. Declaration of Faith, or shahada (witness, testimony)
2. Prayer (salat)
3. Purification (zakat)
4. The Fast of Ramadan
5. Pilgrimmage, or Hajj

Muslims demonstrate their faith in God through prayer. The prayer rituals they follow are exact, and exacting. There are five daily prayer periods—daybreak, noon, midafternoon, sunset, and evening. The prayers offered during these periods are considered "contact prayers"—a means for remembering God and for staying on the right path. The prayers must be recited in Arabic. They can be performed individually or in a congregation.

The rough translation of *Islam* is "submission." A Muslim, or adherent to Islam, translates to "submitters" in English. This refers to the Islamic belief that a true follower fully submits his or her self to God.

In many Muslim countries, followers of the faith are called to prayer by a mosque official called a muezzin who sits in a mosque's minaret, or tower. As they prepare to pray, Muslims face Mecca, the holy city. Before approaching God, Muslims must cleanse both the mind and body to ensure they are spiritually and physically pure. While Muslims can pray in any clean environment—alone or together, in a mosque or at home, at work or on the road, indoors or out—it is preferable to pray with others, if possible, as one body united in the worship of God. Doing so demonstrates discipline, brotherhood, equality, and solidarity among the people of Islam.

The Sequence of Movements

The prayers Muslims recite consist of readings from the Quran interspersed with phrases that glorify God. Each time of prayer begins with the declaration, "God is most great" ("Allahu Akbar"), and is followed by fixed prayers that include the opening verse of the Quran. They're accompanied by a sequence of movements, followed in exact order:

- standing
- bowing
- kneeling
- touching the ground with one's forehead (prostration)
- sitting

Muslims aren't the only people who prostrate themselves during prayer. In fact, prostration is a common posture in many world religions, and is assumed both by clergy and laypersons at various times as part of their prayer life.

Both the words that are spoken and the movements that accompany them reflect humility, submission, and adoration of God. After all the required prayers are said, there is a brief period for personal prayer, during which time private petitions can be offered to God. Pray-ers can pray in Arabic, assisted by recommended texts. If they prefer, they can address God in words and language of their own. At the end of the prayer period, a declaration of faith is again recited, and the peace greeting—"Peace be upon all of you and the mercy and blessings of God"—is repeated twice.

The Path to Enlightenment

Buddhism was founded by a Hindu named Siddhartha who lived 2,500 years ago in what is now Nepal. His father was a king, and he was a prince. However, Siddhartha gave up his princely role in his early twenties and went out to seek understanding. The result of his search became the basis for Buddhism.

What Siddhartha saw on his journeys was a great deal of pain and suffering, disease and death. It made him despair of finding fulfillment on earth. This meant that fulfillment had to lie elsewhere. His quest for knowledge led him to the leading Hindu masters of the day. He also studied with a band of ascetics, with whom he tried to gain the knowledge he sought by going on what amounted to a fast. In so doing, he believed he would break the hold his body had on him, which would allow him to then be enlightened. He ended up sick and weak, and no more enlightened than he had been when he started out.

The title "Buddha" means the "Enlightened One" or the "Awakened One." It is based on the Sanskrit word *budh*, which means both "to wake up" and "to know." In Buddhism, enlightenment also refers to a person attaining nirvana, or a state of no care or concern.

In the final stage of his quest, Siddhartha took up a form of yoga that taught mystic concentration. One evening, he sat down under what has come to be known as the bodhi tree, or tree of enlightenment. There, he sensed that he was on the verge of an enlightenment breakthrough, and he pledged to himself that he wouldn't move until he had grasped the golden ring. He remained in that spot—which Buddhists call the Immovable Spot—for forty-nine straight days. And he got what he was after.

After the Buddha received his enlightenment, he began to preach it to others. He taught them the Four Noble Truths, which remain the basis for Buddhism:

1. Life, as typically lived, is suffering, unfulfilling, and filled with insecurity
2. Human beings suffer because we live in an almost constant state of desiring private fulfillment
3. We know how to train our minds to cure our selfish cravings and reach new levels of satisfaction and cravings
4. We can end our suffering by following a specific course of treatment

Buddha believed that the way to end suffering was to live fully in the moment, in the here and now. He taught his followers not to project into the future, nor to carry the past forward. Instead, one should face all thoughts that flow through the mind and then just simply let them go. Doing so would allow a return to one's "true nature," or "Buddha nature." It also allows entering into a blissful state called nirvana. This state is what the spiritual practices of Buddhism are directed toward and is the ultimate goal of Buddhist worship.

Do not pursue the past. Do not lose yourself in the future. Looking deeply at life as it is in this very moment, the meditator dwells in stability and freedom.

—Buddha, in *The Bhaddakaratta Sutra*

Chapter 4

From the Good Book

Some of the greatest testimonies to the power of prayer can be found in the Bible. It's also one of the best resources you could ask for when it comes to the things that can help you live a prayerful life. People often turn to the Bible in times of trouble because it makes them feel good. But you don't have to be in a bad spot to benefit from what the Bible has to offer.

Getting to Know God's Word

References to prayer and examples of prayer can be found throughout the Bible, which is why many people consider it an essential component in their prayer life. If you're like most people, you probably own at least one copy of the Bible.

FACT

According to a 1996 survey conducted by Barna Research, 91 percent of American adults own one or more Bibles, but only one in five reads the Bible at least once a week. Forty-five percent rarely or never read their Bibles.

And, if you're like a lot of people, your Bible probably spends more time on the bookshelf than it does in your hands. If you're not very familiar with the Bible, you might feel somewhat uncomfortable about reading it, especially if you don't know your way around it very well.

But the best way to learn about the Bible, and mine the riches that it holds, is to simply start reading it. You can use this chapter to get you started. We'll sketch the journey for you by telling you how the Bible came about and how it is put together. We'll also point you to some of the pithiest prayer spots within its pages.

Bible Background

The book that we call the Bible is a compilation of many texts that reflects the creative work of a whole host of people—most of whom are anonymous except for their writings—dating back some 4,000 years. It is a stunning literary work, truly unlike any other with its potpourri of historical narrative, teachings, poetry, philosophy, exhortations, and prophetic visions of the future.

The English word *Bible* comes from the Greek *biblia,* a variation of Byblos, the ancient Phoenician coastal city where the Phoenicians exported the papyrus, or paper, used to copy early books. *Biblia* originally meant papyrus; however, since all early books were written on papyrus, *biblia* eventually came to mean "book."

The Bible tells the story of the people of the ancient world with their warts on, as they really were, with all their strengths and faults. In it, people cry out to God in joy and in sorrow. They both worship the Almighty and question whether He exists at all. The Old Testament books that chronicle the life of David contain stirring narratives that detail his military and political genius. You'll also see passages of an intensely personal nature where a king overwrought with emotion asks God to rescue him from his persecutors, pleads for God's forgiveness after he steals another man's wife (and then sends her husband to certain death in the frontlines of battle).

> *Be merciful to me, O God, for man would swallow me up;*
> *Fighting all day he oppresses me.*
> *My enemies would hound me all day,*
> *For there are many who fight against me, O Most High.*
> *Whenever I am afraid,*
> *I will trust in You.*
> *In God (I will praise His word),*
> *In God I have put my trust;*
> *I will not fear.*
> *What can flesh do to me?*
> *All day they twist my words;*
> *All their thoughts are against me for evil.*
> *They gather together,*
> *They hide, they mark my steps,*
> *When they lie in wait for my life.*
> *Shall they escape by iniquity?*
> *In anger cast down the peoples, O God!*

You number my wanderings;
Put my tears into Your bottle;
Are they not in Your book?
When I cry out to You,
Then my enemies will turn back;
This I know, because God is for me.
In God (I will praise His word),
In the Lord (I will praise His word),
In God I have put my trust;
I will not be afraid.
What can man do to me?
Vows made to You are binding upon me, O God;
I will render praises to You,
For You have delivered my soul from death.
Have you not delivered my feet from falling,
That I may walk before God
In the light of the living?

—Psalm 56

Some of the world's greatest storytelling takes place in the Bible. If you're looking for meaty morality tales and passionate love stories, you'll find them on the pages of this great book. Some of what the Bible contains rivals the best television miniseries. You'll also find a spirited blend of historic fact, myth, and legend that reflect how the ancients perceived the wonders and mysteries of the world around them.

Both the Christian and Jewish faiths accept the Bible as having been inspired by God and of Divine authority, which is what places the Good Book at the center of both religions.

FACT

The Quran, the sacred text of the Islamic faith, contains many verses that mirror those in the Bible. What is interesting about this is that it is very unlikely that Muhammad was ever exposed to the Bible.

Beyond this, there are varying opinions on how the Bible came to be. Some people believe that it is the divinely inspired word of God, which He delivered directly to men who worked as his scribes. Others say that the authors of the Bible were divinely inspired in their writings, but that what they wrote were not God's literal words.

QUESTION?

Is the Bible the literal word of God?
The Bible's authenticity—that is, its authority and authorship—has been debated for centuries. We'll never know the answer to this question, but we do know that the Good Book was written by a number of people, and that the writing was inspired. Some say the inspiration came from the authors' need to reach out to God; others say that God was reaching out to them.

It really doesn't matter what you choose to believe about how the Bible became what it is today. Whether you think it's the word of God dictated verbatim, divinely inspired, or merely a fanciful grouping of fairy tales devised to educate the ancient masses, it still serves as one of the best resources on prayer ever written.

The Bible consists of two parts: The Old Testament contains the Jewish scriptures, which are also called the Hebrew Bible. The New Testament contains the Christian scriptures, and tells the story of Jesus Christ's life and ministry, and how the Christian church was formed.

The Books of the Old Testament

The actual process of writing down the Bible dates back to approximately 1500 B.C.E., which was when the earliest Hebrew scriptures—the first five books of the Bible—were written. In total, the Hebrew Bible contains twenty-four books in three groupings: Torah, or Law; Nevi'im, or the Prophets; and Kethuvim, or the Writings.

Books of the Torah

Consisting of five books—Genesis, Exodus, Leviticus, Numbers, and Deuteronomy—the Torah is the oldest part of the Bible, dating back to approximately 1000 B.C.E.

These five books are often called the Mosaic books in honor of the belief, now disproven, that held that Moses was their author. They are also known as the Pentateuch. The Torah tells the rich story of the earliest days of Judaism and reflects a time when God was experienced on a highly personal level. You'll see various facets of Him in scripture detailing:

- The Creation
- Adam and Eve
- Moses and the Ten Commandments
- The parting of the Red Sea

FACT

The scripture of the Jewish Bible, also known as the Old Testament, was originally written in Hebrew and Aramaic. The books of the New Testament, which detail the life of Jesus Christ and the establishment of the Christian church, were written in Greek.

The Prophets

The next section of the Bible, the prophets, consist of two subdivisions: the Former Prophets (Joshua, Judges, 1 and 2 Samuel and 1 and 2 Kings) and the Latter Prophets (Isaiah, Jeremiah, Ezekial, and The Twelve, which includes Hosea, Joel, Amos, Obadiah, Jonah, Micah, Nahum, Habakkuk, Zephaniah, Haggai, Zechariah, and Malachi).

These books reflect the experiences of men and women who had received Divine messages and who passed them on to others, either verbally or symbolically. They delivered their messages to individuals, groups, the entire nation of Israel, and to foreign nations.

While the prophets often had important messages to convey, the messengers themselves weren't always held in the highest regard. Kenneth Davis, author of *Don't Know Much About the Bible*, notes that they were "itinerants who roamed the countryside, sometimes in bands." Some of them were fairly powerful; many were considered troublemakers.

The Writings

The writings consist of three subdivisions: the Poetical Books (Psalms, Proverbs, Job), the Five Rolls (Song of Songs, Ruth, Lamentations, Ecclesiastes, Esther), and the Historical Books (Daniel, Ezra, Nehemiah, Chronicles).

Of the books contained in the writings, the Book of Psalms is the one that people are often the most familiar with. Psalms, the largest book in the Bible, is a compilation of 150 hymns, or poems, with almost every one containing some words of praise to God. They cover a wide time span and were written to different audiences under many different conditions. For this reason, they run the gamut on emotion and themes, ranging from jubilation to lamentation.

In the Christian Bible, the books of Hebrew scripture are rearranged, and in some cases, split, into seventeen historical books (Genesis to Esther), five wisdom or poetical books (Job to Song of Solomon), and seventeen prophetical books.

The Psalms served as the hymnbook and devotional guide for the Jewish people, and continue to play a role in both Jewish and Christian worship services to this day. Because virtually every psalm contains words of praise to God, it is a rich resource for prayer. Everyone has his favorite psalm. Psalm 23 is one of the more famous:

The Lord is my shepherd;
I shall not want.
He makes me to lie down in green pastures;
He leads me beside the still waters.
He restores my soul;
He leads me in the paths of righteousness
For His name's sake.
Yea, though I walk through the valley of the shadow of death,
I will fear no evil;
For You are with me;
Your rod and Your staff, they comfort me.
You prepare a table before me in the presence of my enemies;
You anoint my head with oil;
My cup runs over.
Surely goodness and mercy shall follow me
All the days of my life;
And I will dwell in the house of the Lord
Forever.

—*Psalm 23*

While the Psalms make for great reading, there are other books in the writings that are worth spending some with. Proverbs is a wonderful book of wisdom, with pithy sayings like, "When pride comes, then comes shame; But with the humble is wisdom" (Proverbs 11:2). The Book of Job is a morality story that tells the tale of a man whose faith in God couldn't be shaken, no matter what. Song of Solomon is a love song written by King Solomon that depicts his courtship and marriage to a Shulamite sheperdess. No one is quite sure whether it's a piece of fiction, an allegory, or an historical account. Read it, and see what you think. Be prepared for some erotic metaphors when you do. Here's an example:

Awake, O north wind,
And come, O south!
Blow upon my garden,
That its spices may flow out.

*Let my beloved come to his garden
And eat its pleasant fruits.*

—Song of Songs 4:16

The Books of the Apocrypha

One of the things you'll notice if you compare different Bibles is that some versions contain more books than others. This doesn't mean that these Bibles are any better than others, or that some versions are incomplete because they don't have as many books as others. The differences exist because some religious traditions recognize certain books as holy or authoritative, and include them in their canon, while others do not.

The word *canon* is Greek, meaning "rule." The canon can refer to the religious laws themselves, the book that contains the laws, or even the members of the council that creates the laws.

Going by "The Rules"

The various biblical canons comprise scriptures that have been deemed authoritative according to certain rules. When compiling its canon, the Protestant church rejected some books, as well as parts of books, that had long been part of the Greek translation of the Old Testament. Church leaders did so because they didn't feel these works belonged to what they believed to be the authentic canon of scripture. In doing so, they sided with Jewish religious leaders, who had come to the same conclusion sometime before when they excluded all works from the canon of the Jewish Bible that they believed to be written after the age of Ezra, the great sage of the fifth century B.C.E., at which time it was believed that inspiration or prophecy had ceased.

The collection of fifteen religious writings rejected by the Protestant church were part of the Septuagint, the ancient Greek translation of the Hebrew scriptures, and were preserved in the Vulgate, the first Latin translation of the Bible. They are commonly referred to as the Apocrypha, which means "things hidden away," although they were never really hidden, just removed from the Jewish and Protestant canons. In the Roman Catholic church, they are referred to as deuterocanonical, which translates to "secondary rule," meaning that they belong to a second layer of the canon but aren't of lesser value than the other books of the Bible.

Pick up anything other than a Protestant or Hebrew Bible, and you'll see that some or all of these books have been included, usually inserted between the Old and New Testaments. The Bible used by the Roman Catholic church, for example, includes Tobit, Judith, the Wisdom of Solomon, Sirach, Baruch, the Letter of Jeremiah, and 1 and 2 Maccabees, as well as Greek additions to the books of Esther and Daniel, including the Prayer of Azariah and the Song of the Three Jews, Susanna, and Bel and the Dragon. The Orthodox churches, which primarily stick to the books that were included in the Greek Septuagint, include a few more, such as 1 Esdras, 3 and 4 Maccabees, and Psalm 151.

QUESTION?

Why is the Old Testament included in the Bible that Christians use?
Jesus often quoted Jewish scripture when he taught. After his death, his followers turned to these scriptures to better understand his life and his teachings. To this day, the Christian church honors the role that the Old Testament played in the formation of Christianity, and considers the Jewish scriptures a cornerstone of Christian life, thought, and worship.

The Value of the Apocrypha

There has never been much agreement among the various religious traditions on the value of the Apocryphal books. The Calvinists discouraged their use and felt they were no better than anything written by any other human. The Church of England requires their inclusion in Bibles distributed for public use, and includes them in its lectionary, but also directs its followers to disregard them as doctrine. Lutherans have decided that these books aren't as important as the other books of the

Hebrew Bible, but they may also study them along with other scripture.

For a long time the majority of Bibles didn't include the books of the Apocrypha. Modern discoveries of ancient texts gave new insights on how the Jewish canon was established, however, and it became clear that the writings, which comprise the third part of the Hebrew Bible, weren't as engraved in stone as they were previously thought to be. This put into question the argument against including the books of the Apocrypha as they are also considered to be part of the writings.

As interest in biblical research and interpretation grew, the Apocryphal books began to appear more frequently. Various stand-alone editions of the Apocrypha have also been published. They provide interesting historical narrative not found in other parts of the Bible, much of it covering the period between the Old and New Testaments. They also contain a number of morality tales, ethical teachings, and apocalyptic revelations.

The Books of the New Testament

In contrast to the thousands of years that are detailed in the books of the Old Testament, the New Testament contains writings that cover a very short period of time—just about 100 years. It tells the story of Jesus' life—his birth, works, teachings, execution, and resurrection. It also details the beginnings of Christianity and documents its early growth.

The New Testament falls into two main divisions. The first five books tell the story of Jesus' life and how his followers established Christianity. The twenty-one books that follow contain letters written by various leaders of the early Christian church that expand upon or interpret Jesus' teachings.

FACT

The Book of Revelation, the last of the twenty-seven books of the New Testament, contains a fantastic account of the days leading to Jesus' revelation. It is written in apocalyptic language, warning of the destruction and devastation accompanying the end of the world, and the resulting triumph of good over evil.

The Gospels

The writings of Matthew, Mark, Luke, and John describe the career of Jesus Christ from four similar but different viewpoints. Also contained in these books are details on Jesus' teachings and the healings he performed.

FACT

At the time that the New Testament was compiled, there were some thirty variations of the Gospel in circulation. Of the four that were included in the New Testament canon, three are believed to have similar roots—the authors of Matthew and Luke used the gospel of Mark along with a second outside source. John was believed to have drawn on other contemporary sources.

Acts

Also known as Acts of the Apostles, this book records the earliest history of the Christian church, covering a period of about thirty years after Jesus' death and resurrection. Written by the same author as Luke, it was originally written as a sequel to the gospel of Luke.

Letters

Paul, one of the Christian church's earliest missionaries, was also quite a letter writer. Many of the twenty-one letters contained in the New Testament are believed to be his missives to the early churches and other missionaries. They are full of encouragement to the new churches and instruction for Christian living.

The Book of Revelation

The last book in the Bible is rich with symbolism and imagery depicting the second coming of Christ. It is apocalyptic literature, meaning that it warns about and predicts the future. In it are a series of divine revelations made by a prophet named John that detail the events leading to the establishment of God's kingdom on earth.

New Testament Apocrypha

Other works related to the New Testament are also considered apocryphal. They were written by various authors and for various reasons. In some cases they were meant to shed additional light on writings already in circulation; other works were penned merely as entertainment. Still others were written to spread practices and beliefs that were contradictory to church doctrine. None of these works are included in any official versions of the Bible, although they have been published in various forms.

One Bible, Many Translations

Over the years, the Bible has been translated into many different versions and into many different languages. In the English-speaking world, the King James Version, first published in 1611, was for many years the translation used in most Protestant churches. To this day, it remains the most widely circulated Bible in existence.

As the Elizabethan-style Old English contained in the King James Version became increasingly out of date, many people found it difficult to read. To make the Bible more accessible, new translations were produced. Today, the following are in wide use:

- **King James Version/New King James Version**—Still "the Bible" to many, especially those who love the poetry of its words. The New King James Version, published in 1982, retains much of the phraseology of the original, but in a modern and updated format.
- **New Revised Standard Version**—Published in 1990, this Bible is a revision of the earlier Revised Standard Version. It is similar to the King James Version in tone and feeling. Unlike the King James, it includes the Apocrypha. It is a gender neutral Bible, with words like people and humankind substituted for man and men.
- **New International Version/New International Reader's Version/ Today's New International Version**—This Bible, in all its versions, is the best selling Bible today. Easier to read than the previous versions, it uses contemporary English and is gender accurate, meaning that it

doesn't eliminate distinctions between genders as some modern translations do. There is also a gender-neutral edition available.

- **Living Bible**—This version of the Bible is actually a paraphrase that was written to help children understand the scriptures. Its simple, everyday English makes the Living Bible very easy to read, which makes it popular among people who are new to reading the Bible or whose first language isn't English.

- **New Living Translation**—One of the newer translations of the Bible, published in 1996, it too uses vocabulary and language structures that are familiar to today's readers. Although considered a new translation, it's also a revision of the Living Bible. A team of biblical scholars went back to Hebrew, Aramaic, and Greek texts to revise the previous version. In so doing, they also made some accuracy and style changes that sets the NLT apart from its predecessor. This translation is also gender neutral.

- **New American Standard Bible**—This Bible's formal tone is off-putting to some, but it's said to be the most exact English translation available.

- **Amplified Bible**—This popular translation uses a system of brackets and parentheses to convey the original meanings of Greek and Hebrew words.

- **New American Bible**—This is the Catholic version of the Bible, published under the direction of Pope Pius XII. All editions include the deuterocanonical books.

Choosing Among the Translations

With so many different Bible translations available, it can be difficult to know how to choose the one that best suits your needs. If you're new to reading the Bible, you may want to stick with a paraphrase as they're often easier to understand. However, if you want a Bible that more closely reflects the original language in which it was written, you'll want to avoid paraphrases.

Beyond this, find a Bible that speaks to you when you read it. If you're serious about studying it, definitely consider a literal translation such as the New King James, the New International Version, or the New Revised Standard Version. If you're a rookie, you might prefer a study Bible, which combines text and study materials in one volume. Other options would be a text and reference Bible, which cross-references passages for easy comparison, or a parallel Bible, which contains different Bible translations placed side-by-side for easy comparison between versions.

QUESTION?

Is any one translation of the Bible better than others?
Not necessarily, although Bible scholars will tell you that they're not all of the same quality or theological level. The translations are written to different reading levels, and some were created at different points in time, which can also alter the reading level of the text.

Studying the Bible

There are many ways to mine the Bible's resources. Some people crack it open randomly and look for inspiration on the pages that happened to open up. Others take a more structured approach and use study aids like an index or concordance to search for passages that deal with specific issues or that are attributed to certain authors. There is really no right or wrong way; only the one that works the best for you.

Martin Luther compared Bible study to gathering apples. First, he said, study the Bible as a whole and shake the whole tree. Then shake every limb and study book after book. Then shake every branch, paying attention to the chapters. Then shake each twig by carefully studying the paragraphs and the sentences. Finally, ". . . you will be rewarded if you look under each leaf by searching the meaning of the words."

The very best way to study the Bible is simply to read it daily with close attention and with prayer to see the light that shines from its pages, to meditate upon it, and to continue to read it until somehow it works itself . . . into the very warp and woof of one's being.

—Howard A. Kelly, a scientist and medical doctor

If you're serious about studying the Bible, however, it is best to have a direction or plan of attack so you know where you're going and how to get there. Along these lines, there are various tried-and-true approaches, each with its own particular merits. Study guides are available for you to follow if you need direction, and many houses of worship offer Bible study groups you can join.

Regardless of the approach you take, read prayerfully. Let God speak to you through His words. And don't rush things. You'll gain a better understanding if you read slowly and reverently.

By the Book

One of the most popular ways of studying the Bible involves reading each book, in order, from cover to cover. Members of the Christian faith sometimes prefer to start with the New Testament first. Either way, this is a good method for getting a feel for the majesty and scope of the Bible if you're unfamiliar with it.

If you're reading the Bible for the first time, focus more on your general impressions of the purpose of the book and its ideas rather than on its details. You can get more specific on subsequent readings.

Studying for Knowledge

Another popular approach involves identifying a specific idea, subject, or doctrine and studying it throughout the Bible. Also called doctrinal Bible study, you'll need a study Bible or concordance (if your Bible doesn't have a good one) to help you find the relevant passages.

QUESTION?

Is it okay to write in or underline passages in my Bible?
If you're new to Bible study you might feel uncomfortable doing it, but there's nothing wrong with marking your Bible. As you grow in your prayer practice, you'll come to cherish the notes and underlining as marks of your spiritual journey.

These are just a few of the many ways you can study the Bible. For information on other methods, check any of the many books available on the subject. Online Bible study resources exist as well. Some study Bibles even contain their own study outlines. Regardless of the method you choose, it's a good idea to take a different approach on occasion. It will keep your study fresh and lead to new insights and discoveries.

Chapter 5

Books of Prayer from Around the Globe

The Bible is a great prayer resource, but it's by no means the only one. There are many other written works, ranging from holy scripture to prayer books to devotionals, that can also help you learn more about prayer as well as help you develop your relationship with God. We'll give you a taste of the various types in the following pages.

Tapping into Wisdom from Other Faiths

You might be wondering why you should read other books about spirituality and prayer, especially those that don't relate to your own spiritual background. You may also wonder if it's all right if you do. Is it all right to read the Quran if you're not Muslim, or the siddur (prayer book) if you're not Jewish? Yes, it is.

There is a great piece of wisdom from the Bible that says, "All Scripture is given by inspiration of God, and is profitable for doctrine, for reproof, for correction, for instruction in righteousness, that the man of God may be complete, thoroughly equipped for every good work" (2 Timothy 4:16–17). To put this piece of wisdom into secular terms, it tells us that there is something of value in the spiritual writings of other faiths, and that reading these works may give us a fuller understanding of our relationship with God.

One of the benefits of exploring the history and culture of other religions through their writings is that it allows us to be more informed and tolerant in our global society. This isn't to say that you are going to agree with everything you read, or that you'll find everything you read enjoyable. On the other hand, you might find some surprises. The Quran, for example, contains many references to people and events central to both Judaism and Christianity. Interesting parallels are to be found between the teachings of Buddha and Jesus.

ESSENTIAL

When reading holy books that are outside of your spiritual background, it can be helpful to put the words into context by reading texts that explain some of the concepts within the religion itself.

One of the great things about the world today is that many of us have a great deal of control over just about every area of our lives. There is no one standing over us telling us what we can and cannot do. We can choose to believe what we want to believe, pray how we want to pray, read what we want to read. In this context, it's good to step out of your own belief system and see what someone else has to say once in a while. You might find something really beautiful there.

With this said, you'll find the suggestions that follow to be somewhat eclectic. Don't take our selections, or lack thereof, as a reflection of any bias. Some of what is here is included because we have personally enjoyed these books and have found them helpful in our own prayer lives. Others reflect works that form the basis for a well-rounded spiritual education. They all lead to a better understanding of how God is experienced in the world religions.

The Book of Common Prayer

Often referred to as "the BCP" by those who use it on a regular basis, The Book of Common Prayer (its full title is The Book of Common Prayer and the Administration of the Sacraments and other Rites and Ceremonies of the Church) is the official prayer book of the Anglican and Episcopal churches.

If you belong to one of these churches, you get to know this book pretty well as it's what you pray with whenever you attend a church service. But The Book of Common Prayer is also a great guide for individual prayer.

FACT

The term common prayer refers to the shared cycle of services of the Anglican and Episcopal churches, which include the Daily Office, the Litany, and the Eucharist. You don't have to be an Anglican or an Episcopalian to use it. In fact, the BCP is a cherished guide to prayer for many Christians of many denominations.

How the BCP Came About

The BCP was the work of Archbishop Thomas Cranmer, who produced it in 1549 as a service book for the new Church of England—a church that he played a hand in bringing about. Remember King Henry VIII and his six wives? Cranmer had gained the king's favor by suggesting ways to implement Henry's much desired divorce from his first wife, Catherine of Aragon. In fact, Cranmer ended up granting the annulment himself on the grounds that the king and his wife were relatives—her first husband, who had died, was Henry's brother—and therefore could not be legally married.

Grateful for Cranmer's assistance, King Henry VIII made Cranmer the Archbishop of Canterbury in 1533. He couldn't write his service book while Henry was alive, however, as the two didn't see eye to eye on many theological matters. After Henry died, Cranmer penned the first version of the BCP as a part of the reforms that were being introduced by the church during the reign of the new king, Edward VI.

If you are interested in seeing how the BCP has changed over the years, do an Internet search on it. You'll find many editions of the BCP, including the full text of the 1559 edition as well as one written in Hawaiian by King Kamehameha.

That first attempt at the BCP was revised many times, first by Cranmer, and then later by others. The book Cranmer first came up with was based on medieval Catholic prayer books and on the liturgies written by the early fathers of the Orthodox Church. Cranmer revised much of the other liturgies, and in doing so emphasized the reading of scripture over elaborate ceremonies as the basis for the new church's worship services. He removed other elements of Catholic ceremonies as well, and wrote the service in English instead of Latin to make it easier for more people to follow. But there were problems with this first effort, and many felt it didn't reflect the reformed nature of this new church. In 1552, Cranmer produced a rewritten version of the first book.

It's been said that no other prayer book or missal includes as complete a collection of worship services and devotional materials as The Book of Common Prayer. If you're looking for a way to put some order into your prayers, and you want to do so by following formal, written prayers, the BCP is a top pick.

What You'll Find in the BCP

Thomas Cranmer set out to write a book of prayer that would serve all the needs of the church and its members. For this reason, much of the book is devoted to corporate prayer and worship. You'll see references to "the officiant" and "the people" throughout the BCP, even in the prayers that can be said individually. If you're praying alone, consider yourself to be both parties—you read (or think) both the officiant's and the people's parts.

The Daily Office is the order of service followed by the church. It also contains prayers that can be said privately:

- The Morning Prayer, which, as its name suggests, is to be prayed in the morning.
- The Evening Prayer, which is said in the early evening.
- Compline, which is said in the final hours of the evening, usually before going to bed.

FACT

The Daily Office has its roots in Judaism, with its ancient traditions of gathering for corporate prayer (and sacrifice) in the morning. Members of the early Christian church followed the traditions of their ancestors and continued to worship together regularly.

You'll find two versions of many of the prayers in the BCP. Rite I is written in Elizabethan English. Rite II uses more contemporary wording. You can use either one. If you're new to the BCP, you may prefer the more contemporary styling of Rite II.

In addition to the prayers from the Daily Office, the BCP also contains daily devotion services. These follow the same pattern as the Daily Office prayers, but are shorter and have the psalms and readings included right in the service, which makes for much less flipping around. There is also a section called Prayers and Thanksgivings, which can be said during the Morning or Evening Prayer as well as separately. They cover just about every subject you can think of, ranging from prayers for the world to general thanksgivings.

Praying with the BCP can be somewhat confusing at first. While the prayer service itself follows a specific order, the readings vary from day to day. You'll have to get used to flipping back and forth from the service to the parts of the BCP where those readings appear. After you've done it a few times, however, it begins to make sense. The Daily Office also calls for readings from scripture, which aren't included in the book, so you'll need a Bible to pray the full office.

The Siddur

Another example of a prayer book that orders one's prayers, the siddur is the prayer book used by followers of the Jewish faith. The word *siddur*, which means "order" in Hebrew, is a good reflection of what this prayer book is all about: it specifies the order of the set prayers for the various Jewish services.

As previously mentioned, Jews say set prayers at home and in the synagogue. The siddur contains both the basic form of Jewish prayer—the blessings, when they give thanks to God at various times during the day, always prefaced with "Blessed art Thou, O Lord our God, King of the Universe"—and the three set services that are prayed in the morning, afternoon, and evening. Like the BCP, there are many versions of the siddur. Many siddurim (the plural of siddur) are printed in both English and Hebrew. Some contain transliterated text, which consists of Hebrew sounds spelled out using the English alphabet, to assist people who can't read Hebrew.

FACT

Jews treat their siddurim with great reverence as they contain the name of God. If one is dropped, it is kissed when it is picked up. Some people kiss the siddur when they're done praying with it. When a siddur is no longer usable, it is buried, not casually thrown away.

Prayers in the siddur fall into four categories: prayers of petition, prayers of thanksgiving, prayers that praise God, and prayers of soul-searching and confession.

The Quran

Revered by Muslims as the eternal and literal word of God, the Quran is Islam's key book of faith. It contains God's revelations as they were delivered to the prophet Muhammad through the angel Gabriel.

The Quran's 114 chapters, called surahs, were revealed to Muhammad over a twenty-three-year period, from the time he was forty until his death in 632 C.E. About fifteen to twenty years after Muhammad died, the entire text of the Quran was gathered into a format and order that Muslims believe was commanded by divine revelation.

People outside of the Muslim faith often avoid reading the Quran for a variety of reasons. Many feel its contents aren't relevant to their own faith. Others think they shouldn't read it because they're not Muslims. And there are those who don't want to read it and never will because they mistakenly believe that it advocates violence.

ESSENTIAL

The Quran can be difficult to get through as the text loses something in translation from Arabic to English. However, it's not necessary to read the Quran itself to gain a fuller understanding of Islam or to mine its philosophies. Plenty of books are available that explore the Quran's main literary themes and its theological perspectives without getting too heavily into the text itself.

Inside the Quran

The Quran isn't a very long work, only about four-fifths the size of the New Testament. Chapters are organized by length instead of chronologically or thematically, with the longest chapter first. Each paragraph within each chapter is considered an individual lesson to be learned and reflected on.

Similarities to the New Testament

One of the things you'll notice if you read the Quran is that parts of it parallel biblical scripture. There are references to names from the Old Testament, including Adam, Noah, Abraham, Ishmael, Isaac, and Moses, as well as references to the Garden of Eden, the parting of the Red Sea, the David and Goliath story, and the story of Joseph. Even Jesus' mother Mary appears, the only woman to do so in the Quran. These similarities are interesting because Muhammad never met Jesus Christ, and certainly never read the Bible. Nor did he have the Bible read to him. You'll also see a different interpretation of how Jesus began his life than what you'll see in New Testament.

FACT

Ramadan, the holy month in the Islam faith, is important for Muslims because it is believed to be the month during which the Quran was revealed to Muhammad (all the revelations would later be recorded by scribes, a process that took twenty-three years). Ramadan is the ninth month of the year in the Islamic calendar.

The Quran contains language that is meant to instruct Jews and Christians as well as Muslims, such as this passage:

> *Surely Those who believe, Those who are Jewish, The Christians, the converts; anyone who*
> *1) believes in God, and*
> *2) believes in the Hereafter, and*
> *3) leads a righteous life,*
> *will receive their recompense from their Lord, they have nothing To fear nor will they grieve.*
>
> *—Quran 2:62*

Such writing reflects the shared heritage of the three monotheistic religions as well as Muhammad's belief that the revelations he received were an extension of Jewish and Christian scripture.

The Imitation of Christ

Revered as one of the greatest Christian devotional works of all times, The Imitation of Christ was written in the fifteenth century by the German monk Thomas à Kempis as a means of teaching monastery novices about spirituality.

Although Thomas à Kempis is given the credit for writing The Imitation of Christ in its entirety, the works were more likely written by several monks who belonged to the same order, and compiled by à Kempis.

The Imitation of Christ remains a spiritual classic for anyone, not just monastics. It is full of good advice that rings just as true today as it has throughout the centuries. It encourages readers to become more like Jesus Christ in all aspects of their lives. But it also gives great advice on how to live a spiritual life in general. Although it's not organized in question and answer format (Book Three, however, takes the form of a dialogue between Jesus and "the disciple"), it often reads like it was written to answer specific questions posed by the novice monks. There weren't advice columnists in the fifteenth century (that we know about, anyway!), but à Kempis and his cohorts came pretty close to being the Dear Abby and Ann Landers of the Enlightenment.

Do not yield to every impulse and suggestion but consider things carefully and patiently in the light of God's will. For very often, sad to say, we are so weak that we believe and speak evil of others rather than good . . . Not to act rashly or to cling obstinately to one's opinion, not to believe everything people say or to spread abroad the gossip one has heard, is good wisdom.

—Thomas à Kempis, in The Imitation of Christ

The Imitation of Christ has been translated into more than fifty languages and thousands of editions. Several versions of this devotional classic also reside on the Internet. If you do a search for them, you'll notice that the language in some is more formal than in others. Translations do vary widely; it's a good idea to take a look at a couple of them before jumping in.

The *Bhagavad Gita*

Bhagavad Gita means "the Song of the Lord." The *Bhagavad Gita* is a Hindu religious poem that details a civil war in India. The participants are the sons of two families—the Kauruvas and the Pandavas—who are fighting over a kingdom that the Pandavas believe was stolen from them by the Kauruvas. This may not seem like the best setting for religious teachings, but it quickly turns into exactly that. During a break in the war, Arjuna, the third Pandava brother, has a chat with Krishna, his charioteer. During the conversation, Krishna gives Arjuna teachings on yoga practice—both physical and spiritual—to lead him to union with God.

The person whose mind is always free from attachment, who has subdued the mind and senses, and who is free from desires, attains the supreme perfection of freedom from (the bondage of) Karma through renunciation.

—from the *Bhagavad Gita*

The *Bhagavad Gita* is actually part of the Mahabharata, one of two ancient historical texts that relate the events that took place in India from 1400 B.C.E. to 1000 B.C.E. The *Bhagavad Gita* contains teachings on the nature of duty and devotion; the Mahabharata details dharma, which in Hinduism relates to the moral code governing the actions of warriors, kings, and anyone else who is seeking immortality. Along with the Upanishads, the *Bhagavad Gita* represents the basic religious scriptures for Hinduism.

The Tao-te Ching

Tao-te Ching means "the Way and Its Power." This sacred text, which is the basis for Taoism, is attributed to a man named Lao Tzu. We know very little about him beyond the fact that he lived in China during the sixth century B.C.E., and that he was a keeper of the archives and sacred books.

According to legend, the Tao-te Ching is the result of a border crossing gone awry. As an old man, Lao Tzu was attempting to enter a different province in China when he was stopped by the guardian of that province and asked to write down his wisdom. In a period of three days, he produced a work of about 5,000 characters.

All the word says,
"I am important;
I am separate from all the world.
I am important because I am separate.
Were I the same, I could never be important."
Yet here are three treasures
That I cherish and commend to you:
The first is compassion,
By which one finds courage.
The second is restraint,
By which one finds strength.
And the third is unimportance,
By which one finds influence.
Those who are fearless, but without compassion,
Powerful, but without constraint,
Or influential, yet important,
Cannot endure.

—Tao-te Ching

The Upanishads

The word Upanishad means "sitting down near" and implies studying with a spiritual teacher. Written by sages of India between the eighth and fourth centuries B.C.E., The Upanishads are a blend of devotions, hymns, opinions, and reflections of holy men regarding the inner meaning of traditional religious truths. They also include some of the earliest ascetic teachings that would become a part of Indian religion.

By whom directed does the mind project to its objects?
By whom commanded does the first life breath move?
By whom impelled are these words spoken?
What god is behind the eye and ear?
That which is the hearing of the ear,
the thought of the mind, the voice of the speech,
the life of the breath, and the sight of the eye.
Passing beyond, the wise leaving this world become immortal.
There the eye does not go, nor speech, nor the mind.
We do not know, we do not understand how one can teach this.
Different, indeed, is it from the known,
and also it is above the unknown.
Thus we have heard from the ancients who explained it to us.
That which is not expressed by speech,
but that by which speech is expressed:
know that to be God, not what people here adore.

—The Upanishads

Chapter 6

First Steps Toward Prayer

Prayer is difficult for many people. Some say it doesn't satisfy them, or they don't see the value in it. Often, what this really means is that they don't know how to pray. While there isn't an instruction manual to follow, there are some things to know that can help you learn how to become an effective pray-er.

Learning How to Pray

Praying—not just going through the motions or mouthing the words, but really getting to know God on a very personal, intimate level—takes some work. It also requires some sacrifices. Hard work? Sacrifice? This may not be what you want to hear about prayer. Ask anyone who prays on a regular basis, however, and he'll tell you that all of his efforts in this particular arena are more than worth it.

The payoff of all that hard work and effort is being able to experience the nearness of God. And that, frankly, is an experience like no other. Those who commit to hearing the word of God do indeed hear His voice, often in some amazing ways.

How to pray? This is a simple matter. I would say: Pray any way you like, so long as you do pray. You can pray the way your mother taught you; you can use a prayer book. Sometimes it takes courage to pray; but it is possible to pray, and necessary to pray. Whether from memory or a book or just in thought, it is all the same.

—Pope John Paul II, in *The Way of Prayer*

The idea that people have to learn how to pray, and that we have to keep on working at it, may seem odd to you. After all, if we're "wired for prayer," as some researchers believe, then we should instinctively know how to do it, right? To a certain extent, yes. One of the wonderful things about prayer is that it's really very simple. However, because we're human and we're concerned about doing things "right," we tend to make a bigger deal out of it than we need to. We read about it, we agonize over it, and we analyze it to death. We spend far more time thinking that we should pray, and wishing that we prayed, instead of just doing it. We forget what we already know, or we simply choose to ignore it.

Mother Teresa, who definitely knew a thing or two about prayer, said the best way to learn how to pray is by praying. There is a certain amount of paradox in her words. But like all paradoxes, there is also truth. Quite simply, while you can read all you want to about praying and how to pray, doing it is the only way you'll really learn how. And keeping at it is the only way you'll become effective at it. While it is possible to gain something from any effort at prayer, even the smallest and briefest dip into it, maintaining a regular prayer practice will move you forward faster and make you better at it. It's like an athlete training for a big event. Working out every once in a while does not make an Olympic champion. But doing a little bit on a consistent basis and building on those efforts can put you into medal contention.

ESSENTIAL

> Even Jesus' disciples had to be taught how to pray. His answer to them was "The Lord's Prayer," which is revered by Christians as the greatest prayer of all.

It can be difficult to move from thinking about praying to actually doing it. However, there's not much to be gained from prayer if it remains an intellectual pursuit. How can you move from thinking to doing? First, by making the commitment to becoming a person who prays. Second, by using that commitment to anchor a plan—call it a prayer plan—to give you a framework for your prayer practice.

Making a Commitment to Prayer

Getting the greatest benefits of prayer does involve making a commitment to it. If you think of prayer as a relationship with God, this makes sense. We make commitments in the relationships we have with people, even the ones we have with pets. The relationship you have with God requires doing so as well.

Making the commitment to pray, however, means more than just saying you'll do it. It means taking some active steps toward it. It also means developing the discipline that will help you honor that commitment. Discipline is a negative word for a lot of people, and it might have negative connotations for you. But, in this context, discipline doesn't mean punishment or regimentation. Instead, it refers to establishing some ground rules for your conduct in your relationship with the Almighty. Or, in other words, a structure for your prayer practice.

Here's the lowdown on why this is important: Without a certain set pattern—a discipline—to govern how and when we pray, our desire to get to know God more fully remains just that. Without being committed to this particular goal, and having a game plan to govern our efforts, we won't get to where we want to go.

FACT

The words *discipline* and *disciple* are both derived from the same Latin word, which means "pupil." In both cases, it refers to a teacher bestowing knowledge upon a student, or pupil.

Prayer itself is considered a discipline in Christianity. As such, it is one of a number of spiritual disciplines, such as meditation, fasting, and spiritual direction, some of which you'll be introduced to in other chapters of this book. When followed, these disciplines allow us to be transformed from within by God's spirit.

Discipline versus Legalism

As important as discipline is, it is also important to keep it in perspective. Discipline is not regimentation. It is not engraving things in stone. It isn't about making laws. Making it so, will only set you up for failure.

Feeling like you've completely blown it if you miss a scheduled prayer session isn't discipline, it's living by fear and shame. You're committing yourself to a lifetime of the same if you take discipline to the extreme. On the other hand, rescheduling a missed prayer session for later in the day, and doing it then, honors both your commitment to God and the discipline you've chosen to govern your time with Him.

Regimentation is not the goal here, but developing a routine and a rhythm to your prayer life can play a significant part in making prayer an ongoing part of your life.

The Disciplines are God's way of getting us into the ground; they put us where He can work within us and transform us.

—Richard Foster, in *Celebration of Discipline*

Commitment as Covenant

Commitment and discipline can also be thought of as making a covenant with God. You'll find many examples of these special agreements in the Bible. There are two types: secular covenants made between leaders and people, and spiritual covenants made between God and man.

As described in the *Oxford Companion to the Bible,* the covenants between God and the people are "all covenants of divine favor or grace. They express God's gracious commitment and faithfulness and thus establish a continuing relationship."

FACT

In the Old Testament, covenants were promises made between God and the Israelites, who agreed to worship no other gods. Throughout the Bible, all serious promises are referred to as covenants.

Some of the best examples of the covenants between God and His people can be found in the Old Testament Book of Deuteronomy. In fact, the entire book revolves around the concept of commitment and obedience. You might find it helpful to take some time to read through it as you are entering into your own covenant with the Almighty. Let the commandment to "fear the Lord your God, to walk in all His ways and to love Him, to serve the Lord your God with all your heart and with all your soul," (Deuteronomy 10:12) guide you in forming your own covenant with Him.

Scheduling Your Prayer Time

If it seems silly to talk about learning how to pray, it may seem even more ridiculous to talk about scheduling the time for doing it. However, honoring your commitment to God means putting aside a certain period of time every day during which you do nothing else but talk to Him. Determining when you're going to pray and how long you're going to do it is part of your plan for success.

I strongly believe that one should have a personal spiritual discipline—whatever it might be—and regularly practice it. I start the day by reading a few verses from the Bible, since that is my tradition. I pray a morning prayer as soon as I get up. I keep a little icon near my bed right at the window so I can look out and see the world. My prayer has a whole series of things I say and it varies a bit from week to week in its pattern. This is a must for me.
—Harvard theologian Harvey Cox, in the journal *Sacred Journey*

It's somewhat of a sad statement about our world today that it's necessary to schedule prayer time, but this is indeed the case. A good majority of the people who pray say that their prayer lives would be sorely lacking if they merely tried to fit prayer into their schedules instead of setting aside a specific time for it.

FACT

According to researchers at the Center for Media Studies at Rutgers, the State University of New Jersey, television has a hypnotic effect. It also acts as a sedative by increasing the brain's alpha waves and slowing its beta waves.

There is no one best time for prayer, but it's a good idea to choose a time when you won't feel rushed. If your schedule is so jam-packed that you don't see how you can avoid hurrying through your prayers, take another look at how you spend your time. There are lots of wasted moments in a day, time that could be better spent doing something else. If, like most Americans, you watch four or more hours of television a day, it's pretty obvious where your time is being wasted. Tuning into the "boob tube" has often been called an addiction, but there is new research that actually supports this claim. One of the best things you can do for your brain and your psyche is to kick this particular habit. What better to replace it with than some good conversation with your best friend?

The second consideration in choosing a prayer time is determining a time at which you can be at your most attentive. Many people prefer to pray early in the morning before they get caught up in the pressures and demands of their everyday lives. Spending time alone with God before the rest of your household is awake, or perhaps as everyone else is beginning to stir, can make a crazy world seem a little saner. However, if you're really not a morning person, don't set yourself up for failure by deciding that the wee hours of the day are for you. Praying at night can have the same benefits as it allows us to look back on the events of the day and reflect on how we experienced God in them.

Many beginning pray-ers feel most comfortable with the traditional times for prayer—upon arising in the morning and before going to bed at night. But they're by no means the only times of day during which praying can be done. If you're working in an office away from home, you might like to break up your day by praying during your lunch hour, or maybe during the ride to or from work. The idea is to find a time that works for you, and that will work for you regularly. If it's in your car during the afternoon rush hour, so be it.

> The work of religion has been compared to the doing of exercises, wherein we desire to have our hearts engaged in God. Metaphors like "running the race," "wrestling with God," "striving for the great prize," and "fighting with strong enemies" are often used to describe the exercises we engage in.
>
> —Jonathan Edwards, in *Religious Affections*

Prayer Duration

The third part of your prayer plan calls for determining how long your daily prayer periods will be. There is nothing that dictates how much time you should spend praying, but there is lots of evidence to support the theory of more being better. The apostle Paul felt that prayer should be unceasing. In the Book of Thessalonians, he exhorted the followers of

Christ to "Pray constantly, and for all things give thanks to God, because this is what God expects you to do . . ." (1 Thessalonians 5:17–18). John Wesley, the founder of the Methodist church, devoted two hours of his day to prayer. Martin Luther did him one better and prayed for three hours a day.

More, however, isn't necessarily better. In fact, focusing on God for short periods of time is definitely superior to praying for hours while your mind is elsewhere. Given the choice, it's better to work with less rather than more, and do it right. Emphasize quality over quantity.

If you're new to prayer, keep it short and simple. Start with a few minutes a day. If you feel like extending your prayer time, by all means do so. But don't feel like you have to spend hours in prayer, or that you're letting God down if you can only manage five minutes a day. You won't earn any gold stars if you go longer, or get demerits for brevity. On the other hand, the more time you spend talking to God, the more you'll get out of it. Let God's spirit lead you both into and out of your prayer time, and the amount of time you spend in prayer will be right and perfect.

Determining a Place for Prayer

The next step in your prayer plan is deciding where you're going to pray. Ideally, it should be a place that you can use every day of the year, come rain or come shine. While there's nothing that beats the experience of talking to God in the midst of nature, having to deal with the "come rain or come shine" factor often means praying indoors at home.

There's a basic practicality to home-based prayer, which is why it's the dominant choice for those who pray daily. You can't beat the convenience, and the doors are always open. If you want to visit a Web site as part of your prayer routine, you can do so without your boss or coworkers wondering what the heck you're doing. No one cares if you're in your pajamas and your hair isn't combed. God certainly doesn't, anyway.

On the downside, praying at home can pose real problems if you have young children who don't understand why Mommy or Daddy can't come out and play right now, or you have a particularly pesky pet who insists on being fed at this exact moment and won't leave you alone until you do something about it.

Where you pray can also affect when you pray. If you want to pray in church or at home when everyone else is asleep, you'll have to plan accordingly. The best approach is to find a place and a time that suits you best, is accessible, and lacks distractions.

If you're going to pray at home, do yourself and everyone else a favor and set aside a specific place in which to do it. Preferably, the spot you choose should be far enough away from your house's main traffic pattern so you don't have to deal with noise, clutter, and interruptions. Your space doesn't have to be spacious. In fact, it can be as small as a corner in your bedroom. Even a pantry or a linen closet will do as long as there is enough ventilation.

Room permitting, you might want to spiff up your prayer space by turning it into a sacred space. This can be a real boon to your prayer practice, especially if you live in an area where it's difficult to get away and connect to nature. You can make your space as simple or lavish as you wish. Possible elements include plants, a fountain, a meditation cushion, a table-top Zen-style sand garden, a finger labyrinth—really, just about anything goes. Other options (you'll read more about them in Chapter 8 as well) include candles, icons, a cross, or a crucifix.

We can pray perfectly when we are out in the mountains or on a lake and we feel at one with nature. Nature speaks for us or rather speaks to us. We pray perfectly.
—Pope John Paul II, in *The Way of Prayer*

What you're after is a contemplative environment that supports all aspects of your prayer practice and helps you stay focused. Make it special, and make it yours. After all, this relationship you're working on—the one between you and God—is a pretty special thing. Spending the time with Him in a space dedicated to mindfulness can make what is already a pretty wonderful experience into a joyous celebration of spirit.

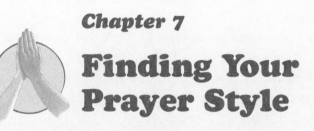

Chapter 7

Finding Your Prayer Style

Each of us experiences God in a different way, and we stand before Him as unique beings. No two people pray exactly alike, but the results are the same. We enter into fellowship with God. We learn more about Him, and in the process, learn more about ourselves as well.

Lots of Ways to Pray

There is no right or wrong way to pray, only different ways—in fact, many different ways—in which to do it. What's more, you can decide the approach you want to take. There are no exact rules to follow, nor any boundaries to mind.

People who are new to prayer tend to think that one method of praying is better than the others, or that there is one specific way of praying that will guarantee that their prayers will be heard. In fact, they may even have been told these things at some point or another. But they are wrong on both counts.

There are no objective or subjective scales when it comes to prayer. In other words, there is no one prayer style that is any better or any worse than the others. This isn't to say that you won't find some methods of praying more to your liking than others. These will be the ones that will be more effective for you. Prayers said while kneeling have no greater chance of reaching God's ears than those said when sitting upright. What's important is that we pray, not that we pray in a way that we think we have to.

A full and balanced prayer life consists of many different kinds and styles of prayer. What's more, the best pray-ers tailor their approach to meet their needs. Since those needs change, so too do their prayer styles. Casual prayers, ones that are offered up to God at all times of the day and night, are the foundation of living a life of prayer. But this doesn't mean that praying casually is the only way in which we should pray. There will also be times when we'll need to talk to God in a more formal manner, both on our own and when we're praying with others.

Private Prayer

Private prayer—spending time alone with God—is the dominant prayer style for most people. It's the easiest style to fit into busy schedules as you can do it anywhere and at any time. You're not constrained by anything other than your own limits. There is no waiting for church doors to open or other people to arrive.

FACT

You can think of private prayers as "instant prayers," as you can do them at any time without constraint. You can pray a private prayer any time you have a spare minute or two. When you do so, you share an intimate moment with God.

If you're going to follow the biblical precept to "pray without ceasing," it stands to reason that you'll spend most of your life praying to God on your own. But there are other reasons beyond unceasing prayer to spend lots of personal time with God.

Private prayer is, more than anything else, intimate. These are the times in which you'll feel most closely connected to the Almighty. When it's only you and God together, wherever and whenever it may be, you can communicate with Him in any way you choose. You can talk out loud or speak your words silently. You can pray whatever is on your mind or follow a set order of prayer. You can sing to Him, laugh with Him, cry with Him, even yell at Him. You can dance with Him or simply sit still and be at rest with Him. Because there are no constraints in place, you can run the gamut of emotions if you need to and not worry one bit about what anyone else might think or say.

ESSENTIAL

Praying without ceasing may be a difficult concept to grasp if you're new to prayer. It doesn't mean that you're going to spend your entire life praying at the exclusion of everything else. What it does mean is carrying out your daily activities with God at your side, and talking to Him on a regular basis.

Praying privately is also a reflection of where you are in your relationship with God. It means you're not afraid to come before Him alone. Since there is no one else to see or hear you pray, it also means that you're praying for the right reasons. You're not praying to please anyone else or to show the world how devout and dedicated you are to prayer. In other words, you're not, as Jesus put it in the Book of Matthew, "practicing your piety before others."

Take heed that you do not do your charitable deeds before men, to be seen by them. Otherwise you have no reward from your Father in heaven. Therefore, when you do a charitable deed, do not sound a trumpet before you as the hypocrites do in the synagogues and in the streets, that they may have glory from men. Assuredly, I say to you, they have their reward. But when you do a charitable deed, do not let your left hand know what your right hand is doing, that your charitable deed may be in secret; and your Father who sees in secret will Himself reward you openly. And when you pray, you shall not be like the hypocrites. For they love to pray standing in the synagogues and on the corners of the streets, that they may be seen by men. Assuredly, I say to you, they have their reward. But you, when you pray, go into your room, and when you have shut your door, pray to the Father who is in the secret place; and your Father who sees in secret will reward you openly.

—Matthew 6:2–6

Private prayer generally takes one of two forms. The first is rational prayer, or prayers of the mind, in which we express our thoughts to God in words and sentences, either out loud or silently. This is the type of prayer that is familiar to most people, and the style of prayer followed by most. When we refer to talking with God, this is the prayer style we're talking about.

The other form of private prayer relies more on connecting to God in a deeper, more holistic or intrinsic way. Instead of using words to communicate with God, we use our hearts. We stay quiet. We listen to Him instead of talking at Him. We open our minds, hearts, bodies, and emotions to God, and allow Him to enter in.

Corporate Prayer

Corporate prayer means coming together with other people to pray. It can be done informally, such as in prayer groups, or formally in houses of worship such as churches, monasteries, synagogues, and mosques. Corporate prayer is also called communal prayer.

The gathering together of pray-ers goes back to biblical times and even before. There are numerous references to it in the Old Testament. While Jesus encouraged his disciples to pray alone, he also recommended that they experience the fellowship of praying together, saying, "For where two or three are gathered together in My name, I am there in the midst of them" (Matthew 18:20). The early Christians clearly took Jesus' words to heart as they prayed together often.

When we come together with others in prayer, we're linking to them by having similar intentions and purposes. We become a community of faith, and we can draw on the resources of that community to help us in many ways. If we need strength, the members of the community can strengthen us. If we need caring, they can care for us. If we need prayer, they can pray for us.

If you are praying in a small group, such as a prayer or Bible study group, your prayers can still be fairly intimate, especially if you are with people you know, or feel you can come to know, and you feel comfortable in their presence.

Doing spiritual practice in the midst of busy activity is like lifting the heavy weights. Just because you can do it only once, for a moment, does not mean that it has no effect. On the contrary, it exercises your spiritual "muscles" as much as doing many repetitions with the light weights, just in a different way.
—Lewis Richmond, in *Work as a Spiritual Practice*

Praying with larger groups, such as those in churches and other houses of worship, however, is often a very different ballgame. You may be with a group of people that you know well, you like, and you feel comfortable with. Then again, you may be surrounded by complete strangers. Because of this, prayer in large groups is oftentimes much less personal in nature. Instead of praying for your own needs, you're praying for the corporate body—the church, the synagogue, and its people. This kind of prayer is important as it takes you out of yourself—it shifts your focus to the interests and needs of your prayer community, and it makes you a part of the community's concerns.

The hallmark of public or corporate prayer are worship services, or liturgies. They range from informal to very formal. You'll find the greatest range of style in Christian churches, which fall into two basic categories:

1. Churches that follow a traditional liturgy, consisting of written prayers from a prayer book, a short sermon, and the sacraments. This is the worship style followed by Roman Catholic, Episcopal, Orthodox, and Lutheran churches, as well as some Methodist and Presbyterian churches.
2. Churches that follow a free form, or free-worship form. Here, the emphasis is less on following a formal liturgy and more on extemporaneous prayers. The sermon, rather than the sacraments, is a big part of the service. Many churches that follow this style don't use prayer books. This is the worship style that you'll find in many Protestant churches, including Baptist, Assembly of God, Church of God, Nazarene, Evangelical Free, and Wesleyan, as well as independent churches that are not affiliated with any particular denomination.

Jewish liturgies also vary in format and style. You'll find the most formal services in Orthodox synagogues. Reform congregations generally have the least formal liturgy, while Conservative congregations are somewhere in between.

Some people find great beauty in the formality of traditional liturgical worship services. To others, they're complete yawners.

One of the advantages of having a written and printed service is that it enables you to see when people's feelings and thoughts have changed. When people begin to find the words of our service difficult to join in, that is of course a sign that we do not feel about those things exactly as our ancestors.

—C. S. Lewis, in *God in the Dock*

What is definitely true is that it can be hard to find a personal connection to God through the words of others, no matter how beautifully crafted and patterned they might be. At the same time, more extemporaneous or free services that allow worshippers greater rein in how they pray during the service can also miss the mark.

On first blush, it may seem like private prayer has a distinct edge over corporate prayer. In many respects, it does. When you're talking to God on a one-on-one basis, you have substantially more control over the situation. You can choose how you want to talk to Him, where you want to talk to Him, and how long you're going to do it. When you pray with a group, you have to follow along with the pack for the most part. However, it's best not to have either form of prayer take precedence over the other in your prayer life. This isn't to say that you should, or need to spend as much time praying with others as you do on your own. However, spending too much time on your own in prayer is also not desirable. There's a certain synergy that develops when you combine corporate prayer with personal prayer. Do one to the exclusion of the other, and you miss out on what the other style has to offer.

QUESTION?

How can I find a church with a worship service that will fit my own prayer style?
There isn't any one type of church that will. Nor will the church that your best friend really connects with necessarily be one that speaks to your heart. Your best bet is to visit a few different churches and experience their worship services for yourself.

Patterning Your Prayer

When you pray as part of a group in a house of worship, your prayers will follow a certain pattern as set by the order of service followed by the group. When you pray by yourself, on the other hand, you don't have to follow a set pattern unless you want to. You can speak extemporaneously, simply saying what's on your mind if you so choose. Or you can be more formal. You can structure your prayers in a certain order or pattern. This can be especially helpful if you're new to prayer and you're not sure what you should pray about.

Acting Up

When we pray, our prayers generally fall into four basic categories. We're either praising God, humbling ourselves before Him by admitting we're not perfect people, thanking Him, or asking Him for His help. ACTS, which stands for Adoration, Confession (or Contrition), Thanksgiving, and Supplication, is a prayer pattern based on these four categories, bringing them together in a neat little bundle.

Adoration

Prayers of adoration are prayers that simply bless God. When we say them, we're both praising Him and telling Him how much we appreciate our relationship with Him. As we bless Him, we in turn are blessed.

Some people have a hard time praising God. They get awestruck and tongue-tied when trying to express their appreciation to God. If you're one of them, know that a simple "Bless you, God," will suffice. You can also rely on the adoration prayers of others, and there are plenty of these to choose from in the Bible. Once again, your greatest resource is the Book of Psalms, as the majority of the psalms praise God in some way. Choose the ones that speak to you.

Confession

Confession, which calls for declaring your sins before God, is a part of prayer that some people have trouble with. Why is this important? Unconfessed sin can stand in the way of your prayer life, and keep you from both wanting to pray and from receiving all that God can bestow upon you. Yes, it is important to come before God in whatever place you're in. But that doesn't mean trying to cover things up that you should be telling Him about. He knows about them anyway, and it's important for you to come before Him and take ownership and responsibility for your actions.

What kinds of things should you confess? Any action or thought that you're not particularly proud of. If you feel bad about yelling at the dog, tell God. If you think you could have been a little more compassionate when a coworker came to you seeking some advice, out with it, too.

Some people change ACTS into CATS so they can begin their prayer sessions by "coming clean" to God.

Thanksgiving

It is always important to give thanks to God, even at times when we don't much feel like doing it. Thanking Him for what we have serves as a reminder of where we are in relationship to Him. It acknowledges God's love for us and our love for Him, and it reminds us of what He has done in our lives. Perhaps most important, taking the time to reflect on the things we have and thanking God for them helps us put into better perspective the things that we do not have.

Praising [God] is not something we do because we feel good; rather it is an act of obedience. Often the prayer of praise is done in sheer teeth-gritting willpower; yet when we persist in it, somehow the power of God is released into us and into the situation.
—Merlin R. Carothers, in *Prison to Praise*

Supplication

Supplication, the last part of ACTS, is when we make requests of God and ask Him for His help on various matters. These prayers are offered for ourselves and for others. Supplication means addressing humble requests and prayers to somebody with the power to grant them—in this case, God.

There are many things that you can pray to God for in this final stage. Here are just a few:

- Yourself, for your physical daily needs and to help you grow in devotion to God.
- Your family, including children, parents, siblings, and so forth.
- Your community, and especially those in power and authority, that they will seek God's counsel in making wise decisions.
- The sick, both for their restoration to health and for spiritual peace and strength.

- The poor and oppressed throughout the world.
- Those who do not know God.

Following the Hours

Another way to order your prayer is to follow the Liturgy of the Hours. Also known as the Divine Office, this is a liturgy with very deep and ancient roots. The Liturgy of the Hours consists of prayers, psalms, and meditations for every hour of every day. If you're looking for a way to pray without ceasing, you'll find it in the Hours. Furthermore, the readings change every day.

While the Liturgy of the Hours is often associated with the Catholic Church, it can be prayed by anyone. Online resources are available to keep you going through the liturgy, as well as a version that can be downloaded to PDAs (personal digital assistants). The basic structure looks like this:

- Lauds, or the Morning Prayer, to be said the first thing in the morning.
- The Little Hours, also known as Prayer through the Day. (These are short prayers said at certain times during the day.)
- Vespers, also known as Evening Prayer or Evensong.
- Compline, also called Night Prayer, which is the last prayer of the day.

The Liturgy of the Hours also includes the Office of Readings, which can be said at any time of the day.

Finding Your Prayer Posture

People pray in all sorts of positions—standing up, sitting down, kneeling, even lying prostrate. They stretch out their hands to God or fold their hands neatly in supplication. They look up to the heavens, or cast their eyes downward.

Where did all of these prayer postures come from? They're ancient as the hills. The custom of praying with the arms outstretched and raised dates back to antiquity and was common to both Jews and Gentiles.

FACT

Among the subjects pictured in the art of the Roman catacombs is that of a female figure in supplication with her arms outstretched. She's known as Orans, or "one who prays."

The posture you choose to pray in is of no great importance in and of itself, but it is important in that it shows respect and reverence to God. In the past, some churches specified that people should stand during public prayer and kneel when praying privately, but most don't get quite so specific anymore. Certain positions are more helpful for some people than for others. Some simply work better at certain times than at others. Kneeling and prostration, for example, are appropriate when we are saying prayers of petition, confession, or repentance. Raising our hands to God just comes naturally when we're praising Him or giving Him thanks. Sitting in a lotus position (or as near as you can get to one) is the classic position for more meditative forms of prayer.

How to choose which prayer position is right for you? Try the ones that appeal to you, and maybe add one that doesn't. Pick one that allows you to be relaxed, yet attentive. And don't be afraid to mix them up. There is nothing that says that one prayer position is more effective than any other.

Here are a few to consider, along with passages from the Bible that talk about them:

- **Kneeling—**"Now when Daniel knew that the writing was signed, he went home. And in his upper room, with his windows open toward Jerusalem, he knelt down on his knees three times that day, and prayed and gave thanks before his God, as was his custom since early days" (Daniel 6:10).

- **Sitting**—"Then King David went in and sat before the Lord; and he said: Who am I, O Lord God? and what is my house, that You have brought me this far." (2 Samuel 7:18)
- **Bowing**—"Then the man bowed down his head and worshiped the Lord." (Genesis 24:26)
- **Standing**—"Then Solomon stood before the altar of the Lord in the presence of all the congregation of Israel, and spread out his hands toward heaven." (1 Kings 8:22)
- **Hands raised**—"Therefore I desire that the men pray everywhere, lifting up holy hands, without wrath or doubting." (1 Timothy 2:8)
- **Face down**—"So Moses and Aaron went from the presence of the assembly to the door of the tabernacle of meeting, and they fell on their faces. And the glory of the Lord appeared to them." (Numbers 20:6)
- **Walking**—"And what does the Lord require of you But to do justly, To love mercy, And to walk humbly with your God?" (Micah 6:8)

QUESTION?

Is it okay to pray in bed?
Absolutely. Many people spend a few minutes in prayer before they go to sleep at night and in the mornings when they wake up. If you find yourself falling asleep while you're praying, simply resume your prayers when you wake up.

Some people feel that you should stay in one position during your prayer time, as moving around may be disruptive to your prayers. Others will tell you that there is nothing wrong with moving around at will when you're praying. Contemplative prayers, however, do call for staying very still and in one position throughout the prayer period. The best approach to take is to match your prayer position with the kind of prayer that you're doing.

Chapter 8

Prayer Tools

Getting into a prayerful state often entails removing ourselves from the distractions that sight and sound can create. This is just one way in which we can more closely focus our efforts on prayer, but it's by no means the only one. Sometimes that focus can be found by keeping our eyes and ears open and treating them to prayer aids that delight the senses. In this chapter, we'll discuss various aspects of the more sensual side of prayer, and how these tools can be used to enhance your prayer experience.

Visual Prayer Tools

The world's religions are rich in visual imagery, symbols, and icons, with many of them dating back to the earliest recorded history. The Christian church used paintings and mosaics to teach and enlighten followers from its earliest times. Images from the Old and New Testaments have adorned most aspects of church architecture, including ceilings, walls, altars, and windows. They are also used to decorate furniture, liturgical vessels, and books. Other commonly used images were inspired by the lives and legends of the saints and from mythology.

The various tools of prayer—crosses, icons, candles, prayer beads, and such—are meant to enhance the prayer experience, not supplant it. Thinking about how much you love God while you're lighting some incense doesn't substitute for spending some time in prayer with Him.

Visual symbols were also not foreign to ancient followers of Judaism. God had forbidden the creation of graven images in the Second Commandment—"You shall not make for yourself any carved image, or any likeness of anything that is in heaven above, or that is in the earth beneath, or that is in the water under the earth; you shall not bow down to them nor serve them" (Deuteronomy 5:8–9). However, God's directive only prohibited making images of anything in heaven or earth for the purposes of worship. In other words, there was a distinction made between graven images that would be worshipped, and graven images in general.

Images of bull calves, cherubim, palm trees, and flowers covered the walls and the doors of the temple. Two cherubs decorated the top of the Ark of the Covenant. Biblical figures dating back to 235 C.E. were also found on the walls of a synagogue in Syria that was discovered in the 1920s. Such Old Testament scenes as Moses descending from Mount Sinai, the parting of the Red Sea, and David in scenes of battle, often rendered in stained glass, grace some modern synagogues. However, in keeping with Jewish tradition, there are never any physical representations of God.

But remember to be careful when adding visual elements to your prayer space. Adding so many visual aids to your prayer space that they distract you rather than help you focus on God makes them, rather than God, the object of your attention. When adding prayer aids to your prayer practice, remember their proper place, and keep their use in perspective.

FACT

In biblical times, cherubim were supernatural creatures associated with the presence of God. Today we think of them as angels. They are often depicted in artwork as beautiful young children with wings.

Crosses and Crucifixes

One of the key symbols of faith, the cross is today associated almost wholly with the Christian faith. In reality, however, this particular symbol predates Christianity. Primitive cruciform signs can be traced back to early Oriental and Indian religious practices, where, it is believed, they represented the sun or the sacred fire of the ancestors. In ancient Egypt, a form of the cross called a tau, which looks like a capital "T," was the symbol of life. The Greeks were also familiar with the form of the cross, and associated its four points with the four elements—earth, water, fire, and air. Cruciform signs have also been found in pre-Columbian ruins in North America, and in ancient Western European megaliths.

Unlike other ancient civilizations, the Romans never viewed the cross as a symbol of faith or spirituality. Instead, they used it as an instrument of torture. It was, of course, used to crucify Jesus, and it was also used to punish many others, in particular individuals who could not prove their Roman citizenship or who stole or committed other crimes. In many respects, it's ironic that an object with such a history would become such an important symbol of faith. Soon after Christ's death, however, it became symbolic for all that Jesus stood for. Early followers of Christianity placed crosses in their homes to symbolize their dedication to their beliefs, and the cross soon became a key element in Christian worship.

As the leading symbol of Christian faith, crosses and crucifixes abound. They come in a variety of forms. The Latin cross, with its single longer vertical element, is the most commonly seen. The Greek cross, which has four arms of equal length and looks like a "+" sign, is also a familiar version.

Other cross forms include:

- **The St. Andrew's cross**—One of the most ancient, and often seen in ancient sculpture; it resembles the letter "X".
- **The Celtic cross**—First used in sixth-century Ireland by Celtic Christians, it is essentially a Latin cross with a circle in its center overlying the axis of the horizontal and vertical elements. The circle signifies eternity.
- **The Eastern Orthodox cross** (also called Byzantine Cross, the Eastern Cross, and the Russian Orthodox Cross)—This cross of early Christianity has three horizontal bars of different lengths crossing one vertical bar. A short bar at the top represents the inscription that Pontius Pilate posted above Christ's head. Close to the bottom is a tilted lower bar that is a bit longer than the top bar, which represents a footrest.
- **The Maltese Cross**—The arms on this cross are all equal in length. Each arm looks similar to an isosceles triangle, with the single points meeting in the middle of the cross. The eight points formed by the arms represent the eight Beatitudes of Matthew.

When a cross is affixed with a representation of the body of Christ it is called a crucifix. The carved figure of Christ's body is called the corpus.

According to church legend, the St. Andrew's cross leans on its side because St. Andrew didn't feel worthy of being crucified in the same manner as Jesus was and asked that his cross be made differently. However, more modern sources identify this cross form with the saint only from the fourteenth century onward.

Icons

An integral part of the traditions of the Orthodox church, icons are depictions of holy figures—often the Holy Trinity, the Holy Family, or Jesus and Mary—and religious events. They can be and often are beautiful works of art, but they are meant to do much more than merely delight the eyes. To followers of the Orthodox faith, they are the means through which the kingdom of God can be experienced on earth. For this reason, icons are often referred to as "windows into heaven."

Jesus himself is believed to be the first iconographer, having created an image of his face on a linen cloth as a healing gift for a king. This icon, known as "Not Made by Human Hands" or the "Holy Face," no longer exists in its original form, but copies of it are still being produced to this day. A similar story credits the first icon as having appeared on a cloth given to Jesus by Veronica, one of the women who comforted him as he was carrying the cross. According to church history, the apostle Luke was the first to actually paint an icon. He painted a living subject—the Virgin Mary—whose face he had seen for himself. When he presented the images he had created to her, she gave them her blessing and said that Christ's grace would be imparted to them.

FACT

At least three of the icons that Luke created of the Virgin Mary are still in existence, including a portrait of the Virgin Mary holding Jesus as an infant (the first such depiction). Luke is also credited with painting icons of Peter and Paul.

Many early church leaders kept icons front and center to inspire them during their studies and devotions. Over time, the practice was embraced by laypeople as well. Throughout the centuries, people have contemplated icons and have prayed before, with, and to that which the icons represent. In so doing, they have accessed the spirit of the saints they portray in order to deepen their connection to God.

Icons were traditionally created by monks who lived in seclusion. Instead of canvas, which was deemed too fragile to withstand the hard use that icons are often subjected to, the monks painted on solid blocks of wood, using as many as thirty layers of paint and lacquer to create the holy images. As opposed to other forms of sacred art, in which subjects are often depicted in more natural or representational styles, the rules of iconography dictate that the saints not be portrayed as they appeared in real life. Instead, their images are meant to reflect their spirit, and especially that spirit as experienced and interpreted by the iconographer.

To this day, iconographers create their images using specific artistic devices that are unique to iconography. To a casual observer, these techniques may seem rather odd and rudimentary. Faces and bodies are highly stylized and flat, bearing no shadowing or shading to make them look three-dimensional, and therefore lifelike. Details are minimal, with scenery and other settings, and are rendered as simply as possible. Perspectives are placed in such a way that the viewer's eye is drawn into and toward the subject of the icon. Clothing takes the shape of geometric forms—triangles, rectangles, and ovals—that demonstrate a heavenly order.

Orthodox icons were originally meant to be used only for religious veneration. In the twentieth century, however, they became highly sought after as collectible works of art, especially after the fall of communism and the resurgence of the Orthodox faith in many Eastern European countries where its practice had been prohibited.

Even the colors used in icons are dictated by tradition to a large extent, although there will be some differences based on local traditions, the materials available, and the iconographer himself. Blue, the color associated with heaven, mystery, and the mystical life, is primarily used for Christ's outer garment or mantle as well as the clothing of Mary. Red, associated with life and vitality, is used for Christ's tunic or inner garment. A deeper red or wine color is used to depict the Virgin Mary's outer garment.

Candles

With their warm flames leaping and dancing with life, candles have long been used to enhance religious ceremonies, worship, and prayer, far beyond their basic function of bringing light into darkness. It's hard to think of a religion where candles, flame, or fire don't play a role in one way or another.

In Judaism, the flame symbolizes the soul. A special candle called a yartzeit candle (meaning "year" and "time" in Yiddish) is customarily lit on the anniversary of a family member's death to commemorate the travel of the individual's soul from its earthly plane. Candles are lit both at the beginning of the Sabbath observance and at its end. Some families light a candle for each member of the family, or for each person who is present at the beginning of the Sabbath. The candle that closes the Sabbath—the Havdallah candle—is braided and has more than one wick, which symbolizes harmony, love, and the coming together of the souls during the Sabbath remembrance. During Hanukkah—the Festival of Light— the rededication of the Temple in Jerusalem in 165 b.c.e. is symbolized by eight days of candle lighting.

Blessed are You, Lord, our God, King of the Universe, who sanctifies us with his commandments, and commands us to light the candles of Shabbat.

—The blessing said over the Sabbath candles

Flame, or fire, is a common symbol for God's presence in scripture. In 1 Kings, Elijah tells the children of Israel that the God "who answers by fire" is the true God (I Kings 18:24). In Hebrews, God is described as a "consuming fire" (Hebrews 12:29). In Deuteronomy, God's voice is described as "speaking out of the midst of the fire" (Deuteronomy 4:33).

For Christians, the flame also symbolizes Christ's divine presence. Candles are used to symbolize him as the "true light," and to remind those who follow him of their commitment to their faith. Candles are also lit in memory of the dead and in other special devotions. Catholics light candles as part of the veneration of saints. When praying privately, many Christians light a candle when they pray to signify Christ's presence in their lives.

The Sweet Smell of Incense

Fragrancing is as old as history itself, and the use of fragrance—primarily as incense—in worship dates back to the earliest times as well. The people of the ancient Near East used it both cosmetically and in religious ceremonies, and its application spread widely from there. Both Ovid and Virgil document the use of incense in early Roman worship.

Frankincense and myrrh, the two main types of incense used in ancient times, come from two types of resinous trees that grow in parts of the Middle East, Africa, and India. Both are obtained by cutting or peeling the bark of the tree and harvesting the resins and gum that flow out.

The ancient Egyptians were particularly fond of incense and used it widely for fragrancing, in religious rituals, and in preparing bodies for entombment. Images of kings burning incense in censers similar to those that are still used today in Roman Catholic, Orthodox, and Anglican churches can be seen in the carvings on Egyptian tombs and temples.

FACT

A censer is a fireproof vessel, usually suspended from chains, used for burning incense. Also called a thurible, a censer consists of a cup or bowl, which rests on a firm base, and a hollow movable pan for holding ignited charcoal, plus a lid.

Over time, incense was used to both enhance prayer practice and to symbolize prayers as they traveled upward to God. Incense also factored heavily in ancient Jewish rituals, and there are numerous references to its use in the Old Testament. In the Book of Exodus, Moses was commanded by God to "take sweet spices, stacte and oncycha and galbanum, and pure frankincense with these sweet spices . . . You shall make of these an incense, a compound according to the art of the perfumer . . . And you shall beat some of it very fine, and put some of it before the Testimony in the tabernacle of meeting where I will meet with you. It shall be most holy to you" (Exodus 30:34–36). In Leviticus, Moses' brother Aaron was instructed to present a bull to God as a sin offering. To protect himself from the presence of God, he was also told to ". . . take a censer full of burning coals of fire from the altar before the Lord, with his hands full of sweet incense beaten fine, and bring it inside the veil. And he shall put the incense on the fire before the Lord, that the cloud of incense may cover the mercy seat . . . lest he die." (Leviticus 16:12–13). According to the gospels of the New Testament, frankincense and myrrh mixed with gold were given to the infant Jesus by the Magi, or the Three Kings.

The use of incense in Christian worship services also dates back to ancient times as many of the church's rites and ceremonial observances were based on Jewish worship forms. However, there aren't many references to burning incense in the New Testament, and its use fell out of favor when the practice of blood sacrifice was halted after the destruction of the Jewish temple in 70 c.e. It's not known exactly when or why incense was reintroduced to Christian worship, but its use is documented from the fifth century on and most believe that it played a role in Christian ceremonies earlier than this.

QUESTION?

Can the same kind of incense that's burned while praying be used at other times during the day?
While reserving the incense you use during prayer to these periods can add a special significance to the practice, there is nothing that says you can't use your prayer incense at other times of the day. Many people like to light some incense to create a sense of calm and peace when they get home from work or before they go to bed.

Incense continues to play a key role in the spiritual practices of many of the world's faiths. Buddhists burn it during festivals and initiations in addition to daily prayer. The Hindus use it for ritual and domestic offerings. In China incense is burned to honor ancestors and household gods. In Japan it is part of many Shinto rituals. Many American Indians burn fragrant herbs as part of their prayer rituals, either as an element of cleansing or as an offering to the Great Spirit.

Incense is also a wonderful adjunct to home worship. It engages a very ancient part of the brain called the limbic system, which is the brain's emotional and memory center and also houses the sense of smell. Depending on the type of incense burned, the practice can be healing, soothing, or uplifting.

FACT

Resin incense, such as that used in ancient times, comes in small chunks or powdered form. If it's in chunk form, users typically grind it into a powder using a mortar and pestle. The powder is then sprinkled on a piece of long-burning charcoal that is held in a heat-resistant container. Stronger forms of resin incense, such as frankincense and myrrh, are often combined with milder forms like copal and benzoin, or with other additives.

Prayer Counters

Another prayer tradition shared by Eastern and Western faiths is the use of beads or other objects to count or focus prayer. This, too, is an ancient tradition, with evidence of it dating back to the Assyrian empire of the Old Testament. In early times, people would drop tiny pebbles into their laps to keep count of their prayers. About 500 years before Christ, it became customary to tie knots in strings. Christians, Buddhists, Hindus, and Muslims today use various kinds of prayer counters to assist them when they're praying repetitive prayers.

Ropes and Rosaries

One of the best-known forms of prayer counters are the rosaries used by Roman Catholics. They consist of a string of 150 beads, divided into groups of ten. Prayers, such as the "Hail Mary" and the "Our Father," are said while fingering each bead. The term rosary comes from the Latin word *rosarius*, which means "garland," "bouquet," or "garden of roses."

According to legend, the rosary was developed by St. Dominic in the thirteenth century, given to him by the Virgin Mary who appeared to him when he was praying for a weapon to use against those who opposed Christianity. In honor of this tradition, Dominican priests still wear a rosary on the left side of their belts in the same place that a knight would wear a sword.

There is, however, more myth than fact to this story. More likely, rosaries came into Christianity from Islam during the Middle Ages, and were used as a tool to help people learn and remember teachings from the Bible. At the time, most people couldn't read, and even those who did could rarely get their hands on a Bible. Instead, they learned their lessons by hearing them and committing them to memory as they fingered the beads on their rosaries.

Primitive prayer beads were made of fruit pits, dried berries, pieces of bone, and hardened clay. The wealthy used precious stones, jewels, and even nuggets of gold to count their prayers.

In the Orthodox church, the rosary takes the form of a prayer rope, which consists of a series of small knots. Commonly referred to as komboskini by the Greek Orthodox and chotki by the Russian Orthodox, prayer ropes are used to say the "Jesus Prayer"—"Lord Jesus Christ, Son of God, have mercy on me, a sinner," or other short prayers. Usually made of black yarn, prayer ropes are marked off at intervals by wooden or glass beads, and come in various lengths, ranging from thirty-three knots (each knot represents a year in Jesus' life) to 100 knots. Prayer ropes are also used to count a silent "breath prayer," with "Lord Jesus Christ, Son of God," prayed on inhalation, and "have mercy on me, a sinner" prayed on exhalation.

Praying the Rosary

The Rosary prayer, which differs from the prayer counters, helps worshippers pay attention to mysteries in the history of their salvation, and to thank and praise God for them. There are twenty mysteries reflected upon in the Rosary, and these are divided into the five Joyful Mysteries, the five Luminous Mysteries, the five Sorrowful Mysteries, and the five Glorious Mysteries. When praying the Rosary, you pick one of the categories of mysteries to pray on. Each of the Mysteries is also referred to as a decade, as each involves the reading of five "Hail Mary's."

Generally, the Joyful Mysteries are said on Monday and Saturday, the

Luminous on Thursday, the Sorrowful on Tuesday and Friday, and the Glorious on Wednesday and Sunday (with these exceptions: Sundays of Christmas season—the Joyful Mysteries; Sundays of Lent—the Sorrowful Mysteries).

The Five Joyful Mysteries

The Five Joyful Mysteries are as follows:

1. The Annunciation of Gabriel to Mary
2. The Visitation of Mary to Elizabeth
3. The Birth of Jesus
4. The Presentation of Jesus
5. Finding Jesus in the Temple

The Five Luminous Mysteries

The Five Luminous Mysteries are as follows:

1. The Baptism of Jesus
2. The Manifestation of Christ
3. The Proclamation of the Kingdom of God
4. The Transfiguration
5. The Last Supper

The Five Sorrowful Mysteries

The Five Sorrowful Mysteries can be found in the following verses:

1. The Agony of Jesus in the Garden
2. Jesus Scourged at the Pillar
3. Jesus Is Crowned with Thorns
4. Jesus Carries the Cross to Calvary
5. The Crucifixion of Jesus

The Five Glorious Mysteries

The Five Glorious Mysteries are reflected in the following:

1. The Resurrection of Jesus
2. The Ascension
3. The Descent of the Holy Spirit at Pentecost
4. The Assumption of Mary into Heaven
5. The Coronation of Mary as Queen of Heaven and Earth

Saying the Prayers

Every bead on the rosary corresponds to a prayer. To properly pray the Rosary, first you make the sign of the cross and recite the Apostles' Creed:

I believe in God, the Father almighty, creator of Heaven and earth.
I believe in Jesus Christ, his only Son, our Lord.
He was conceived by the power of the Holy Spirit and born of the Virgin Mary.
He suffered under Pontius Pilate, was crucified, died, and was buried.
He descended to the dead.
On the third day he rose again.
He ascended into heaven, and is seated at the right hand of the Father.
He will come again to judge the living and the dead.
I believe in the Holy Spirit, the holy catholic church, the communion of saints, the forgiveness of sins, the resurrection of the body, and the life everlasting.
Amen.

Following the "Apostles' Creed," say the "Lord's Prayer" (Our Father):

Our father, who art in heaven
hallowed be Thy name
Thy kingdom come
Thy will be done on earth as it is in heaven.
Give us this day our daily bread
and forgive us our trespasses as we forgive those who trespass against us,
and lead us not into temptation; but deliver us from evil.
Amen.

Following the "Lord's Prayer," pray three "Hail Mary's":

Hail Mary, full of grace,
the Lord is with thee
blessed art thou among women,
and blessed is the fruit of thy womb, Jesus.
Holy Mary, Mother of God, pray for us sinners,
now and at the hour of our death.
Amen.

Following the three "Hail Mary's," say the "Glory Be to the Father":

Glory be to the Father,
and to the Son,
and to the Holy Spirit.
As it was in the beginning,
is now, and ever shall be,
world without end.
Amen.

Next, announce the first Mystery followed by the "Lord's Prayer." Then say ten "Hail Mary's" while keeping the mystery in your mind. Following this, say the "Glory be to the Father," and then say:

O my Jesus,
forgive us our sins,
save us from the fires of hell,
lead all souls to Heaven,
especially those who have most need of your mercy.

Do the same for the second, third, fourth, and fifth mystery. When you have completed the entire rosary, pray the "Hail, Holy Queen":

Hail, Holy Queen,
Mother of Mercy, our life,

our sweetness and our hope!

To thee do we cry, poor banished children of Eve;

to thee do we send up our sighs, mourning and weeping in this valley of tears.

Turn then, most gracious advocate, thine eyes of mercy toward us,

and after this our exile, show unto us the blessed fruit of thy womb, Jesus.

O clement, O loving, O sweet Virgin Mary!

Other Prayer Counters

Buddhists and Hindus also use prayer counters called malas to count mantras, typically in 108-bead cycles. For Buddhists, the usual mantra is "om mani padme hum," meaning "Jewel in the heart of the lotus," which is one of the names of the Buddha. For each mantra that is uttered, the fingers advance one bead. Followers of Islam use prayer beads strung in thirty-three- or ninety-nine-bead strands to give glory to Allah in several prayer forms or simply to pray the ninety-nine names of Allah.

FACT

Mantra is the practice of using specific "sacred sound" syllables for spiritual and material transformation. The power of the mantra is believed to come not from what the syllables specifically mean, but from their vibrational effect on the body's physiological and energy systems.

Although not a universal tradition in the Episcopalian church, prayer beads are also becoming a popular prayer tool for members of this denomination. Developed in the 1980s, Anglican prayer beads are ropes of thirty-three beads, divided into groups of seven. The thirty-three beads signify the number of years that Jesus lived on earth. The divisions of seven relate to the seven days of creation, the seven days of the week, or the seven seasons of the church year. A large bead called a cruciform bead separates each set. There is no official set of prayers for these beads as the practice is still too new. Popular choices include the "Jesus Prayer" and excerpts from The Book of Common Prayer.

Music to the Ears

Music is a powerful expression of human emotion, and it has long enhanced prayer and worship services. References to music abound in the Bible, and scripture from the Bible has formed the basis for some of the world's most beautiful songs. It is a cornerstone of all major religions, taking a variety of forms ranging from chanting to hymns to ringing bells and singing bowls. Researchers have found that soothing music induces states of deep relaxation. Simply chanting "om" can affect metabolic rate, heartbeat, and respiration rate.

Many people feel a special connection to God through music, and for some, prefacing their personal prayer time by listening to music helps them get into a prayerful state. What they listen to runs the gamut from Gregorian chant to contemporary instrumental music composed especially for prayer and meditation. Other choices include Sufi or Native American chanting, music from the Celtic tradition, modern sacred music, and classical music.

The resonant tones of Tibetan bells and singing bowls have long been used by Buddhists to help spiritual seekers enter into meditation. They can also be used at the beginning of a prayer session to cue the start of the session and as a focus for quieting the mind. The bowls are struck with a padded mallet or a soft piece of wood, or rubbed around the rim to produce a harmonic ringing. Each produces a different sound, with smaller ones usually pitched higher. Tibetan bells, also known as ghantas, are played by ringing or by rubbing a stick around the rim. Tingshaw, another type of Tibetan bell, come in matched pairs coupled together with a leather cord. They are played by striking them against each other.

You can buy recordings of singing bowls and bells, or you can buy the real thing and learn how to play them yourself. You'll find resources for both in Appendix B, along with some suggestions of music to use before or during prayer.

Chapter 9

Praying Simply

All relationships have to start at the beginning. So, too, does our relationship in prayer with God. Simple prayer, or beginner's prayer, honors our newcomer status by sticking to the basics. What could be easier?

Starting with Fits and Starts

Stepping out in prayer can be as nerve-wracking as going out on a first date. It shouldn't be, but there's something about starting a relationship with God that can be, well, tongue-tying. We might think we know what to say, or what we want to say, but when we start talking the words either don't come, or they don't come the way we'd like them to. We can't just sit down and have a heart-to-heart talk with the Almighty—which, by the way, is what simple prayer is all about. Then the self-doubt kicks in. "I'm not doing it right," we think. "Boy, God must think I'm one heck of a dodo. Why did I ever want to do this in the first place?"

Blush, blush, stammer, stammer, end of first date. Maybe there will be another one. Maybe not.

Negative Tapes

There are lots of reasons why there are fits and starts at the beginning of a life of prayer. The one that seems to be the biggest is that our rational minds are often too much in control. In other words, we spend too much time thinking about what we're doing instead of just doing it. Because of this, there's usually some pretty negative chitchat going on inside our heads. You might replay every old tape you've ever heard about prayer—it's dumb, it's silly, it's ineffective, it doesn't work, it's archaic, it has to be exactly right or God won't answer—you name it, while you're trying to pray. If prayer is all these things, your brain is saying, "Then why are you even remotely thinking about doing it, much less trying to do it? Give this up, go back to something that makes sense." The only problem is, we don't know what that "something that makes sense" would be.

Prayer does make sense. If it didn't, we wouldn't feel called to do it. Nor would the billions of other people who make a conscious effort to connect with God on a regular—if not daily—basis. This isn't to say that there won't be times when you'll have some of the same feelings. In fact, you can expect to.

Don't let anything you've heard, anything that anyone says to you now, or any of your past experiences convince you that prayer doesn't make sense or that you're less of a person for wanting to pray. Your rationale for wanting to get to know God through prayer—whatever it may be—is what justifies your actions now. Honor whatever it was that made you decide to start moving toward God in prayer. Don't let negative self-talk hold you back.

Being in Control

When we first start out in prayer, we often try to control the outcomes. While we might go to God with the greatest of intentions and desires to get everything we can out of the time we spend with Him, we can't help trying to anticipate what the outcome should be. In other words, we won't hand over the controls to God. However, as the following words from the Book of Proverbs point out, this is exactly what needs to happen:

Trust in the Lord with all your heart,
And lean not on your own understanding;
In all your ways acknowledge Him,
And He shall direct your paths.
Do not be wise in your own eyes;
Fear the Lord and depart from evil.
It will be health to your flesh,
And strength to your bones.

—Proverbs, 3:5–8

As human beings, we often think we want things to be different. At the same time, we tend to resist change. Our status quo, the place we're in at the moment, is vastly more comfortable to us than the unknown is. Even if the place we're in isn't that great, if we've been there for a while we've grown comfortable with how it feels and we're reluctant to see if anything else could or would be better. Or, we tell ourselves that a little bit of change is okay. We don't want to be made anew. That would be too drastic. Instead, we just want to be a little different.

Prayer, however, is all about change. In fact, change is prayer's inevitable outcome. What's more, we can't control how things will change, when they'll change, or how even much they might change. Much as we might want to have our hands on the outcomes, we can't. We have to turn those controls over to God. If we don't, we'll be stalled out in the same awkward place for a very long time.

Starting from Scratch

Another big stumbling block to getting started in prayer is that we're self-conscious about doing it. Frankly, we're not very good at being beginners at anything. As adults, we're too out of touch with what it feels like to start to learn anything from scratch. We pride ourselves in being good, if not expert, at everything we do, and we tend to avoid the things that we are less than expert at. If we can't sail into a dialogue with God with as much grace and aplomb as anything we've ever heard or read, well, then, we'll just let that one sit for now. Or maybe we'll try again later, when we're better at it.

The problem is, the expertise we want to have in prayer doesn't come unless we start praying, and keep at it after we start. In other words, you don't get better at prayer unless you do it. This means that you have to start somewhere. It also means that you have to be a beginner.

Being a Good Beginner

Throughout the long history of humankind talking to God, some of the most effective prayers—if not all of them—have been offered up to the Almighty by people who considered themselves absolute beginners at the process. In fact, no matter how much they prayed, how long they prayed, or how fervently they prayed, they never thought of themselves as being experts at it. You might find this hard to believe, but it's absolutely true. Mother Teresa sure knew a thing or two about talking to God, but in her eyes she was always a beginner. To her dying day, she communicated with God very simply, like a child would talk to a parent. She always felt that there was something new to be learned from Him, and the best way to learn it was to keep things simple. In her words, everyone who prayed should, ". . . go to God like a little child. A child has no difficulty expressing his mind in simple words that say so much."

Other spiritual greats also valued the simple prayer of the beginner.

Prayer is strange in being an activity where no success is possible. There is no perfect prayer—except insofar as it corresponds to one's real situation and represents a total turning toward God.

—Michael Casey, in *Toward God*

Jean-Nicholas Grou

An eighteenth-century Jesuit priest, Grou spent most of his time writing and speaking about spiritual growth and especially about how the practice of prayer furthered it. In *How to Pray*, he wrote, "Every Christian ought to say to the Savior as humbly as [the disciples]: "Lord, teach us to pray." He went on to say, "God must teach us everything concerning the nature of prayer: its object, its characteristics, the disposition it requires, and the personal application we must make of it according to our needs. In the matter of prayer we are as ignorant of the theory as of the practice."

Brother Lawrence

Brother Lawrence (given name Nicholas Herman) was a lay brother in a monastery in seventeenth-century Paris. He lived the simplest life, focusing his efforts on living every moment in the presence of God. As such, he also valued the importance of simplicity when praying, and wrote, "I have since given up all forms of devotions and set prayers except those which are suitable to this practice (conversing silently with God). I make it my business only to persevere in his holy presence wherein I keep myself by a simple attention and a general fond regard to God . . ."

Thomas Merton

Thomas Merton, a Trappist monk for twenty-seven years, wrote *The Seven Story Mountain*, an autobiography that dug deep into his own soul and ended up becoming a spiritual bestseller. As a Trappist, he spent his entire life in prayer, and understood the paradox of always being a beginner in prayer very well. As he put it, "We don't [enjoy] being beginners but let us be convinced of the fact that we will never be anything except beginners, all our life!"

Learning to Be Humble Before God

Allowing ourselves to be beginners activates one of the fundamentals of a successful prayer life. Admitting that we know very little, perhaps even nothing, about what we're about to do is a pretty humbling experience for most of us. However, being able to do so also signifies our intention, and our desire, to open ourselves to God and allow Him to work with us. And that's a good thing. As Benedict of Nursia put it: "The fifth step of humility is to keep no secrets from the one to whom we confess. We must humbly confess all of our evil thoughts and all of our evil actions."

Keeping no secrets means coming before God just as we are. It also means:

- Not trying to speak to God in the Queen's English. No one really does this.
- Not trying to make things pretty for God. In other words, you're going to blurt out exactly what's on your mind, no matter how ugly it is.
- Not trying to be anything that you aren't. Remember, God knows you better than you know yourself.

Pretty simple, right? If you can stick to these rules . . . well, you'll be praying. Now, how simple could that be?

But wait, you're thinking. Surely, it can't be this easy. I mean, after all the stuff I've read about ordering my prayer life, structuring my prayers, deciding where to pray, how to pray, and whether I should sit, stand, or kneel when I'm doing it, now you're going to tell me that praying is this simple? That all I have to do is follow these guidelines and I'll be okay with God? That I'll be praying?

Absolutely.

And you shall remember the Lord your God, for it is He who gives you power to get wealth, that He may establish His covenant which He swore to your fathers, as it is this day.

—Deuteronomy 9:18

The Power of Praying Just as You Are

As previously mentioned, one of the things that tends to trip us up when we go to pray is that we think we have to come before God in our Sunday best. We think we have to look our best, act our best, and pray our best. But this isn't what God wants. Not by a long shot.

All God wants us to do is come before Him just as we are. This is what simple prayer is all about. As Richard Foster described it in *Prayer: Finding the Heart's True Home:*

In Simple Prayer, we bring ourselves before God just as we are, warts and all. Like children before a loving father, we open our hearts and make our requests. We do not try to sort things out, the good from the bad. We simply and unpretentiously share our concerns and make our petitions.

As you can see, simple prayer is the easiest kind of prayer that you can do. All you have to do is open your mouth and say what's on your mind. Just talk about the ordinary events of your everyday life. If you're unhappy with things at work, you can talk about them. If someone in your life just threw you a curveball, out it comes. If you're beside yourself because you just got an unexpected raise, tell God how you feel. If you're disappointed beyond words because you didn't get that raise, tell Him too. Everything and anything that's on your heart is fodder for simple prayer. Simple prayer is what we can do when we think we can't pray. Another word for simple prayer is expository prayer, meaning that it sets forth facts.

You don't have to put a lot of thought into your words when you're praying simply. Instead, you just let the words tumble out, however they want. If you're a linear thinker, your words might align themselves in a fairly logical way. If you're not, they might be all over the place in a mad, free-association jumble, and they might not make sense at all. It simply doesn't matter.

Simple prayer is the kind of prayer that you see most often in the Bible. Some of the best examples of it can be found in the Psalms of the Old Testament. The following psalm, a psalm of David, reflects about every form that simple prayer can take. It also illustrates how praying simply allows us to air all our emotions, and all our dirty laundry, before God:

> Be merciful to me, O God, be merciful to me!
> For my soul trusts in You;
> And in the shadow of Your wings I will make my refuge,
> Until these calamities have passed by.
> I will cry out to God Most High,
> To God who performs all things for me.
> He shall send from heaven and save me;
> He reproaches the one who would swallow me up.
> My soul is among lions;
> I lie among the sons of men
> Who are set on fire,
> Whose teeth are spears and arrows,
> And their tongue a sharp sword.
> Be exalted, O God, above the heavens;

Let Your glory be above all the earth.
They have prepared a net for my steps;
My soul is bowed down;
They have dug a pit before me;
Into the midst of it they themselves have fallen.
My heart is steadfast, O God, my heart is steadfast;
I will sing and give praise.
Awake, my glory!
Awake, lute and harp!
I will awaken the dawn.
I will praise You, O Lord, among the peoples;
I will sing to You among the nations.
For your mercy reaches unto the heavens,
And your truth unto the clouds.
Be exalted, O God, above the heavens;
Let Your glory be above all the earth.

—Psalm 57

You can also get very angry with God during simple prayer, which is
something that we are often afraid to do when praying in other ways.
The following psalm is entitled "A contemplation of Heman the Ezarhite."
Whoever he was, he had clearly experienced better days in his walk with
the Almighty:

O Lord, God of my salvation,
I have cried out day and night before You.
Let my prayer come before You;
Incline Your ear to my cry.
For my soul is full of troubles,
And my life draws near to the grave.
I am counted with those who go down to the pit;
I am like a man who has no strength,
Adrift among the dead,
Like the slain who lie in the grave,
Whom You remember no more,

And who are cut off from Your hand.
You have laid me in the lowest pit,
In darkness, in the depths.
Your wrath lies heavy upon me,
And you have afflicted me with all Your waves.
You have put away my acquaintances far from me;
You have made me an abomination to them;
I am shut up, and I cannot get out;
My eye wastes away because of affliction.
Lord, I have called daily upon You;
I have stretched out my hands to You.
Will you work wonders for the dead?
Shall the dead arise and praise you?
Shall Your lovingkindness be declared in the grave?
Or Your faithfulness in the place of destruction?
Shall Your wonders be known in the dark?
And Your righteousness in the land of forgetfulness?
But to You I have cried out, O Lord,
And in the morning my prayer comes before You.
Lord, why do You cast off my soul?
Why do You hide Your face from me?
I have been afflicted and ready to die from my youth up;
I suffer your terrors;
I am distraught.
Your fierce wrath has gone over me;
Your terrors have cut me off.
They came around me all day long like water;
They engulfed me altogether
Loved one and friend You have put far from me.
And my acquaintances into darkness.

—Psalm 88

Psychologically my relationship with God varies. There are better days, when we seem to get along well. Occasionally I get mad at him. I get bored with God often. Sometimes I wonder if I have any relationship with him at all and whether this whole business is not one big illusion.

—Jerry Ryan, in "Desiring Prayer," *America* magazine

Simple prayer is also the most dominant prayer form among modern-day pray-ers. It has so many fans because it's so simple to do. Because it follows no specific style, it appeals to people who don't like more formal prayer styles. It allows you to pray about what you want, when you want, and wherever you want to do it. You don't have to worry about carrying a prayer book or a devotional along with you. Other reasons why simple prayer is so popular:

- It allows us to experience God in a very personal way.
- The words you speak in personal prayer are yours and yours alone.
- You can speak to God about exactly what's going on in your life at any time.
- You can let your emotions run the gamut.

It's a good idea to balance the freedom of simple prayer with some structured prayer time to keep your walk with God from getting too casual. Doing daily Bible readings, following the readings in a daily devotional, or using written prayers on occasion are all ways of keeping simple prayer from becoming too "me focused."

The Benefits of Simple Prayer

When we speak frankly and honestly with God through simple prayer, we're inviting Him into our hearts and allowing Him to walk with us in all aspects of our lives. As we do, something pretty wonderful happens. We get to know God better. We learn to trust Him with all of our thoughts, feelings, and emotions, even the ones we're not particularly proud of. We get a better feeling for what it's like to be in His presence, and it no longer intimidates us as it once did. We get over our feelings of inadequacy. Performance anxiety becomes a thing of the past. In other words, we learn how to pray.

Is simple prayer for everyone? While anyone can pray simply, this prayer form may be too undisciplined and spontaneous for some people. Taken to the extreme, it can perhaps lead to a fairly careless prayer life because it doesn't call for much effort. However, if you're moving forward in your spiritual walk, your desire to experience God in other ways will deepen, and you'll keep simple prayer in its proper perspective. It will always be a part of your prayer life, but it won't be all of it.

Each person brings himself along when he comes to pray; and if he is inexperienced in prayer, what he brings with him will mostly bear the stamp of his personal problems and daily life.

—Attributed to Adrienne Von Speyr,
a writer and convert to Catholicism

How to Do Simple Prayer

Simple prayer starts right where you are, with exactly how you're feeling at the moment you begin to talk with God. All you have to do is say something like this:

"God, it's really a great day today and I'm in a fantastic mood. Boy, the world you created is a wonderful spot. I'm having such a great time with it right now. I wish everyone could. It troubles me that everyone doesn't. There are hurting people in this world. I don't understand why. I wish I did. That Tom guy I work with—boy, he's a hurting person. He'd like to hurt me, no doubt about it. He sure shoots me the old evil eye whenever he can. Boy, I'd like to understand him better. Maybe I need to think about that one for a while. Things could be pretty crummy in his life. As a matter of fact, I think they are. I think his kid is having problems. He's taking them out on the family, and Tom's taking them out on the people around him. Hmmm . . . God, I don't know what to do about him. I'd like to be able to help him, but I don't like him very much, so I keep my distance. Oh well. Time to get back to work. Talk to you later, God. Oh, and thanks."

That's all there is to praying simply. Let your thoughts flow. Don't work at it. Let God do the work. Ⓔ

Chapter 10

Praying in Times of Trouble

Trouble in all its various forms is a pretty big part of the human condition. When we're kids we sometimes revel in being little troublemakers, but as adults we usually try to avoid it like the plague. Still, trouble can find us. Going to God in prayer can help us get through the times when a little—or a lot—of trouble comes our way.

Dealing with Difficulties

Times of crisis can turn life upside down. They're the times when the bottom falls out of our world. The things we may have believed to be true might no longer be. We may not know what to do, how to cope, or where to turn. We may be gripped with fear so great that we feel paralyzed and unable to do anything. We might even be afraid to ask anyone for help for fear of exposing our problems. Nothing seems right. Nothing feels right.

Crisis times can literally flip your world over and put it on its ear. The word *crisis* comes from the Greek *krisis*, meaning "decision." For many people, these are the times at which it's toughest to pray. But they are the times at which prayer can do the most good. In fact, some of the most powerful praying happens when it seems like prayer is the last resort. Not only can talking to God about our problems bring us peace and relief, it can also bring greater clarity and understanding to the situation at hand.

Let me not pray to be sheltered from dangers but to be fearless in facing them.

Let me not beg for the stilling of my pain but for the heart to conquer it.

Let me not look for allies in life's battlefield but to my own strength.

Let me not crave in anxious fear to be saved but hope for the patience to win my freedom.

Grant me that I may not be a coward, feeling your mercy in my success alone; but let me find the grasp of your hand in my failure.

—Rabindranath Tagore, Fruit Gathering

Being prayerful, staying with God, talking to Him, and telling Him what is going on, is what we should do at all times. When crisis strikes, however, it can sometimes be difficult to do so. For this reason, crisis also tends to redefine our prayer life and make us approach it in a very different way. For many people, times of trouble tear them away from prayer. Others draw closer to God and spend more time in prayer with Him than ever before.

Why Bad Things Happen

It is often said that times of trouble are tests of faith. This doesn't mean that the problems we face are God-sent, although some people do believe that they are, or can be. Why would God intentionally send trouble our way? Here are a few of the possible explanations for it:

- He is making us better people by repairing our character faults.
- He is trying to teach us a lesson.
- He is trying to punish us.

These may seem like plausible answers to the question; however, they are patently untrue. We may become better people, and learn some lessons as we travel through adversity, but God doesn't intentionally create problems for these reasons. He does not cause our suffering. Nor does He punish us.

If you're still looking for an explanation of why bad things happen, one of the best comes from Rabbi Harold S. Kushner's book *When Bad Things Happen to Good People.* In it, he offers a very simple answer: Sometimes they just do. However, because of our innate nature, we try to make sense of it by looking for reasons why they do.

Can you accept the idea that some things happen for no reason, that there is randomness in the universe? Some people cannot handle that idea. They look for connections, striving desperately to make sense of all that happens. They convince themselves that God is cruel, or that they are sinners, rather than accept randomness.

Understanding that problems can just happen for no particular reason may not bring you much comfort. You might still be wondering, "Why me?" What this understanding can do, however, is put adversity into better perspective.

Trouble's "Good" Side

No one in his right mind would ask for trouble to come his way, but when it does arise it can actually end up working for the good. It can sometimes take a while to realize the benefits, but they do manifest in time. They can include:

- Finding strength and courage that we never knew we had.
- Learning how to rise to the occasion in ways we never would have expected.
- Finding compassion and support from sources we never knew existed.
- Gaining a greater sense of how God works in our lives.

As odd as it may sometimes seem, the challenges that life presents are what make us better people. When we stand up to the bad times, we learn that we have the capacity to do so, and that we can continue to do so. We learn, as Eleanor Roosevelt said, to "do the thing you think you cannot do."

You gain strength, courage, and confidence by every experience in which you really stop to look fear in the face. You are able to say to yourself, "I lived through this horror. I can take the next thing that comes along. . . ." You must do the thing you think you cannot do.

It is never easy to face adversity. It's not meant to be. Psychiatrist and author M. Scott Peck notes that being on unfamiliar ground or doing things differently is always going to frighten us, but that it is necessary for all types of growth, including spiritual growth. Fear, he says, is "inescapable if they [people] are in fact to change."

Individuals who have gone through periods of immense difficulties will often say that their experiences during these times, and what they learned from them, are what made them who they are now. While they would never wish for dire things, in retrospect they're actually thankful that they happened. Through them, they learned their mettle, what they're really made of. Such times also made them more aware of their weaknesses, fears, and faults.

It is good for us to have trials and troubles at times, for they often remind us that we are on probation and ought not to hope in any worldly thing. It is good for us sometimes to suffer contradiction, to be misjudged by men even though we do well and mean well. These things help us to be humble and shield us from vainglory. When to all outward appearances men give us no credit, when they do not think well of us, then we are more inclined to seek God Who sees our hearts. Therefore, a man ought to root himself so firmly in God that he will not see the consolations of men.

—Thomas à Kempis, in *The Imitation of Christ*

The Fear Factor

Fear often plays a key role in times of trouble. This is an emotion that can take many forms, but the one that pops up the most often is fear of the unknown. When the parameters of life have been shifted without our consent, we begin to sail uncharted waters. Like the seafaring explorers of centuries ago, we don't really know what is out there or what to expect. There could be monsters on the edges of the world. And they could be pretty awful indeed.

Dear Lord,
be good to me . . .
The sea is so wide
and my boat is so small.

—Irish fisherman's prayer

Some of the most legendary figures in the Bible knew firsthand what it was like to deal with fear of the unknown. The first time that Moses came into contact with God—in the form of a burning bush—he did so with a certain amount of trepidation. In fact, he turned away from what he did not know and chose not to "see this great sight." The children of Israel, whom Moses led to the Promised Land, were afraid to enter it because it was new territory—it was unknown and it frightened them. Even though the land offered the Hebrews all the abundance they could ever wish for, they found lots of reasons why they just didn't want to go there. After listening to a night's worth of crying and complaining, God had had enough.

Then the Lord said to Moses: "How long will these people reject Me? And how long will they not believe Me, with all the signs which I have performed among them?

—Numbers 12:11

Maybe the signs that God had sent weren't enough for the children of Israel, but they were enough for Moses. He trusted God, and he finally convinced his people that they needed to trust God as well if they wanted to get to where they needed to go.

We, too, need to remember to put our faith in God in all things. This means turning to Him when we fear the unknown. Simply telling God that we're afraid, even if we don't know what we're afraid of, can bring blessed relief, both physically and emotionally.

Suffering in Silence

People sometimes resist praying to God when they're troubled because they feel it's inappropriate to bother God with their problems. Instead of turning to a source of strength for comfort and guidance, they suffer in silence and bear the burden on their own.

As compassionate as we can be toward others, we often don't treat ourselves kindly at all. We are reluctant to expose our vulnerabilities. Instead, we often walk a pretty stoic walk. We maintain a stiff upper lip. We tough it out. Taking this approach, however, tends to make our problems worse. It isolates us from the people who could help us, and it isolates us from God, who will.

The belief that it is inappropriate to turn to God in times of trouble has no basis in any form of scripture. If you were to search the sacred writings, you wouldn't find anything to support this notion because there isn't one religion that considers God anything less than supremely compassionate. Instead, you would find some powerful words that attest to the fact that God will listen, no matter how large or small the problems we bring to Him.

Now that evening has fallen,
To God, the Creator, I will turn in prayer,
Knowing that he will help me.
Knowing that he will help me.

—A Dinka prayer, Sudan

The belief that it is inappropriate to pray our problems to God has its basis in some pious thinking that many believe is simply wrong. If you've been raised in religious traditions that espouse these beliefs, it might be difficult for you to take the first step. But there's an easy way to do it: talk to God. Keep talking to God. As you do, you'll realize that the benefits of doing so outweigh any concerns you might have about your prayers being "inappropriate."

Stopping the Spin Cycle

It can be difficult to think straight when our minds are spinning with problems. Prayer can stop the spin cycle long enough to let us begin to see what's really going on. We might not be able to determine what's at the root of the problem, but going to God in prayer can help us see beyond our immediate situation and start sorting out the details.

How to Pray in Times of Trouble

The prayers we pray when we're hurting, scared, or troubled for any reason can be some of the most fervent we'll ever voice. They can be emotional, beseeching, even pleading. This is as they should be. Simple prayer can be a good way to pray during these times as it allows you to get everything out in the open, all your thoughts and all your feelings. However, it is fine to pray in whatever manner works for you. If you're so overwrought that you can't even think straight, just find a quiet place where you can simply sit in God's presence for a while. Just listen, and let Him do the talking.

As much as we don't like to let others in on our problems, it can be helpful to do so in times of adversity. Ask a close friend, someone you love and trust, to pray with you. You might also find comfort by attending a healing prayer service, or by praying with a group. You don't need to give out any details about what's going on unless you want to.

What should you pray for? Some people believe that it is best to be very specific about telling God what you want. However, this approach takes more of a "my will be done" than a "thy will be done" tone, and can lead to disappointment if the things you pray for don't come about. A better approach, often, is to simply turn to God, admit we can't manage things on our own, and ask for His help.

People who pray for miracles usually don't get miracles . . . But people who pray for courage, for strength to bear the unbearable, for the grace to remember what they have left instead of what they have lost, very often find their prayers answered . . . Their prayers helped them tap hidden reserves of faith and courage which were not available to them before.

—Attributed to Rabbi Harold S. Kushner

When the Prayers Won't Come

There are times when the words won't come when we try to pray. It happens to everyone at some time or another. But it seems to happen especially often when we want to pray our way through a crisis.

What can you do when the words won't come? Praying scriptural prayers is always a great way of communicating with God. Finding some verses that speak to your heart when things aren't going well can be especially helpful. Psalm 23—"The Lord Is My Shepherd"—is one of the best known. Here is another from the Book of Psalms:

Hear my cry, O God;
Attend to my prayer.
From the end of the earth I will cry to You,
When my heart is overwhelmed;
Lead me to the rock that is higher than I.
For You have been a shelter for me,
A strong tower from the enemy.
I will abide in Your tabernacle forever;
I will trust in the shelter of Your wings.
For You, O god, have heard my vows;
You have given me the heritage of those who fear Your name.
You will prolong the king's life,
His years as many generations.
He shall abide before God forever.
Oh, prepare mercy and truth, which may preserve him!
So I will sing praise to Your name forever,
That I may daily perform my vows.

—Psalm 61

Leaning on the words of God and the experiences of those in the Bible can give you strength when you have exhausted your own supply of it. The stories of courage can help drive away your fears. If nothing else, focusing on someone else's problems for a while can give you a break from obsessing over your own.

The Story of Job

The story of Job, in the Old Testament, speaks volumes about human suffering. In the Book of Job, we learn about a man who was "blameless and upright, and one who feared God and shunned evil." In other words, he was so good and so perfect that there was no question that he walked in God's favor. But Job's goodness and perfection were put to the test.

One day, Satan appears before God to taunt Him about all the evil and sinful things that His people were doing. God holds up Job to Satan as an example of how wonderful His people could be. Satan then tells God that Job's piety and perfection were the result of God's having made it easy for him to be.

Lord, hear my prayer, and listen when I ask for mercy. I call to you in times of trouble, because you will answer me.

—Psalm 86:6–7

To prove Satan wrong, God allows him to wreak havoc in Job's life without giving him so much as a clue that trouble was coming his way. In short order, Job's house is destroyed and his cattle, servants, and children are killed. But Job continued to bless God's name. Next, Job's health is attacked and he develops boils "from the sole of his foot to the crown of his head." Job's wife can't take it and urges him to curse God, even if doing so would cause God to strike him down. Job's friends come to comfort him, but then side with his wife. "Curse God," they tell him, "even if it means death." But Job won't budge. He remains devoted to God.

As long as my breath is in me,
And the breath of God in my nostrils,
My lips will not speak wickedness,
Nor my tongue utter deceit.
Far be it from me
That I should say you are right;
Till I die I will not put away my integrity from me.
My righteousness I hold fast, and will not let it go;
My heart shall not reproach me as long as I live.

—Job 27:3–6

Finally, God appears to Job and the two have a long talk. At the end, Job again proclaims his faithfulness to God, and the test is over. God rewards Job for remaining faithful, and restores his life to where it was before, giving him a new home, a new family, and a new fortune.

The story of Job is, of course, a morality tale, and it shouldn't be taken literally. In a literal sense, it is a "God giveth, and God taketh away" story, and the problems sent Job's way are of God's making, via Satan. Look beyond this, however, and the story of Job is a strong testimony to the power of faith. What it tells us is this: When disaster strikes, don't let it shake your faith in God. Ⓔ

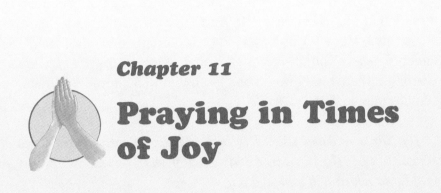

Chapter 11

Praying in Times of Joy

We often pray big and heavy prayers when we pray to God. We pray these prayers so often, in fact, that we sometimes forget to talk to Him when all is well with the world. We forget to say thanks, to tell Him we're grateful, or praise Him for His works. While we often wait until times of joy to pray these prayers, the truth is that we should be doing so on a regular basis.

Giving Thanks and Praise

Joy can take many forms. We can have feelings of great happiness or pleasure tied to our life on earth. And, joy can also be more elevated and spiritual. Many religions speak to God being the source of joy. The main message in Hindu scriptures is that of joy. In the *Bhagavad Gita*, we are told that when one comes to know the Supreme Brahman one becomes fully joyful.

The Supreme Lord said: My dear friend, mighty-armed Arjuna, listen again to My supreme word, which I shall impart to you for your benefit and which will give you joy.

—Bhagavad Gita, 10:1

Many of the prayers in the Bible are of thanks and praise. David was almost a ceaseless thanker of God, and the Book of Psalms is full of his prayers of thanksgiving and praise.

Make a joyful shout to God, all the earth!
Sing out the honor of His name;
Make His praise glorious.
Say to God,
"How awesome are Your works!
Through the greatness of Your power
Your enemies shall submit themselves to You.
All the earth shall worship You
And sing praises to You;
They shall sing praises to Your name."

—Psalm 66:1–4

The Bible contains many other messages about joy. Among them:

• There is great strength in joy—". . . for the joy of the Lord is your strength" (Nehemiah 8:10).
• Being joyful helps those around us to be joyful as well—". . . having

confidence in you all that my joy is the joy of you all" (2 Corinthians 2:30).

- God's mercy is a source of great joy—". . . I will be glad and rejoice in Your mercy" (Psalm 31:7).
- Being joyful is important to remaining strong—"A merry heart does good, like medicine, But a broken spirit dries the bones" (Proverbs 18:22).

Why Praying with Joy Is Difficult

There is so much that we can be joyous about in our everyday lives. However, it is a strange truth that many people find prayers of joy, thanks, or praise the most difficult of all to pray. This is somewhat understandable when we are feeling unhappy, or when things aren't going well in our lives, as it's hard to feel joyous during times of trouble. When you go through tough times, praying prayers of joy and thanksgiving can be extremely difficult, as they can seem almost irrational. It can seem extremely crazy to think of thanking God for something in the midst of tragedy. Doing so, however, can lift you out of the depths of despair and sorrow. But the reluctance to express joy to God, and praise Him for His role in creating that joy, even extends to the good times when it should be easy for us to do so.

Try to find the time for giving thanks on a regular basis—daily, if possible. Learning how to pray joyously at all times can help you maintain feelings of gratitude when things aren't going as well as you would like them to.

The Myth of "Praying Correctly"

You might find prayers of joy or gratitude difficult to pray, too, especially if you were taught that "praying correctly" meant offering only prayers of petition or supplication. There isn't much room for expressing joy, or for thanking or praising God, when our prayers are focused on pleading to Him or petitioning Him.

As previously noted, believing that prayers should only take the form of petition or supplication is a formal, old-fashioned notion of prayer that should have been tossed out a long time ago. If it lurks in the back of your mind when you're praying, it's time to exorcise it, once and for all. Having some old, negative patterns is to be expected—after all, none of us comes into a life of prayer as empty slates just waiting to be written upon. We all have baggage. But thoughts like these can, and usually do, hinder your spiritual growth. It's important to recognize them so you can work on them, and it's important to work on them so you can put them aside.

FACT

The word *thanks* is used more than thirty-five times in the Psalms. Hymns of thanksgiving and songs of appreciation are sung by followers of most, if not all, world religions, in recognition of God's greatness and the gifts He bestows.

Afraid of Feeling Joyous

Even for people who embrace prayer in all its forms, praying for joy can be difficult. We understand prayers of adoration and thanksgiving, but joyful praying—praise praying—does not come naturally for many. In *When in Doubt, Sing: Prayer in Daily Life*, author Jane Redmont noted that prayers of sorrow or anger seem to come more easily than joyous prayers, and wondered if "sometimes whether our fear of pain is matched only by our fear of joy."

Perhaps the problem is that we are not so much afraid of joy as we are afraid of admitting that we feel joyous. We live in a hurting world, a world in which there is a great deal of pain and suffering. Being outwardly joyous can seem a bit vain, egotistical, even cocky, especially when we are surrounded by so many other people who are suffering. Isn't keeping our mouths shut when we're happy the kind and compassionate thing to do? Perhaps you feel that expressing your feelings of joy would make people around you feel worse. But this doesn't mean that we should try to hide our feelings when we are talking to God. Doing so denies God the opportunity to know us in all ways. Not only that, not feeling comfortable in voicing feelings of joy during prayer is a poor reflection of what our relationship with God is all about, as so much of the joy we feel is a result of knowing Him.

If you feel as though negative patterns or beliefs from your past are holding you back on your spiritual journey, consider talking with a spiritual adviser or director. Doing so can help you sort out your feelings and develop ways to replace negative patterns with more positive ones.

Another possible reason why many people find it so difficult to pray joyously is because they are afraid that doing so will somehow cause an end to their happiness. In other words, they are somehow afraid that being "too joyous" will put a hex on the source of their joy and derail their happiness. This concern might also be rooted in some old experiences or beliefs. "You shouldn't be too happy because it could end tomorrow" is unfortunately some negative programming that propagates this idea.

Being afraid of ending our happiness by paying attention to it has somewhat of a self-defeating aspect to it. If we don't pay some attention to the happy times in our lives, and recognize them by praising God for them, we end up not being able to appreciate them fully, or at all.

Being Unaware of Joy

In fact, one of the biggest reasons behind the lack of joyous praying may very well be that we are not very good at recognizing the joy that is present in our lives. In other words, we tend to be a bit ungrateful, whether we are aware of it or not.

The very act of praise releases the power of God into a set of circumstances and enables God to change them if this is his design . . . I have come to believe that the prayer of praise is the highest form of communication with God, and one that always releases a great deal of power into our lives.

—Merlin R. Carothers, in *Prison to Praise*

Most people don't mean to block out or ignore all that is wonderful about life. Instead, they simply forget to pay as much attention to the grace notes, the good moments that come their way, as they should. Buddhist scripture tells us that "The worthy person is grateful and mindful of benefits done to him," yet we often take things far too much for granted.

In the whirlwind of activity that constitutes so much of what it's like to live in the twenty-first century, this can be easy to understand to a certain extent. It can be difficult to "stop and smell the roses" when life seems like one big to-do list. But being too busy is a poor excuse for not being grateful, or for not taking time to notice all the things that we should and can be grateful for. When we don't take the time to experience joy in life, and express that joy in prayer, we don't feed our souls.

Let joyous prayer lapse long enough, and hearts harden. Instead of being compassionate toward others, we feel miserable and sorry for ourselves. We allow ourselves to get too hung up on our feelings of joylessness. As we do, we become pretty miserable people to be around, and we wreck other people's joy. Rumi, the Sufi poet, put it well when he wrote, "Your depression is connected to your insolence and refusal to praise! Whoever feels himself walking on the path and refuses to praise— that man or woman steals from others every day—is a shoplifter!"

The basic response of the soul to the Light is internal adoration and joy, thanksgiving and worship, self-surrender and listening.
—Thomas Kelly, in *A Testament of Devotion*

Being grateful calls for a shift in attitude, a shift in perspective. It calls for recognizing that life—in whatever shape it takes—is a gift. It means looking for silver linings in storm clouds, as pious as this might seem. It calls for being a little Orphan Annie-ish. You don't have to go about life skipping and singing "The sun will come out tomorrow," but the feeling that you could do so if you wanted to is pretty much what you are after.

If your take on the world is naturally a little dour or cynical, if the glass you see is half empty instead of half full, making the shifts in attitude necessary to see the bright side of life can take a great amount of effort. Herculean, in fact. However, if you can learn to do it—yes, it is a learning process, and it will take some time—you will see more positive things in your life. You will be able to find the good in the bad. As you do, you will find it easier to give thanks to God.

Developing an Attitude of Gratitude

Gratitude thinking, or having an attitude of gratitude, has received a lot of attention in recent years. We have been encouraged to work at gaining a better appreciation of what we have, and if we don't know how to do this, we have been encouraged to learn how. We have been told that we have "shut down or ignore[d] our authentic impulses" in order to conform to the world around us, and that happiness and joy lie in getting back in touch with our authenticity. According to author Sarah Ban Breathnach in *Simple Abundance Date Book of Comfort and Joy* (2003), this involves "appreciating everything that's right about you right now and giving thanks for it."

Gratitude is the most passionate transformative force in the Cosmos. When we offer thanks to God or to another human being, gratitude gifts us with renewal, reflection, reconnection. It is a choice of mind-set. When we put ourselves in a grateful frame of mind, we recognize all the blessings life has granted us.

If as a child you were told to "count your blessings" every time you seemed ungrateful about something, or wished you had something that you didn't have, gratitude thinking might have negative connotations for you. But there is good advice in this often pious-sounding directive. Sometimes we get so focused on the future, so intent on setting goals and pushing forward to meet them that we forget to be thankful for the things we already have. In other words, we forget to pay attention to the moment, and be mindful of where we are right now.

The Gifts of Gratitude Thinking

Gratitude thinking offers a great framework for praying joyously. It calls for making a habit of thanking God every day for the little things as well as the big things—our health, a beautiful sunrise, the love of family and friends, getting a college paper done on time, the small grace of a soft dog paw on your knee.

QUESTION?

Aren't we always supposed to give thanks when we pray to God?
Yes, thanksgiving is a part of the ACTS prayer formula—adoration, confession, thanksgiving, and supplication. Prayers of joy, however, can also take the form of praise or adoration, where we acknowledge God's work in our lives in addition to thanking Him.

When you focus on giving thanks, and giving thanks for all that you have in life, an interesting thing happens. The more you exercise your "abundance muscles," the more you will get back. The results are often subtle or intangible. They may take the form of feeling more peaceful, happier, or just more content with life in general. But they can be tangible as well. There are numerous stories that describe the riches bestowed upon individuals who consistently go to God with prayers of thanks. Again, the Book of Job in the Old Testament is a good biblical example. No matter what life threw at him, his faith in God remained constant, and he continued to thank God for that which was good. Job lost everything he had at one point, but God restored it all to him, plus more.

The Benefits of Brakhat

In the Jewish faith, the spiritual practice of offering brakhat, or blessing prayers, is seen as a way to bring the sacred into every aspect of life. Praying brakhat serves both as a constant reminder of God's presence and increases the awareness of all the little blessings that are constantly being bestowed on us.

According to author Marcia Prager in *The Path of Blessing: Experiencing the Energy and Abundance of the Divine,* prayers of blessings and thanks made to God are part of a "sacred cycle of giving and receiving," and are necessary to keep this cycle in balance. Offering them completes our energy exchange with God. When we don't offer them, or forget to offer them, the energy exchange is thrown out of whack. "When we fail to praise," Prager says, "it is we who suffer. Without gratitude we become bored and depressed."

FACT

Blessing prayers are central to Jewish prayer. These prayers always begin with "Blessed art Thou, Lord our God, King of the Universe." They may be prayers giving thanks to God, praising Him, or petitioning Him. They can also be offered in acknowledgment of His creation, such as blessings said over food, or in preparation for performing a mitzvah, or a good deed.

Journaling Joy

One of the ways in which we can become more aware of joy in our lives—and, in turn, find it easier to let God in on the things that make us joyful—is by jotting down the things that make us happy, or that we are grateful for, on a regular basis. What we write doesn't have to be much, maybe a line or two on a daily planner or in a prayer journal. Just little notes, like:

- I am grateful for my talent.
- I am grateful for my muscles.
- I am grateful for peace.
- I am grateful for new beginnings.

Other things you might wish to note are the little kindnesses that come your way ("Gee, didn't expect so-and-so to be so nice") and the times when you notice God's work ("Great sunrise!" "Beautiful day!" "Made the right decision," "Feeling like I'm walking in grace").

These simple notes can in themselves be prayers of joy and thanksgiving. Perhaps more important, writing things down that you are thankful for helps you to be more mindful of them. Doing so will also help foster a spirit of thanksgiving that makes it easier to pray joyously.

There are also special abundance journals available that can help you keep track of the things you are thankful for. One to take a look at is the *Simple Abundance Datebook of Comfort and Joy* by Sarah Ban Breathnach. Published annually, it includes thoughts on gratitude and abundance.

Reviewing the Details of the Day

Another way to increase awareness of the joyfulness of everyday life is to review the gifts of the day. Here are some steps you might take:

1. Pick a time—evenings are good, so you can go through the full events of the day. (In fact, this is a great exercise to practice right before you go to sleep as you'll fall asleep thinking of good things.)
2. Let your mind wander through the events of the past twenty-four hours. Don't judge them or sort them into good and bad. Review everything. Even if the day was really rotten, this will help you identify some good moments, even if they're along the lines of "I didn't get too wet in that downpour," or "That new door ding on my car could have been a lot worse."
3. As you remember the grace notes, the events of the day for which you can be grateful, thank God for them.

How to Pray Joyous Prayers

Prayers of joy can take many forms. They can be short quick prayers ("Thanks, God!") or lengthy colloquies. They can be simple or formal. They can be blessings to God offered before meals. They can take the form of songs, and of dance.

Praise the Lord!
Praise God in His sanctuary;
Praise Him in His mighty firmament!
Praise Him for His mighty acts;
Praise Him according to His excellent greatness!

Praise Him with the sound of the trumpet;
Praise Him with the lute and harp!
Praise Him with the timbrel and dance;
Praise Him with stringed instruments and flutes!
Praise Him with loud cymbals;
Praise Him with clashing cymbals!
Let everything that has breath praise the Lord.
Praise the Lord!

—*Psalm 15*

Some people write down everything they have to be thankful for on a daily basis and meditate on their lists as part of their regular prayer time. Others say prayers of joy and thanks on the fly, whenever and wherever they experience or see something that makes them happy and thankful.

If you're not in the habit of praying joyously, start simply. All it takes is a quick "thank you God" to let Him know when you're grateful. It's been said that if the only prayer you say in your entire life is "thank you," it would be enough.

If you have children, you can help them get into the habit of praying joyfully by offering a prayer of praise and thanksgiving before mealtimes. Ask everyone around the table to come up with a couple of things that made them happy during the day, or that they were thankful for, and thank God for these things, too.

Chapter 12

Praying for Special Needs

Throwing our hearts open before God and asking for His assistance can be some of the most difficult prayers to pray. These prayers, however, are also some of the most important. Our need to ask God for His help never goes away, no matter how well we think we can manage things on our own.

Going to God for Help

God likes to hear our calls for help. Not only this, He likes to answer them. Unfortunately, prayers that ask for help from the Almighty have received a bit of a bad rap over the years. Not from God—remember, He likes us to come to Him for assistance—but from humankind.

Some people believe that there is no need to ask God for help if they are living their lives as they should be. They believe that the people who do so are only interested in their own needs and wants. Because of this, the assumption goes, these selfish people focus on prayers that reflect their desires when they should be praying more exalted prayers.

Those opposed to asking for God's help often believe that the only kinds of prayers that should be spoken to God are prayers of adoration and thanksgiving. Asking Him for help is considered crass, crude, or the mark of an inexperienced or beginning pray-er.

FACT

Prayers that ask God for help are called prayers of supplication—a humble appeal to someone who has the power to grant the request; petition—an appeal or request to a higher authority or being; and intercession—a prayer made on behalf of someone else.

While it is a bit of a stretch to characterize all pray-ers who ask for help as being unsophisticated or greedy, there are some people who are guilty as charged. Their prayers take the form of petition more than they should because they allow themselves to get too wrapped up in their own needs.

The Guilt Factor, Part 1

More often than not, however, the reverse is true. Many people who pray feel that it is only appropriate to ask God for help on behalf of others. When they do petition God on their own behalf, their prayers are accompanied with a good dose of guilt. There are a variety of reasons for why they feel this way. Among them are the following:

- A crisis in faith, resulting from not fully believing that God can help or is powerful enough to help in all situations.
- Feeling shameful about needing help.
- Not wanting to admit to needing help.
- Not wanting to believe that help is available.
- Feeling uncomfortable about bothering God with "little" problems when other people are in greater need of His help.
- Feeling that it is selfish to ask God for help.

What causes people to feel shame or guilt over petitioning prayer? There are no easy answers to this question, but we do know that part of the problem is cultural. We live in a society that values independence, self-reliance, and individualism, often at the expense of human emotion and need. These beliefs are reinforced by the messages we are sent through the media, either directly or indirectly. Magazines feature page after page of beautiful and happy celebrities who look like they haven't got a care in the world, or strong and forceful-looking business and political leaders who look like nothing would shake their confidence. Flip through the channels on your television and you'll see more of the same. The message? The "best people"—the most powerful and the most successful people—are beautiful, strong, and self-reliant, and they don't need anyone's help.

ESSENTIAL

Although God does encourage us to ask Him for help, it is important to remember that petitioning is just one form of prayer. To be most effective, prayers of petition should be balanced with prayers of adoration, confession, and thanksgiving.

This is an immensely powerful message, but it has both a positive and a negative side. On the positive side, we always need role models to look up to. Today, thanks to global communications networks, we not only are aware of more individuals that we can respect and admire, we know more about them than we ever did before. On the flip side, the negative message goes something like this: If you aren't like these individuals, or you can't be as strong or self-assured as they are, then you are weak, needy, and inferior. And, if indeed you are weak, needy, and inferior, you had better not let anyone else know it.

The Guilt Factor, Part 2

Another reason why many people feel guilty about asking God for help is because they've been raised in families that put a high value on self-reliance and independence. From an early age, the children in these families are encouraged to work things out on their own, to be strong, to "tough things out." When they grow up, these individuals are often some of the world's biggest success stories, but their success also often comes at a great personal price. Since they weren't allowed to admit that they needed help when they were growing up, they find it difficult or impossible to do so as adults. Many of them don't believe that anyone— including God—could help them even if they did ask for assistance. Because of this, they often experience problems at work and in relationships, and are often perceived as being aloof, cold, or as having a "mightier-than-thou" attitude. When they crash—and they almost all do at some time or another—the fall is often catastrophic.

One of the best things that parents can do for their children is to encourage them to seek help from others when they've reached the limits of what they can do on their own. If this lesson wasn't taught to you as you were growing up, you can learn it as an adult. In fact, you can ask God to help you do so.

Getting Beyond the Guilt

While feelings of guilt or shame about asking for help are understandable, living a full spiritual life necessitates overcoming them as they stand in the way of developing that life. These feelings don't allow us to be humble before God, which is one of the essentials of a successful prayer life. Not being willing to admit that we need help, and not feeling that we can ask God for it, is the antithesis of humility. It is false faith as it puts us in control instead of God. If it is allowed to continue, it will lead to a shallow prayer life and a superficial relationship with the Almighty.

> What are the things that we should lay before the Almighty God in prayer? Answer: First, our personal troubles . . . The greatest trouble we can ever know is thinking that we have no trouble for we have become hard-hearted and insensible to what is inside of us.
> —Attributed to Martin Luther

There are many passages in the world's sacred scriptures that warn against relying on one's own power, and that underscore the need for people to admit their weaknesses before God. And, there are many passages that talk to what the benefits are of doing so. *The Bhagavad Gita* says, "United with me, you shall overcome all difficulties by my grace." The Quran tells us, ". . . If you help God's cause, He will help you and will make your foothold firm."

Have you not known?
Have you not heard?
The everlasting God, the Lord,
The Creator of the ends of the earth,
Neither faints nor is weary.
His understanding is unsearchable.
He gives power to the weak,
And to those who have no might He increases strength.
Even the youths shall faint and be weary,
And the young men shall utterly fall,
But those who wait on the Lord
Shall renew their strength;
They shall mount up with wings like eagles,
They shall run and not be weary,
They shall walk and not faint.

—Isaiah 40:28–31

Not only can God not help us until we acknowledge our needs and ask for help, we deny ourselves the benefit of experiencing all that He can do for us until we turn to Him. As the Tao te Ching puts it: "To those who have conformed themselves to the Way, the Way readily lends its power. To those who have conformed themselves to the power, the power readily lends more power."

If you feel guilty about asking God for assistance, it might help to know a little more about the basic dynamic of these prayers. They are the classic embodiment of the parent-child model. God is our father; we are His children. In His eyes, we are always His children, and it is always appropriate to ask for His help. If going to a parent for help has negative connotations for you, try to remember that God is a parent like none other. There is no judgment, no blaming, no scolding, and no admonishments in our relationship with Him. There is only love.

Prayers of Petition

As mentioned, the prayers that we pray on our own behalf are prayers of petition. These are some of the most important prayers we can offer as only we know what is in our hearts. Only we know what we want to bring to God. We can't hope for God to hear our concerns unless we offer them to Him.

When we move from petition to intercession we are shifting our center of gravity from our own needs to the needs and concerns of others. Intercessory Prayer is selfless prayer, even self-giving prayer.
—Richard Foster, in *Prayer: Finding the Heart's True Home*

What to Ask For

Prayers of petition acknowledge that we need God's help. For this reason, it is appropriate to pray them whenever we need God to help us do something we can't do for ourselves. People often say prayers of petition when they face obstacles or challenges that are new to them or larger than they have dealt with in the past. They pray for strength, courage, or simply the resolve to help them last through whatever it is that they are facing. As the late J. Robert Ashcroft, an Assemblies of God minister and educator put it, "Prayer is not just asking God to do things—it is helping him bring them to pass."

But asking God for His help can be as simple as saying "God, help me," when you are completely frustrated and almost out of strength after wrestling with something as simple as a tight lid on a jar. Silly? Maybe. But the next time you are in a similar situation, try it. Just taking a brief moment away from the object of your frustration can have surprising results.

FACT

Many people pick and choose among their concerns, and only bring the ones they feel are the most meritorious to God. They forget that God wants to hear all prayers, not just the ones we think are most important.

Feelings You Might Get

If you haven't prayed for yourself before, you might feel somewhat self-conscious and maybe even a little smarmy about doing it at first. It can be hard to get over feeling uncomfortable about being the center of your own attention. Other negative thoughts that might arise include:

- Feeling that God has much better things to do.
- Feeling that God has people who are far worse off to listen to.
- Feeling that your needs are small and petty.

Again, remember that God wants to hear what is on your heart and mind, and that nothing is too small to bring to Him. Getting into the habit of petitioning Him will help you get over the negative feelings you might have about doing so. It will also help you better discern the results of your prayers. As is often the case in prayer, they may not be exactly what you think they would be, or would like them to be.

Whosoever keeps his duty to God, God will appoint a way out for him, and will provide for him in a way that he cannot foresee. And whosoever puts his trust in God, He will suffice him. Lo! God brings His command to pass. God has set a measure for all things.

—*Quran 65:2–3*

Keeping Track of Long-Term Petitions

If you are asking God's help regarding an ongoing concern, or an issue that has recently arisen in your life that you feel might turn into a larger one, it can be helpful to keep track of your concerns and your prayers—and their results—by writing them down. Keeping a prayer journal is one way to do this. For more information on prayer journals, and their role in an ongoing life of prayer, turn to Chapter 20.

Another way to keep track of long-term petitions—both yours and the ones you pray for others—is to make a list of them to refer to when you are praying. Following a list of prayer requests may sound like praying by rote, but it's better than wondering whether or not you remembered to include a specific request.

Intercessory Prayers

Intercessory prayers are very different than petitioning God on your own behalf. When you say these prayers, you are praying for someone else's needs. You are asking for God to step in and do something good for another person.

Kinds of Intercessory Prayers

There are many examples of intercessory prayers in the Bible. Moses interceded on behalf of the Israelites more than once, and was even willing to give up his own life so that his people could live. Abraham made an intercession when he pleaded to God on behalf of his son Ishmael. He also interceded on behalf of the people living in the wicked cities of Sodom and Gomorrah because they were his neighbors and he felt it was right to do so:

And Abraham came near and said, "Would You also destroy the righteous with the wicked? Suppose there were fifty righteous within the city; would You also destroy the place and not spare it for the fifty righteous that were in it?"

—*Genesis 18:23–24*

Many of the prayers that Jesus made were on the behalf of other people, including the one he prayed on the cross: "Forgive them, Father, for they know not what they do." Paul was another earnest intercessory pray-er, and offered up many prayers on behalf of the new church and its followers.

Therefore I also, after I heard of your faith in the Lord Jesus and your love for all the saints, do not cease to give thanks for you, making mention of you in my prayers.

—*Ephesians 1:15–16*

FACT

People often refer to the act of intercessory prayer as "standing in the gap." This refers to their being willing to stand up for others before God, and to ask God for help on the behalf of others.

Matching Prayers to Needs

Many people believe that intercessory prayers should address specific concerns or requests in order to be most effective. Others feel that it is better to offer intercessory prayers of a more general nature, such as those that ask for strength, peace, or an overall resolution of whatever it is that is causing problems or concerns.

While it can be helpful to know exactly what you should pray for when you intercede for someone, it isn't always possible. Many people feel uncomfortable asking for prayer on their own behalf for the same reasons they find it difficult to pray their own petitioning prayers. When they finally muster whatever it takes for them to ask someone else to pray on their behalf, they might be uncomfortable discussing the specifics and will only ask for prayer of a general nature.

If you have been asked to pray for someone, but you don't know what you should pray for, it is perfectly all right to ask the person. Doing so shows that you are truly concerned about this person's needs, and that you want to provide the best help you can. If you don't feel comfortable asking, or you don't get an answer, it is also fine to bring the person's concerns before God in a more general manner. You can simply hold the person in your heart and pray that he or she finds relief through God's help.

Developing Your Intercessory Prayer Muscle

While intercessory prayer comes easily to some people, not everyone embraces it with zeal. If you fall into the latter group, don't feel guilty. It doesn't mean that you're a bad person, or a bad pray-er. It just means that praying for others isn't a prayer style that comes naturally to you. Some people get so many requests for prayers from others that they feel burdened by them. A heavy prayer load can diminish just about anyone's enthusiasm.

If you don't like to pray intercessory prayers, or you simply don't feel the desire to do so, it might help to ask for God's help on your own behalf first. *In Prayer: Finding the Heart's True Home,* Richard Foster suggests starting by praying for an increase in your ability to care and love others. "As God grows your capacity to care," Foster writes, "you will very naturally begin working for the good of your neighbors, your friends, even your enemies." In other words, you'll be praying for them.

When Intercession Goes Awry

As strange as it may seem, there are times when it may not be wise to pray for someone else. As mentioned in Chapter 2, we might have the very best of intentions in mind, but what we think is best may not be in line with the desires and beliefs of the individual we're praying for.

What should I do if someone asks me to pray and I don't feel comfortable praying for him or her?
It can be difficult to pray for someone you don't know very well, or about whom you have mixed feelings for some reason. In these situations, just tell God what is on your mind. Tell Him that you know someone who needs His help and you're turning it over to Him. This is all you need to do.

There are times when we can pray for someone with assuredness, knowing that we are doing what is right for the person we're concerned about. If you get a request for prayer directly from the person who desires it, you can bet that this is exactly what he or she wants you to do. Even still, it is a good idea to ask exactly what you should pray for. Make sure that your prayers align with the individual's needs and desires.

Intercessory prayer is also appropriate in the following situations:

- When a friend asks you to pray on behalf of someone he or she knows who has asked for prayer.
- When you are part of a prayer group and you are praying as a body for individuals who have requested it.
- When you belong to a prayer chain and you are praying over requests submitted to the entire chain.
- When you are addressing the concerns of individuals as part of congregation.

Mary Baker Eddy, the founder of Christian Science, also believed that it was all right to pray for others without their knowledge if other means of intercession had failed. In these situations, she said, the end result could justify the intrusion into someone's privacy. She also believed that such prayer was warranted if the situation were so dire that there was "no time for ceremony and no other aide is near." As she put it, "It would be right to break into a burning building and rouse the slumbering inmates, but wrong to burst open doors and break through windows if no emergency demanded this."

As for the faithful friends and acquaintances who pray so assiduously for my stained soul, I know it sounds churlish to say, "Please don't." But it's a somewhat queasy feeling, knowing that someone is praying for me to think differently or act differently or embrace a different God. Sort of like Mormons baptizing reluctant ancestors. If people are so convinced that prayer has magical powers of efficacy, how dare they use it to impose a change of their own devising?

—Jeannette Batz, "Be Leery of Anyone Who Wields Prayer as a Spiritual Weapon," in *National Catholic Reporter*

Asking for Specific Outcomes

Like healing prayers and discernment prayers, petition and intercessory prayers often revolve around our desire to receive specific answers to our prayers. The question then becomes: Should I ask for specific outcomes? Or should I keep my requests more general? There are several schools of thought on this. Some people believe that it is better not to be too specific with such prayers as it can be so disappointing if the outcomes don't match our requests. Others feel that God can't answer our prayers unless we tell Him what we want. Still others feel that it's important to believe that miracles can happen, and that specifically asking for them does not diminish the possibility of them taking place.

While the best prayer is always a variation of "Thy will be done," the ultimate decision regarding how specific to make your prayers is up to you.

For You O God know that which we need and want before we have thought of it and better than we can ever imagine.

—A prayer from the Armenian church

Perhaps the best way to approach the issue of specific outcomes is to remember that God already knows what is on our hearts and minds. If you desire specific outcomes, or you are praying on behalf of someone else who desires them, it isn't in the spirit of an honest prayer life to keep them from Him.

Chapter 13

Praying for Guidance and Wisdom

Living a full life calls for making decisions. We always want to make good ones, but it can be hard to know which direction we should take when we only rely on our own thoughts and feelings. Going to God and asking for His leading can help us get a better idea of the road we should travel.

Seeking God's Wisdom

One of the greatest joys of becoming an adult is the ability to make decisions on our own. The freedom of being able to decide where we want to live, what we want to do for a living, even what we want to eat for lunch—it can all be pretty wonderful. Even intoxicating at times.

Ask God for what you want, but you cannot ask if you are not asking for a right thing. When you draw near to God, you cease from asking for things. "Your Father knows what things you have need of, before you ask him." Then, why ask? That you may get to know Him.

—Oswald Chambers

When we first step into the adult world of decision-making, we often do so knowing that we have a safety net to catch us if we should fall. We have the support and confidence of our parents or other older and wiser folks to fall back on should we need it. However, as we grow wiser and more mature during our spiritual walk with God, we gain an even greater safety net. In fact, it's the best fail-safe system we could ever hope for.

Getting a Grip on the Big Picture

If you are looking for the big picture, the macro view, on how to approach and handle life's turning points, you couldn't ask for a better guide than God. Here's why: When we ask the people around us—our friends and family members—for their opinions on what we should do, the responses they give us are going to be shaped and colored by their own experiences and their own belief systems. When we ask God for His advice, there are no such temporal filters. We don't get answers based on other people's experiences and beliefs. We instead are guided toward the proper course of action through the insights we gain as a result of asking His opinion.

This isn't to say that other peoples' opinions aren't worth anything, or that you should never ask anyone for an opinion or a piece of friendly advice. There is nothing wrong in doing so, and there is nothing about your relationship with God that would prevent you from doing so. What it does mean is that it can be a good idea to take the answers you get with a grain of salt.

Vain is the man who puts his trust in men, in created things . . . Do not be self-sufficient but place your trust in God. Do what lies in your power and God will aid your good will. Put no trust in your own learning nor in the cunning of any man, but rather in the grace of God Who helps the humble and humbles the proud . . . for God's judgments differ from those of men and what pleases them often displeases Him.

—Thomas à Kempis, in *The Imitation of Christ*

The Folly of Following Your Own Advice

Taking matters into your own hands and following your own advice can be just as troublesome as leaning on the wisdom of others to help you make your decisions. The decisions you come up with on your own, without seeking God's wisdom and help, are just as biased as the ones you get from other people. They too are colored by your own experiences and feelings. The better answers, the ones that will serve you the best in the long run, will come when you have made them with the help of God's counsel.

Trust in the Lord with all your heart,
And lean not on your own understanding;
In all your ways acknowledge Him,
And He shall direct your paths.
Do not be wise in your own eyes;
Fear the Lord and depart from evil.
It will be health to your flesh,
And strength to your bones.

—Proverbs 3:5–8

Grant to me, O Lord, to know what I ought to know, to love what I ought to love, to praise what delights Thee most, to value what is precious in thy sight, to hate what is offensive to Thee. Do not suffer me to judge according to the sight of my eyes, nor to pass sentence according to the hearing of the ears of ignorant men; but to discern with true judgment between things visible and spiritual, and above all things to enquire what is the good pleasure of thy will.

—Thomas à Kempis, in *The Imitation of Christ*

Asking for Guidance and Wisdom

When we ask God for His guidance and wisdom, we pray prayers of discernment. These are prayers that help us see things that we can't see on our own, that help us gain a better understanding of the issues we face, or that help us make wise choices between the various courses of action that are open to us.

Discernment prayers are important because we can't predict the future, as much as we would often like to be able to do so. We also don't know what the future holds for us from God's point of view. Because of this, we need to ask for His help so we can better figure out what we should do and where we should go. It is important to seek His wisdom so that we can better align our decisions with what He has in mind for us, or what He wills for us. In other words, God's will.

FACT

Discernment prayers help us better see things that are not very clear or obvious, to understand things better, or to be able to tell the difference between two or more courses of action or decisions. Another word for discernment is judgment, which describes the ability to form sound opinions and make sensible decisions or reliable guesses.

Bugging God

We can ask for God's help in making many different kinds of decisions. In fact, there really isn't an area in which we can't ask for His help. Some people believe that it's not a good idea to bug God all the time, however, to run to Him with every decision we need to make. Doing so, they say, activates something akin to a "chicken little" syndrome. In other words, God gets so tired hearing about all of our little questions that He doesn't pay attention to the big ones when they come His way.

Well, God is all-powerful, and He certainly knows a great deal more about things than we do. However, there is no evidence to suggest that He makes judgment calls when it comes to the issues in the lives of His people. He doesn't pick and choose, nor does He toss aside one question for another based on a scale of importance. In other words, He hears them all. If something is important enough to you that you want to ask God's opinion about it, it is important enough for Him to hear your request.

ESSENTIAL

Everyone has his own sense of what is important to him, and his own comfort level in asking for God's help in making decisions. While there are many reasons to seek God's counsel, you might feel it unnecessary to ask Him to sweat the small stuff. However, most people seek God's advice and assistance far too infrequently. It's better to ask too often than not to ask at all.

Knowing When to Ask for Advice

The best times to seek God's advice is when you are facing decisions that pertain to some aspect of how you live your life, or how you wish to live it. Other times when it is wise to ask God's opinion is when your decision will affect the lives of the people you care about—family members, coworkers, friends—more than slightly. Examples of these decisions include:

- Caring for an elderly parent
- Job changes that may require relocation
- Relationship changes
- Starting a new business

These are broad brushstroke decisions, ones that can have a significant effect both on your own life and the lives of the people you care about. Making these decisions often calls for extending your field of inquiry beyond where it has been before. In other words, you are venturing into unknown territory, and these voyages almost always carry with them a certain amount of trepidation. Feelings of unease can too easily be translated into decisions if you try to make them in a vacuum. Pulling God into the process may not ease your butterflies, but it can help you recognize them for what they are.

Taking God's Point of View

If you still think that you need to filter your requests to God, and that you should only ask His advice on matters that you feel are important enough for Him to consider, think for a moment about what this says about your relationship with the Almighty. In effect, when you pick and choose the issues that you want God's advice on, you are taking matters into your own hands. In other words, you are playing God. You're assuming you know what He wants to hear. In so doing, you are also assuming that you know more than He does. This, of course, isn't the case, nor can it ever be.

The greatest wisdom is not ours, it is that which we receive from God. If we ask Him for it, we will receive it.

If any of you lacks wisdom, let him ask of God, who gives to all liberally and without reproach, and it will be given to him.

—James, 1:5

Hearing God's Voice

When we say prayers of discernment, we are asking God for His advice. We want Him to give us His opinion. But how do we hear what He has to say? Will He speak to us? If so, what will He sound like? Will His words be those we can understand? How will we know that it is God speaking to us and not someone else? How can we tell that it is His voice, and not ours?

ESSENTIAL

> When asking God for advice, it is important to step back and let Him do His work. Don't start trying to guide the outcome by searching for signs of God's direction. Be patient, and let it come to you.

The truth is, it can be extremely difficult to discern God's voice. Unlike biblical times, His words aren't accompanied by dramatic natural phenomena. The heavens don't open when He speaks. We don't hear His voice in a burning bush. The seas don't part. These days, God mostly speaks to us in ways that we can only learn to understand through talking—that is, praying—to Him.

A Bang or a Whisper?

Even in biblical times, however, God sometimes made His feelings known in much more subtle ways. In the Book of Elijah, God speaks in a "still, small voice" instead of in an eardrum-shattering revelation accompanied by earthquakes and thunderstorms. Other world scripture underscores the fact that God, as it is often said, is in the details.

> *Eye cannot see him, nor words reveal him;*
> *by the senses, austerity, or works he is not known.*
> *When the mind is cleansed by the grace of wisdom,*
> *he is seen by contemplation—the One without parts.*
>
> *—The Upanishads*

Much is said about hearing the still small voice of God. It is the manner in which He usually speaks to us today. However, this isn't to say that you won't get a good old-fashioned revelation when you ask Him for His opinion. They do—and can—happen. Sometimes God's answer comes in a big "aha" moment. It might even be accompanied by something—a voice—that has no earthly presence. It may be a voice that you don't hear but you somehow sense deep inside of your being. On the other hand, you could possibly hear it loud and clear, just like you would when someone is talking to you.

To be honest, these types of revelatory experiences don't happen very often. Many people live their entire lives hoping to hear the voice of God, striving to hear Him, and yet they never do. You might not as well, but you can learn how to recognize the other ways in with He does answer you.

How to Recognize an Answer from God

As much as we might yearn and pray for definitive answers to the questions we throw up to God, He rarely issues concrete directives. He won't tell us to take one approach over another. He won't plant a road sign that says "Turn here," or put up a barrier that says, "Stop." Instead of words, we get nuances. And they can be very, very subtle.

While God's answers can take the form of external signs, His answers more often manifest themselves deep within our bodies and souls. In prayer, we turn our hearts and minds toward God. As we do, we become attuned to His presence. The more often we pray, the greater our sense of attunement becomes. It's as if we develop a special little antenna that picks up God's signals. What we sense or hear might be faint at first, but as we keep on praying, the signals get stronger. We become better able to sense how our actions do or don't line up with His will. In other words, we get our answers.

Answers from God are often described as feeling like being on the right path, even if it is a difficult one. Other indications of getting an answer from God include:

- An overall feeling of calm or peace
- Feeling like you've reached a resolution
- Feeling a sense of relief
- Feeling free of any need to second-guess your decision

Patience, Patience

It can take some time, and a great deal of prayer, to reach a resolution on important issues. God rarely works on the same schedule as we do, which can be a source of immense frustration at times. Although we know we need to be patient and wait for God, it is difficult to do so when we are seeking answers from Him. Because of this, we sometimes try to force God's hand. We search for specific signs or signals—often external—that we think could be an indication that He has answered us, and we use these signs to justify the actions we want to take. Or, we try to connect the lack of such signals to God's assent. If something doesn't happen, or we don't see a specific sign, it means that our plans meet with God's approval.

You must be nothing but an ear which hears what the universe of the Word is constantly saying within you. The moment you start hearing what you yourself are saying, you must stop.

—*The Maggid of Mezerich*

Seeking "Yes" or "No"

Searching for signs of God's answers can get a little silly at times. It can be amazingly easy to ascribe even the tiniest things to a yes or no answer from the Almighty. Here is one example of how it's possible to go a little overboard while seeking answers from God: Let's say you have been diligently asking God's advice regarding a relationship you'd like to pursue. You have been talking to Him for a while about it, and you don't feel like you've received much guidance either way. The person you're interested in hasn't changed in behavior toward you, or may not be aware that you even exist.

One day you happen to hear through the grapevine that this person has just ended a long-term relationship with someone else. "Aha," you think. "There is my answer from God. It's a divine intervention, and it's been set up just for me. Green light, I'm good to go."

Or are you? Did God send a message? Did He intervene on your behalf and break up this person's relationship so you can step in? Or are you taking things into your own hands and reading something into the situation that has nothing to do with it?

There is no sure answer to this question beyond—you guessed it—continuing to seek your answers by turning to God in prayer. As you do so, you may sense a very different set of emotions than the ones previously described. Instead of feeling calm and peaceful, things might not seem right. You might feel confused and conflicted. Perhaps you are no longer sure that the events that have transpired have anything to do with God's will. That's good, because chances are pretty good that they don't. Instead, you made them fit what you wanted God's answer to be.

"My Will" Instead of "Thy Will"

When we look for God's answers instead of allowing them to come to us, we are again engaging in "my will" instead of "thy will" thinking. Even though it may not seem like we're taking things into our own hands, we are.

A better way of learning how to discern God's answers is to stick to the internal discernment approach described earlier. Pay close attention to how you feel when you are in His presence. As you do, you will gain a better sense of what God is doing in your life. You learn how to discern, or recognize, the messages He sends you. The more you go to Him, and the more attention you pay to how you feel, the better you will get at recognizing His answers when you get them. You won't have to go looking for them.

Getting to "Yes"

One of the biggest problems people have with discernment prayers is that they feel like God never gives them a clear answer. He is speaking, they sense something, but the message is garbled with static. Or, they get conflicting answers. God seems to be saying different things on different days. One day it's yes. The next day it's no.

In situations like these, the problem lies not with God but with us. As long as we continue to ask the same questions, His answers will be the same. Only our perceptions of what they are change. Problems with conflicting answers often arise when we are dealing with complex issues, and we are tossing up a lot of questions. It can also happen when the issues that we are dealing with are emotionally charged. It is always difficult to discern God's answer when your head is spinning.

The Master said, "Danger arises when a man feels secure in his position. Destruction threatens when a man seeks to preserve his worldly estate. Confusion develops when a man has put everything in order. Therefore the superior man does not forget danger in his security, nor ruin when he is well established, nor confusion when his affairs are in order. In this way he gains personal safety and is able to protect the empire. In the I Ching it is said: 'What if it should fail? What if it should fail?' In this way he ties it to a cluster of mulberry shoots [makes success certain]."

—I Ching, Great Commentary

Sorting Out the Questions

When you can't get a firm handle on God's answers, it usually means that you need to sort out the questions that you are asking Him. The following six steps may help you to do so:

1. Write down the issues on which you are seeking God's leading.
2. Do a pro and con list for each. For example, if you are trying to figure out if you should accept a job offer, list all the reasons why you think you should accept the offer, and all the reasons why you think you shouldn't.
3. Next, list all the things you think might happen if you accept the job, and the things you think might happen if you don't.

4. Finally, list your concerns, your hopes, and your fears.
5. Find a quiet space, and spend a few moments just resting in God's presence. Then, ask for His help.
6. Read through your lists. As you do, pay attention to how you feel. Do some issues make you uneasy? Did you list some fears that now seem unfounded? Make note of your feelings.

After you are done with this process, you might find it helpful to simply let your thoughts stay in your head and heart for a while. As you do, you might get a sense that they are somehow moving around and shifting in importance. What may have seemed like a huge concern when you started your lists might now be at the bottom of the pile. Little things might have come forward. You might even have come up with some new feelings that you hadn't been aware of before. If they unsettle you, add them to your list.

You may have to repeat this process several times, if not more, before you feel like you've gained the clarity you're after. You'll know you've got it when you quit feeling unsettled and you start feeling at peace.

Seeking God's Voice in Sacred Literature

Another way to sort out the answers God is giving you is to read spiritual literature. Seek out both the words of others who have struggled with the same issues that you're facing, and words of wisdom from those they sought help from. Pay attention to how you feel as you read. As before, feelings of peace or calmness may be indications of God's answers for you.

Scripture from the Bible is an obvious choice for this, and you'll find some of the best words of wisdom you could ask for in the Book of Proverbs. Chapter One in Proverbs contains some especially good words of wisdom. But don't forget the sacred texts of other religions. There is wonderful guidance to be gained from these works as well. Ⓔ

Chapter 14

Praying for Healing

Healing prayer is controversial. Many people misconstrue what it is or reject it as nothing more than a placebo because they say it doesn't work. To a certain extent, such skepticism is understandable, especially in a world where science rather than spirit usually gets the credit for working miracles. But this doesn't mean that praying to God for healing doesn't also fit into the equation.

The Ancient Tradition of Healing Prayer

Prayer has played a significant role in healing since ancient times. In the earliest civilizations, people believed that gods, demons, and spirits both caused and cured diseases. Since they couldn't explain why disease happened, the only explanation for it had to lie in the unseen. So, too, did the cure. Because of this, priests and temples were the doctors and hospitals of the ancient world.

In ancient Greek and Egyptian civilizations, supernatural causes and cures for disease intermingled with more rational approaches. The Greeks believed that the god Apollo was the inventor of healing, and that he passed his sacred knowledge to Asclepius, a priest and medical practitioner who was eventually worshipped as a god. Temples and shrines to Asclepius were being built at about the same time that Hippocrates, the father of medicine, was practicing a more rational form of medicine, one that was based more on the powers of observation than on the supernatural powers of god and spirits. Hippocrates's refusal to blame the gods for causing illness and disease led to healing being thought of as a science instead of a religion.

FACT

The Bible documents four major types of healing that can be experienced through prayer: forgiveness, physical healing, emotional healing, and deliverance from evil. Other things to pray for healing over include addictions and relationships.

Egypt, one of the ancient world's more advanced societies, was also the first to regard medicine as a specialty. Egyptian physicians treated people with plants, herbs, oils, magic charms, and surgery. However, they continued to both blame the gods and ask for their help when the treatments failed.

The belief that the supernatural was both responsible for and could cure disease is well documented in the Bible. There are numerous examples of God inflicting illnesses and curing them in the Old Testament. There are fewer examples of God-sent diseases in the New Testament, and the ones that are here are vastly overshadowed by the healings that were such a significant part of Jesus' ministry. Healing of both the body and the spirit is a key theme in the New Testament. During his ministry, Jesus healed the lame, lepers, blind men, a hemorrhaging woman, and the demon-possessed. He even raised the dead. More than 20 percent of the Gospels are about the healings that Jesus did.

Healing, in fact, was so important to Jesus that he spent more time making people well than doing anything else. The early Christian church also emphasized physical healing, and considered it a component crucial to Christian life and faith. Some of the earliest monasteries built had hospitals where treatment relied on prayer and medical remedies. Later on, these monasteries housed some of the first medical schools.

By the fourth century C.E., however, medical practice began to overtake prayer for treating disease. A number of Christians now believed that illness was sent by God as a way to punish or correct people. Since they couldn't go to the same entity who had caused the problem and ask for help, their only defense against it was to seek treatment from a physician. Faith became secondary to science. Still, there were some who believed that prayer could heal. Others, including St. Augustine, witnessed God's healing firsthand and became believers. Despite growing skepticism in the secular world about the power of prayer, the ministry of healing continued in the Christian church. Many people continued to seek—and receive—God's grace in matters of health as the debate over body versus spirit continued.

Ever since at least Moses was born . . . [divine medicine] has healed so many human beings; and not only has it not lost its proper power, but neither has any disease ever yet overcome it.
—St. John Chrysostom, in *Homily Against Publishing the Errors of the Brethren, or Uttering Against Enemies*

To this day, many churches include requests for healing as part of their services. A growing number hold special healing services where prayers for healing are offered. Jewish healing services, held in synagogues and other settings, are also blossoming. Prayer is also regaining its place in medical practice as part of a growing emphasis on treating the mind, body, and spirit together. Not only are people praying to God for healing, they're doing so with the support of modern medicine.

FACT

In 1992, only three medical schools in the United States were offering courses on spirituality and healing. Today, as many as two-thirds of all medical schools offer some kind of program that combines healing and spirituality. Even though there are some people who do not believe that prayer and spirituality have powers of healing, most everyone acknowledges that the peacefulness and serenity often achieved through prayer and spirituality can have tremendous benefits for the ill and injured.

The Nature of Healing Prayer

Like other types of prayer, we don't know exactly how praying for healing works. Skeptics, of course, will tell you that it doesn't, and that any healing that comes about through prayer is coincidental and more the result of good medicine than of good faith. That's fine, but what about healings that happen in the absence of medical intervention or treatment? Are they just a matter of coincidence, too? If a woman diagnosed with cancer recovers by doing nothing more than praying, and asking others to pray on her behalf, what is the basis for the recovery?

Healing prayer requires, more than anything else, the willingness to believe that anything—and everything—is possible. That requires a good amount of faith in God's abilities, including His ability to work miracles, which is something that an effective prayer life develops. It also means having an open heart. This isn't always easy when we're afraid or hurting, but not having one is one of the greatest obstacles to any kind of prayer.

The Faith Factor

Faith in God is clearly a big part of healing prayer. It is also the factor that gets blamed when prayers for healing don't deliver the hoped-for results. There is no scriptural basis for believing that healing was denied because a person was lacking in faith, or that the people praying for healing were lacking. But this type of causal thinking goes on. We're sometimes guilty of it ourselves.

The truth is that there is no cause-and-effect relationship between the amount of faith that one has and the healing that he or she either receives or doesn't. It is important, however, that our faith is aligned correctly. It's folly to say to God, "Hey Lord, I know you're going to heal so-and-so, so thanks in advance." That's telling God that we want a specific outcome that may or may not be aligned with what He has planned.

Sometimes healing happens as a single miraculous event. More often, however, it manifests in things like finding the strength to stick to a long-term treatment program, or in developing a greater sense of peace about a lingering medical problem. However, if we fully put things in God's hands, we're focusing less on what we think should happen and more on believing that whatever happens is according to His divine plan.

Prayer Plus Medicine

What is also pretty clear about healing prayer is that it works best when coupled with medical practice. Research has shown that religious belief increases the effectiveness of medical treatment. There's no reason to believe that the reverse wouldn't also be true. While at times it may seem to be a good idea to emphasize one approach over the other, it's better to engage in both at the same time, and with the same level of commitment.

How to Pray for Healing

People who don't know much about healing prayer often believe that such prayers can only be offered by certain individuals—ministers and priests, for example—or other exalted beings who have somehow been chosen by God to utter these important prayers. Well, they're wrong. Anyone can pray for healing, both for themselves and for others.

FACT

In biblical times, healing activities were often carried out by people who had a special relationship to God, or whom God had anointed for such service. In modern times, such precepts have often been interpreted as meaning that only people who felt specially called to healing, or who were "indwelt with spirit," could offer healing prayer.

Praying for healing does require certain attributes, such as:

- **The ability to listen**—Both to the needs of others, and to God.
- **The ability to discern**—You need to be able to tell if you're praying for the right thing.
- **Compassion**—Those with caring hearts offer the best prayers.
- **Belief**—Both in God and in His ability to heal.
- **Patience**—Healing doesn't usually happen overnight. If you're going to pray for it, you'll need to keep at it.
- **Humility**—Being able to accept what happens, good or bad.
- **Gratefulness**—The ability to give thanks to God, regardless of what happens.

Being weak in any of these areas doesn't necessarily mean that you shouldn't pray for healing. However, it might require taking a critical look at your current prayer life. Being deficient in any of these areas can indicate that your relationship with God isn't all that it should be. The people who are most effective at praying for others are those who are on solid footing with the Almighty. To help others heal, you may have to heal yourself first. If you're not right with God, it can be real folly to go to Him in prayer for others.

We are all healers who can reach out and offer health, and we are all patients in constant need of help.
—Henri Nouwen, in *The Wounded Healer*

As much as we might not like to think it true, our own problems can be the cause of unanswered prayers. In *Prayer: Finding the Heart's True Home*, Richard Foster identifies lack of faith or sin on the part of the person doing the praying as two possible roadblocks to the flow of God's grace and mercy. Not being able to align yourself correctly with God can also lead to praying for the wrong things, such as physical instead of emotional healing, or to praying for the right things in the wrong way.

Before praying for healing, it's also important to put your efforts into perspective. Remember that you are just a part of the process.

Putting your efforts into perspective can help you understand why your prayers might not get answered. The disappointment of unanswered prayer is most keenly felt when healing is what's being prayed for.

There is no one set form that healing prayer must take. Certain types of healing prayer, such as that which takes place as part of a church service, often follow a specific order. But they can also be offered up very casually by people praying alone. They can be in the form of a prayerful attitude—a going about life in a compassionate, prayerful state—instead of limited to specific times of prayer. Some research suggests that the most effective prayer reflects the personality of the pray-er. If you prefer a more introverted, inner-directed way of praying, the energetic, emotionally charged atmosphere of a charismatic Christian prayer service might not be for you. If you enjoy the camaraderie and fellowship of praying with a group, however, you might like being part of a prayer group or a prayer circle. Many people believe in the scriptural precept that healing prayer is more effective when it's done ". . . where two or three are gathered together in My name . . ." (Matthew 18:20)

Most important, don't let yourself be intimidated by the enormity of what you're praying for. Prayers for healing are some of the most common prayers offered. So jump in and start praying.

FACT

The belief in corporate or communal prayer dates back to biblical times, when it was customary to ask church leaders to pray over people in need of healing. In the New Testament, Jesus tells his disciples that when more than one person prays together, the power of that prayer is greater than the prayer of one person alone.

Where Healing Prayer Takes Place

Healing prayer is done in many different settings and takes a variety of different forms. As previously mentioned, it's a standard part of many church services, but it's by no means the exclusive property of the church. You'll find healing services in synagogues and spiritual centers. Do a search for healing prayer on the Internet and you'll find some Web sites devoted to it as well. You'll find several listed in Appendix B.

Prayer Services

Prayer services generally follow a format similar to a church's regular liturgy. Because of the more intimate nature of a prayer service, however, they're often less formal than a regular service. Many are held in chapels or other small spaces instead of large sanctuaries.

During a prayer service, all participants voice prayers at certain times during the liturgy. Individual prayers, either spoken or silent, are also offered. At some prayer services, lists of people who have asked for prayer are passed around, and each person is prayed for.

A number of services also offer the laying on of hands or anointing with oil. Both are healing practices dating back to ancient times, when they were symbolic of calling upon gods and spirits for supernatural healing. They're also well documented in the Bible. In the Book of James, the writer tells anyone who is suffering to ". . . call for the elders of the church, and let them pray over him, anointing him with oil in the name of the Lord" (James 5:14). In the Book of Acts, a disciple of Jesus named Ananias healed Saul of Tarsus (who later became the apostle Paul) of blindness by putting his hand on him. Special prayers are said for both practices as they are done.

If you're not familiar with these practices, they may seem strange or uncomfortable to you. But they can be a powerful adjunct to prayer. Both signify a special link between the people in need of prayer, those who are praying for them, and God. They make what is already an important act even more important. It may be difficult to see the power in something as simple as a hand laid upon one's body during prayer. But, it can be powerful indeed. Many people who are ill suffer from isolation and rejection. Sometimes, the most basic human contact—touch—is a very welcome gift.

Prayer Groups

Prayer groups are a common fixture in many churches, and are often formed by members of the congregation who feel called to pray in this manner. These groups vary from being very informal to having a pretty specific structure, with prayer leaders and committees and what not. Members might receive specific training in healing prayer as well. Some pray over prayer requests that are submitted to them or that they become aware of in other ways instead of directly over the people in need of healing. Others combine the people requesting prayer with those who wish to pray for them. Laying on of hands may also be done.

Even if you generally prefer to pray alone, participating in a prayer group can be an effective way to practice healing prayer, both for yourself and for others. Not only are you surrounded by a group of people with similar desires, they tend to be a pretty compassionate lot. They're also usually pretty good at what they do. If you're new to prayer, and especially if you're new to healing prayer, there's a lot to be learned from a group of fervent pray-ers who gather together on a regular basis.

Prayer Chains

Another popular type of corporate prayer, prayer chains link together individuals who share the desire to pray for others. Thanks to the Internet, some of these groups extend around the world, which means that a single request for prayer may be prayed over by thousands of individuals. Prayer requests are passed along to members of the circle. Some groups schedule a specific time of day at which prayers are to be offered. Others simply commit to praying daily for the people on the prayer list.

QUESTION?

Is it better to have a specific goal in mind when praying for healing?
Not necessarily. In studies conducted by the Spindrift Organization, directed and nondirected prayers were both proven effective. However, open-ended, or nondirected prayer was shown to be substantially more effective.

Going It Alone

While there is often great strength in numbers when it comes to healing prayer, there's nothing that says you can't do it on your own. If you're praying for someone else, you might find it helpful to have something that reminds you of that person in front of you—a picture, a favorite object, maybe even a letter. Asking the individual for guidance on what you should pray for is also a good idea. Don't assume that you know what's in someone's heart.

Your healing prayer should follow the same or similar pattern you've established for your usual prayer routine. If your emotions overwhelm you and you have a hard time talking to God, simply rest in His presence. He'll understand. You may wish to read scripture that specifically deals with healing. There are numerous examples throughout the Bible. Of them, the Twenty-Third Psalm is one of the best loved.

The very personal nature of the Book of Psalms, and its reflection of just about every human emotion you can think of, makes it a top pick for accompanying healing prayer. Almost every psalm praises God in some way or asks for His help.

At the end of your prayer period, it can be helpful to offer a "thy will be done" prayer. This one by Reinhold Niebuhr may be more familiar to you as the Serenity Prayer, but it is also a good one for this purpose:

God, give us grace to accept with serenity
The things that cannot be changed,
Courage to change the things which should be changed,
And the wisdom to distinguish the one from the other.

—Reinhold Niebuhr

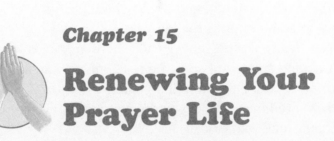

Chapter 15

Renewing Your Prayer Life

There will be times in your prayer life when you'll feel stuck. You may feel worn out, in a rut, or simply bored with prayer. You might have hit a dry spell in your prayer practice during which it seems like nothing much is happening, or when it seems like you're moving farther away from God instead of closer. In this chapter, you'll learn about ways in which you can renew your prayer life and keep it moving forward.

Recognizing the Need for Renewal

Just as with any relationship, your relationship with God will have its ups and downs. There are times when you feel like you're racing along so fast that you're out of breath, and times when it feels like it's stalled out. There are good days of prayer when you feel so close to God that you can physically sense His presence. Then there are times when He feels very far away and you're not sure you're connecting at all. You might feel out of sorts with God, either a little or a lot. Or, you're simply not as happy with where things are as you once were. And you're not as excited about spending time with God.

Our time in prayer is supposed to be something that we look forward to. However, just like athletes who get burned out when they work out too often or too hard, it's also possible to get to the point where you feel like you're dragging yourself into prayer instead of welcoming the time you spend talking to God. If this is the case, you're in good company. Everyone has times when they feel like they have to pray instead of wanting to pray. Even the greatest spiritual leaders have had times when prayer became more of a burden than a blessing. In other words, dry spells happen.

It's important to understand these periods and to put them into perspective. They are never indications that our relationship with God is over. Usually, they're signs that we need to take a look at other factors. Some might be physical. Others will be spiritual.

Body Talk

Sometimes the problems we're having in prayer are more related to our bodies instead of our souls. When we're working long hours or working in demanding jobs, our lives outside of prayer can get way out of balance. Being ill can also throw what is usually a very satisfying prayer life out of whack. When our bodies don't feel right, our physical feelings can distract us from focusing on God. When we're done praying, it just doesn't feel like we've connected with Him very well.

If you feel like your prayer problems are more related to your physical being, listen to what your body is trying to tell you. Body and spirit can both be renewed in prayer, but sometimes the body needs to take precedence.

When you've hit a dry spot in your prayer life, don't stop praying. This is exactly when you don't want to put the skids on your relationship with God. Continue your prayer practice in some way. As long as you continue to go to God, to talk to Him, to lay your fears and your desires at His feet, your relationship with Him will move forward.

Maybe the half hour that you usually spend praying to God in the morning or at night would be better spent catching up on some much-needed shut-eye, at least for the time being. If so, you can find other times during the day to catch up on your conversations with God. You can pray simply throughout the day. Or, take mini prayer breaks—maybe spend five minutes in the morning reading your Bible, another five minutes at lunch doing an online meditation, and another five minutes before dinner simply sitting in God's presence.

Mind Games

Very often, our problems in prayer are related more to our heads than our hearts. For whatever reason, the prayer life we once found satisfying just isn't cutting it any more. God may seem very far away, and the joy we experience in communicating with Him may be gone as well.

In Psalm 42, the psalmist also talks about his feeling that God is distant, and voices his desire to overcome the chasm between himself and the Almighty:

As the deer pants for the water brooks,
So pants my soul for You, O God.
My soul thirsts for God, for the living God.
When shall I come and appear before God?
My tears have been my food day and night,

While they continually say to me,
Where is your God?
When I remember these things,
I pour out my soul within me.
For I used to go with the multitude;
I went with them to the house of God,
With the voice of joy and praise,
With a multitude that kept a pilgrim feast.
Why are you cast down, O my soul?
And why are you disquieted within me?
Hope in God, for I shall yet praise Him
For the help of his countenance.
O my God, my soul is cast down within me;
Therefore I will remember You from the land of the Jordan,
And from the heights of Hermon,
From the Hill Mizar.
Deep calls unto deep at the noise of Your waterfalls;
All Your waves and billows have gone over me.
The Lord will command His lovingkindness in the daytime,
And in the night His song shall be with me—
A prayer to the God of my life.
I will say to God my Rock,
"Why have You forgotten me?"
Why do I go mourning because of the oppression of the enemy?
As with a breaking of my bones,
My enemies reproach me,
While they say to me all day long,
"Where is your God?"
Why are you cast down, O my soul?
And why are you disquieted within me?
Hope in God;
For I shall yet praise Him,
The help of my countenance and my God.

—Psalm 42

It's also important in times like these to remember that God is willing to listen, and that He will guide us in all circumstances. Even though He may seem beyond our reach at times, He really isn't.

> If we neglect prayer and if the branch is not connected with the vine, it will die. That connecting to the branch to the vine is prayer. If that connection is there then love is there, then joy is there, and we will be the sunshine of God's love, the hope of eternal happiness, the flame of burning love.
>
> —Mother Teresa

How can we get back into the swing of things with God? It can be as simple as exchanging your current prayer routine for something new. At other times, you may need to change your attitude about prayer, or readjust your expectations of what you get out of the experience.

In any case, don't let yourself become paralyzed by your feelings. Doing so opens you up for being overcome or defeated by your circumstances. While praying may be the last thing you feel like doing, it's one of the best things you can do. If you're really lacking enthusiasm, make your prayers very simple. The important thing is to keep the lines of communication open. As will be discussed in Chapter 18, all prayer needs to consist of is one word offered up to God with the right intention.

One of the best things you can do when you're feeling lost or unsettled in your prayer routine is to talk to God about your feelings. Whatever is on your mind, praying is one of the best ways to get your thoughts out.

Changing Old for New

If you've been following the same prayer routine for a while, you might simply be bored. It does happen. If you think you're bored, don't stay stuck in your same prayer routine. Try something new. This doesn't necessarily mean completely tossing aside your current prayer practice for something else. Try taking a micro approach first. Consider making small changes such as:

- Praying at a different time of day—If you usually pray at the end of the day, try switching to late afternoon, just before dinner, early morning, or whatever works.
- Praying in a different place—Sometimes a change of scenery can do the trick.
- Praying in a different position—If you always sit in a chair, maybe it's time to try a meditation cushion.

Praying Online

There isn't much you can't do online these days. It might seem a little silly to pray with a computer, but it can be surprisingly effective if you hook up with the right prayer site. If you haven't searched the Internet for sites that offer online prayer experiences, you might be surprised at how many are out there. It may take some time to find one that suits your particular needs, but keep searching as there are sites that offer a truly wonderful experience. Some even have online studies on various facets of spirituality. You'll find a couple of them listed in Appendix B.

Praying with a Group

We're always linked to the community of God when we pray, which means that we're never really alone. However, if your usual prayer practice takes place in physical solitude, you're missing out on the energy that's present when "two or three are gathered."

Prayer groups are often affiliated with houses of worship, and it's usually easiest to find them by checking with local churches and other organizations. Other places where prayer groups meet include monasteries and community centers. While it's usually best to experience group prayer in the physical presence of the people you're praying with, it's also possible to do it through cyberspace. Do an Internet search for prayer sites, and check the site menus to see if they offer group prayer.

If you already belong to a prayer group, think about asking a member of the group for help in revitalizing your prayer life. Having someone who's willing to encourage you and to check on your progress can keep you going forward.

Enhancing Your Environment

If you're a "bare-bones" pray-er, maybe it's time to burn some incense or light a candle when you pray. If you already use tools like these in your practice, try something new. It could be as simple as buying a new candle, or treating yourself to that CD of Celtic music that caught your ear the last time you were music shopping. If you don't have a space set aside in your home for prayer and meditation, this might be the time to do it.

Asking God for Help

If making small changes doesn't get you out of your rut, it might be time to make bigger ones. Before you do, it can be helpful to spend some time in discernment with God and see if you can sense the direction He'd like you take.

Ask Him for guidance, either during a scheduled prayer period or informally as you're going about your normal daily routine. It may take some time to get your answers, so be patient.

What should I do if God answers my question, but the answers aren't what I wanted to hear?
Sometimes God wants us to move in directions that may initially disturb or trouble us. If the direction you received from Him is of this nature, don't panic or dismiss it out of hand. Continue to go to God in prayer, and stay open to letting His spirit work within you.

Getting a New 'Tude

The early stages of a prayer practice can be pretty exciting. Things are fresh and new to us, and every way in which we encounter the Almighty feels wonderful. After a while, however, the newness wears off. We're no longer carried along by the freshness of the experience. The time we spend with God seems more ordinary, less wonderful, not as special. In other words, the bloom has fallen off the rose.

One of the mistakes that is often made in prayer is thinking of it as being different than any other relationship. We tend to think that our communion with God should always be a profound experience, and when it's less than transforming we feel somehow let down, even disappointed.

Just like a relationship with a spouse or significant other, our relationship with God doesn't remain in one place. As God's spirit moves within us, we move to new places and new ways of experiencing Him. There will be times when things will seem academic and you'll feel like you're merely going through the motions. Then, out of the blue, something will happen that will knock your socks off, and you'll be amazed all over again.

Even when it feels like your prayer life is going nowhere, it always is. It can be difficult at times to sense the small changes that God makes within us, but they always lead to great ones.

Stepping Back to Go Forward

Sometimes the best way to renew your prayer life is to take a step back. In other words, we need to retreat. Most people don't think they can afford the luxury of spending time away from their busy schedules, but it's because we are so busy that we need to withdraw at times. No one can keep going full speed ahead all of the time. Sometimes it's necessary to stop and get your bearings, to gain a new perspective on things. One of the best ways to do this is by stepping back for a time of refreshment and renewal.

A retreat is a time for stopping and resting for the purpose of moving forward with renewed vigor and purpose. It's a time for returning to the basics: basic beliefs, basic attitudes, the basic balance of life. Above all, a retreat is a rest in God.

Many people make prayer retreats a regular part of their spiritual walk, no matter how busy their lives are. Spending time away from normal routines in contemplation and quiet affords singular opportunities for drawing closer to God.

The Tradition of Withdrawing from the World

Retreats are well documented in the Bible. In the Old Testament, the prophet Elijah escaped to the desert to pray after his encounters with Jezebel, the Phoenician princess who threatened to kill him after he deposed her priests.

Jesus began his ministry by retreating into the wilderness for forty days of prayer and fasting. He often went into "a mountain apart to pray," and he invited his disciples to come with him. Paul also practiced the discipline of retreat.

Over the centuries, many men and women have followed these early examples of spiritual discipline and have withdrawn from daily life for various periods of time. The desert fathers and mothers of ancient Christianity took to the desert so they could draw nearer to God, and they recommended the practice, in shortened forms, to all who wished to better direct their lives toward the Almighty. St. Francis of Assisi often traveled to hermitages where he spent time in prayer with his followers. And the prophet Muhammad spent much of his time in retreat, communing with God.

Ignatius's Spiritual Exercises

In the sixteenth century, a young Spaniard named Ignatius experienced a religious conversion, after which he spent nine months in a cave talking to God and discerning His will. After his "desert experience," Ignatius wrote a small book that documented what he had learned. Called *Spiritual Exercises*, it emphasized the importance of retreat in spiritual development, and provided a framework for others who wished to pursue this path of knowledge. In it, he detailed a four-week series of exercises and meditations, along with instructions on various spiritual practices, including prayer. The exercises were meant to be completed on retreat.

By the term "Spiritual Exercises" is meant every method of examination of conscience, of meditation, of contemplation, of vocal and mental prayer, and of other spiritual activities . . . For just as taking a walk, journeying on foot, and running are bodily exercises, so we call Spiritual Exercises every way of preparing and disposing the soul to rid itself of all inordinate attachments, and, after their removal, of seeking and finding the will of God in the disposition of our life for the salvation of our soul.

—St. Ignatius, in *Spiritual Exercises*

Ignatius of Loyola later founded the Society of Jesuits. It was the first religious order that required its followers to go on regular retreats. Before taking their vows, followers also went through the spiritual exercises.

As the practice spread, retreat or "exercise" houses were established across Europe as places where clergy, nobility, and common people alike could go to pray and meditate. Today, thousands of retreat centers around the world offer the opportunity to get away from it all and spend time alone with the Almighty.

Modern-Day Retreats

For some, a retreat might simply mean praying as they take a long walk. Most people, however, find longer retreat experiences of a day or more to be most beneficial for rest and renewal. For the most part, retreats like these mean finding a place away from everyday routines. Many people seek the resources of retreat centers for these times, but it isn't necessary that you do so. What is important is that you find a place where you can meet God alone.

Either way, you'll need to do some advance preparation before you depart and the following three steps are recommended:

1. First, and perhaps most important, schedule your time away—Write it into your calendar, just like you would any appointment. And, consider it as important as any other. Don't start thinking about canceling your retreat or rescheduling it unless you absolutely can't avoid it.

2. Find a place for your retreat—As previously mentioned, you can take a retreat just about anywhere. If you like to camp, find a national park where you can enjoy God's majesty in peace. If the comforts of a bed and a warm meal have more appeal, consider a retreat center or spiritual center. Just about every religious organization has these resources. You might want to stick to ones in your own religious tradition, but there's nothing saying that you have to do so. You might enjoy a week at a Zen retreat center, where you can go on a Zen meditation retreat, or a sesshin. You might like a weekend at a Benedictine monastery where you can get a taste of what the monastic life is all about by praying with and working alongside the monks who live there. You'll find some resources to help you locate these and other places for retreats in Appendix B.

3. Make whatever arrangements are necessary that will make it possible for you to spend your time alone with God—This includes finding someone to watch the kids and pets if you need to.

You probably won't need to bring very much with you. The basics include clothing and perhaps a good pair of walking shoes or hiking boots, your Bible, a notebook for journaling your thoughts, and whatever personal hygiene products you'll need. Many people like to bring a devotional book on prayer or another spiritual discipline to read as well. Leave electronic devices such as cell phones, PDAs, pagers, CD players, radios, and laptop computers behind. Most retreat centers won't allow them. Even if you're spending your retreat time elsewhere, you'll welcome the break from them and the silence that fills their absence. Silence is, of course, when you are most likely to hear the voice of God. You might also consider leaving your watch behind.

Most retreat facilities are pretty sparse, although they're usually far from monastic. Single rooms with shared baths are fairly common. Some may have special accommodations for couples, or hermitages or small cabins where you can have complete solitude. Some separate men and women into different facilities.

For the most part, don't expect luxury, or even most modern conveniences during your retreat experience. You'll have a light for reading, but that will be about it. Forget about such things as phones, televisions, and T1 lines, and even radios. Remember, the focus is on spiritual matters, not affairs of the world.

Retreat centers generally provide things like linens and towels, but it's a good idea to find out for sure ahead of time as you may need to bring your own.

Digging deeper refers to internalizing our experiences with God. Some call this "turning our hearts toward God." While we always experience Him in an internal way, this is different. It means creating a quiet space inside ourselves by experiencing Him in our hearts instead of our minds.

Private Retreats

Many people like to go on retreats where they can call the shots, either at retreat centers or other places of their choosing. On these retreats, what you do and how you use your time is completely up to you. You can get up when you want to and stay up as late as you like. You can keep your schedule very loose and allow God's spirit to lead you to times of prayer, meditation, and rest, or establish specific times for prayer and worship. You can eat regular meals or fast. The choice is up to you.

Regardless of the approach you take, be sure to take time to rest. Your desire to be alone with God might be so consuming that you'll lose track of time if you're not careful. It is very easy to spend hours reading and praying to God when you're away from your normal routines. While there is nothing wrong with this, resting with God is just as important. Take naps. Go for walks. Sing. Take a break from the Bible and read a devotional book or a book on living spiritually—or take a break from reading altogether.

Directed Retreats

Directed retreats are more structured and are often a good choice for people who are new to the retreat experience. While you can structure your own retreat virtually anywhere, they're best experienced in the context of a retreat center or camp.

The amount of structure in a directed retreat varies greatly. Some retreat centers are very informal. You'll be able to choose how and when you pray and how you want to spend your free time. You might be expected to join others during meal times, or you may be able to take your meals privately. A daily meeting with a retreat director is usually part of the schedule.

Other retreat facilities take a more hands-on approach and offer formal schedules of classes and services. If you go on a retreat at a monastery, you'll have the opportunity to experience the routine that the members of the monastery follow on a daily basis. While you'll be invited to participate in all activities, you usually aren't required to do so.

To pray is to descend with the mind into the heart, and there to stand before the face of the Lord, ever-present, all-seeing, within you.
—Attributed to Russian mystic Theophan the Recluse

The following schedule is typical of one you might be asked to follow at a monastic retreat. Periods of silence alternate with meals and prayer times—Matins, Diurnum, Vespers, and Compline. These are chant-like services that include scripture readings and sung psalms.

Time	Event
6:00 A.M.	Matins
7:00 A.M.	Breakfast
7:30–10:00 A.M.	Free time
10:00 A.M.	Celebration of the Holy Eucharist

continued

Time	Event
11:00 A.M.–12:00 P.M.	Free time
12:00 P.M.	Diurnum
1:00 P.M.	Lunch
2:00–3:30 P.M.	Free time
3:30 P.M.	Vespers
4:30–6:00 P.M.	Free time
6:00–7:00 P.M.	Dinner
7:00–8:30 P.M.	Free time
8:30–9:30 P.M.	Compline

If you are new to retreats, there may be some activities that you'll find strange or that you don't understand. Monastic retreats, in particular, can seem very strange, especially if you're not familiar with the prayer style that they follow. If this is the case, don't hesitate to ask questions of your retreat leader, a member of the monastery, or of others who are attending the retreat. Make sure, however, that you ask your questions at the appropriate time. It's bad manners—not to mention a little embarrassing—to break a period of silence. E

Chapter 16

Going Deeper into Prayer

At some point along your spiritual journey, you may feel the desire to get to know God in a different way. Your prayer life is going fine, but you're kind of unsettled for some reason. You get a feeling as though there's something more to experience, a mystery door that you haven't yet opened. And it's got you kind of curious.

Understanding Your Feelings

The fact that there is always something else to experience with God is one of the many gifts of a fruitful prayer life. When we open our hearts and minds to God, we go on a journey like no other. We enter into a relationship that knows no boundaries. We might reach points where we are simply dazzled by how far we have come, and we can't imagine going any further. Then we learn that we are just beginning again. We enter into a whole new phase of being with God, walking with God, praying with God. We get to know Him all over again.

There is an inner dynamic in the evolution of all true love that leads to a level of communication "too deep for words." There the lover becomes inarticulate, falls silent, and the beloved receives the silence as eloquence.
—Thelma Hall, in *Too Deep for Words: Rediscovering Lectio Divina*

Like life itself, a prayer life goes through various stages. Some of these stages are pretty painless, and we move through them relatively quickly. We might not even be aware of going through them until some time afterward. At other times, the transit through the stages of our prayer lives can feel a little uncomfortable. Sometimes it can be a lot uncomfortable. Uncomfortable transits—the ones that hurt because they last too long or they move us too far out of our comfort zones—can, in fact, wreak havoc with our spiritual lives. They can strain our relationships with God, or even dry them up for a certain period of time. This can cause a crisis of faith that can be pretty frightening. John of the Cross, a sixteenth-century monk who had experienced a number of these crises himself, gave them a most fitting description. He called them "dark nights of the soul."

At a certain point in the spiritual journey God will draw a person from the beginning stage to a more advanced stage. Such souls will likely experience what is called "the dark night of the soul." The "dark night" is when those persons lose all the pleasure that they once experienced in their devotional life. This happens because God wants to purify them and move them on to greater heights.

There is nothing fun about a dark night of the soul. When you are in a dark night, you might feel alone and emotionally drained. Prayer brings no relief, and might even make you feel worse. Understanding the dynamics behind times like these, although it won't make them pass any faster, can help you get through them. What these feelings of unrest—these dark nights—often indicate is that you are moving into a new phase of your spiritual journey, or that you are just about to. You are becoming more spiritually mature. As St. John put it, God wants to purify you and move you to greater heights.

Going to those heights, however, does not mean that you are an expert pray-er, or that you'll become one once you reach them. Remember, no one ever is, as there is no such thing as a person who prays perfectly. Perfection is never the goal of prayer. What it does mean is that you are ready for some more serious spiritual work. In other words, you are ready to dig deeper. You may be getting good at praying, but you are not obligated—or even advised—to seek perfection in the way you pray.

What does digging deeper mean? Perhaps it is easier to look at what it does not mean first. Digging deeper does not mean spending more time in prayer, although there is nothing wrong with that if you decide to do so. It does not mean praying more fervently, although there is nothing wrong with this either. What it does mean is spending your time with God in a different way. Instead of talking to and thinking about Him, you are going to put your words, thoughts, and feelings on hold. You are going to be quiet, and you are going to listen.

. . . And behold, the Lord passed by, and a great and strong wind tore into the mountains and broke the rocks in pieces before the Lord, but the Lord was not in the wind; and after the wind an earthquake, but the Lord was not in the earthquake; and after the earthquake a fire, but the Lord was not in the fire; and after the fire a still small voice.

—1 Kings 20:11–12

Listening Up

We are so good at filling our lives up with sound. We even fill up our time with God with it. Intentionally or not, we often share our prayer time with the background noise created by life. Sometimes it is of our own creation, sometimes we are at the mercy of the people around us. How many times have you prayed with a television set blaring away in the background? How often have you chattered along in simple prayer so long that when you stop it feels like you are surrounded by the void left by the absence of your words? How often have you said, "I can't hear myself think"?

Rational Prayer versus Silent Prayer

So much of the time we spend with God consists of rational, discursive prayer. We talk to Him in words and sentences, either out loud or silently. Either way, these prayers fill our heads with sound. There is nothing wrong with outwardly directed prayer of this nature. It is the prayer style with which many people feel most comfortable. But, it is important to have moments of silence and quiet with God, too.

Prayer can also consist of being quiet in God's presence. It can take the form of simply coming into His presence, sitting down, quieting our minds, and allowing Him to speak to us. When we are quiet, we allow a space to open up inside of us that God can fill without our going through the usual motions of prayer. We don't have to say a word, yet He comes.

As you will soon see, the quiet times you spend with God can be extremely satisfying and an important adjunct to your regular prayer practice. Author and therapist Bruce Davis describes silence and prayer as "two best friends who take each other on all kinds of journeys."

Problems with Silence

If you haven't spent much time in silence with God, it may not be easy for you to do so at first. Many people are so used to the sounds of words that they actually feel uncomfortable when there are no words being spoken. Some people have a fear of silence, and will do everything they possibly can to avoid it. Instead of listening to the voices of their inner selves, they would rather fill their minds and souls with noise.

If you feel uneasy when you are not surrounded by sound, you may have to ease yourself into silence. One of the best ways to do this is to pick a day of the week for taking a break from sound. On this day, you won't turn on any device that makes a noise. No television, no radio, no CD player, no cell phone. You might also try extending the silence to yourself and others. In other words, no talking.

FACT

To enhance and protect lifelong health, noted holistic physician and author Andrew Weil suggests taking a weekly "news fast"—a day away from the television, radio, newspapers, and magazines. As he writes in *8 Weeks to Optimum Health,* many people take in too much mental junk food. Taking a break from the news can help you better understand the influence it has over you, and help you decide just how much news you want to let into your life.

Many people regularly take a break from the noise in their lives. Sundays are particularly popular days for this practice as silence fits well with a day of rest.

Taking a break from sound might be incredibly difficult if you are used to having a radio or television turned on to keep you company. If you are, do not force yourself to spend too much time surrounded by silence. Doing so will just make you nervous, and you may resent the experience so much that you won't want to do it again. Turn on the noise before the absence of it starts to bother you too much. The next time you take a sound break, try to extend the silence a bit longer than you did the last time.

Going to the Desert

The desire to experience and understand the unknown through our spirit instead of our rational minds can be found in many religions. It is the basis for Buddhist and Zen meditation. Both Christianity and Judaism also have these spiritual heritages. In the early Christian church, individuals who sought these experiences took to the desert, where they could focus their entire lives on God with no interruptions. In so doing, they developed a spiritual discipline based on solitude, silence, and prayer that enabled them to experience God in a deeply profound and organic manner. You will read more about these early mystics in the following chapters.

Solitude allows us to be alone with God when we pray. It leads to something called "prayer of the heart," described by Henri J. M. Nouwen as "the rest where the soul can dwell with God."

Today, it is not necessary to go to the desert (unless, of course, you choose to!) to replicate the experiences of these early spiritual seekers. You can create your own desert—your own solitude—right where you are by drawing on their knowledge and learning how to experience God through a practice called contemplative prayer.

What Is Contemplative Prayer?

Contemplative prayer is a prayer practice that creates interior silence. It is similar to some forms of meditation, but not meditation practices that call for consciously focusing the mind on a specific object or idea and then trying to gain a new understanding of it. Instead, it is similar to meditation styles in which the mind is cleared of thoughts, feelings, and emotions.

Contemplative prayer is also described as resting in God, resting in God's presence, resting the spirit, or gazing lovingly at God. For many people, it is a prayer form that they unconsciously yearn for, and it brings them much joy when they find it.

Contemplative prayer is not a relaxation exercise or self-hypnosis, although it is often compared to or confused with these things. It also is not meant to lead to supernatural experiences of God. It will not knock you to the floor bathed in the Holy Spirit and speaking in tongues. If you are seeking out-of-body experiences, you will not get them through contemplative prayer. Unlike the meditation practices followed by Buddhists and Hindus, contemplative prayer is not a way of learning how to control your mind. Instead, it is meant to still it.

What contemplative prayer will do is put your entire self—your body, mind, and spirit—into a receptive state where God's spirit can inspire your spirit without any interruption or interference caused by your thoughts or actions. In other words, He can enter right in without you doing anything besides being open to Him. To paraphrase the words of the Spanish nun and mystic Theresa of Avila, when you settle yourself in solitude, you will come upon God in yourself.

QUESTION?

Why is contemplative prayer considered prayer?
Although it is not like the more discursive prayer styles that we're usually more familiar with, we do communicate with God, albeit in a very different way, when we practice contemplative prayer.

This interior silence, or receptive state, is created when we clear our minds of thoughts and feelings and allow ourselves to simply be in God's presence. We will explore how this is done later in this chapter.

Who Does Contemplative Prayer?

At one time, long ago, it was believed that contemplation was a special spiritual gift that only people who had directly experienced God's presence could enter into. Over time, however, it became clear that contemplation was not reserved for only those individuals who had heard God's voice, and heard it in such a way that it transformed them. In fact, it became clear that contemplative prayer is itself a transforming spiritual discipline. It is reserved to no one, and it is open to all who desire it.

As previously mentioned, the discipline of contemplation has deep roots in many world religions. Although we often associate it with Eastern religions, like Hinduism and Buddhism, it is also a part of Jewish and Christian prayer traditions.

In the Christian church, contemplation became a way to fulfill the biblical precept to pray without ceasing. Its best-known form—the "Jesus Prayer"—dates back to the sixth century and was developed by monks and others who were seeking a deeper relationship with God to be able to pray wherever and whenever they could.

The Hebrew word *ruach* (pronounced "roo-awk" or "roo-atch"), like the Latin word *spiritus*, means both "breath" and "spirit." Breath prayer, or ruach prayer, the most basic form of contemplation, was used in ancient times to pray the refrains of the Psalms.

Over the centuries, most of the more contemplative prayer styles fell out of favor in Western religions. However, these ancient traditions were revived in the latter part of the twentieth century as people began seeking deeper spiritual experiences. Interest in it continues to grow to this day.

How to Do Contemplative Prayer

Contemplative prayer takes many forms. There is lectio divina, a form of prayer based on the slow, meditative reading of sacred scripture, and centering prayer, which is often done as a prelude to lectio divina or on its own. You can read about these forms of contemplative practices in the chapters that discuss them. Here, we will focus on the most basic contemplative prayer of all—the breath prayer.

FACT

The Yoga Sutras of the Hindus, the oldest surviving text on meditation, describe the spiritual discipline of breathing, or pranayama. Pranayama exercises are still an important part of modern yoga practice, and are included in many yoga sequences.

This prayer style is the most organic and intrinsic of all as it taps into the most basic connection we have with God and that which we can't live without. It is said that every breath we take is a prayer of thanks to God.

The "Jesus Prayer" is also a breath prayer, and is probably the best-known form of it. "Lord Jesus Christ" is said (or thought) while breathing in. "Have mercy on me, a sinner" is said while breathing out. As the body relaxes, the words become fewer, dwindling down to just "Lord" and "mercy." They may even slip from consciousness into the heart, where they are said intuitively.

Beginning Breath Prayer

Breath prayer begins with—you guessed it—simply being aware of your breath. The following method is one of many that you can use to learn it:

1. Find a quiet place—Preferably, one in which you won't be disturbed for a while—and have a seat. Sit in any way you like. Some people prefer sitting in a chair with their feet on the ground. Others prefer a prayer or meditation cushion. Allow yourself a few minutes to adjust to the sound of silence.
2. Focus on taking a breath, and letting it out—As you do, note how all you can think of is how you breathe. Keep breathing. In. Out. Slowly. In. Out. If your mind wanders, return your awareness to your breathing.
3. Next, close your eyes and continue to focus on your breath—In. Out. Stay focused on breathing in and out.

Soon, very soon, you should notice a feeling of calmness begin to build inside your body and mind. Keep breathing. In. Out. Let the silence within you continue to build. Keep breathing. As you do, the rhythm of your breathing will change. It will lengthen, and you'll breathe more slowly. You don't have to consciously focus on changing your breathing, nor should you. It will happen on its own.

As your breaths lengthen, your body will relax and go along with your breathing pattern. Some describe this feeling as sinking into your breathing. You'll be in the flow, or as Sam Keen describes it in *Hymns to an Unknown God,* "After a long while you will feel yourself being breathed. As you surrender to the movement, figure and ground reverse, the gestalt changes. Who you are changes. Where once you were acting, now you seem moved by a power beyond yourself. Your breath tells you that you are of the same substance as the spirit that moves everything."

ESSENTIAL

One of the benefits of breath prayer is that you can do it anywhere you happen to be. You can do it while you are standing in line in the grocery store or while you are waiting for someone to come to the phone. In fact, it is a great way to keep yourself from getting impatient in almost every situation that forces you to wait. The breath prayer can also be done when praying with prayer beads or a prayer rope.

On the face of it, the breath prayer is a great little relaxation method. In fact, as you practice it you may get drowsy. Some people even fall asleep doing it. However, the breath prayer has a deeper meaning than this. Breath prayer symbolizes God's breath, the breath of life that He gave all living beings. When we breathe in, we are taking in all that is possible in the world. When we breathe out, we give it all back to God.

Breath Prayer, Yoga Style

Another form of the breath prayer is based on a yoga position called Savasana (in Sanskrit), or the Corpse Pose. You do it by lying on the floor on your back with your legs stretched out in front of you. Let your feet fall to the side naturally. Don't try to keep your toes pointing upwards. Also let your arms rest naturally along your sides, slightly away from your torso, with your palms facing upward. Now, actively stretch your arms and legs away from you for a few seconds. Then relax them completely. As you do, close your eyes and turn your attention inward. Note how you are feeling—you should be calm and relaxed.

FACT

The Savasana, or Corpse Pose, is deceptively simple but amazingly effective. It is often done at the end of a yoga sequence. It can also be done at any time to soothe the nerves and calm the mind. The state of total relaxation brought out by this pose gives the body renewed energy and determination.

Next, take a few deep, slow breaths. Inhale into your chest while keeping your throat, neck, and diaphragm soft and relaxed. As you exhale, feel your body sink into the floor. Keep your shoulders, neck, and facial muscles relaxed. Try to keep your eyes still as well. As before, focus on your breathing. Become aware of breathing in and out. If your mind wanders, let it return gently to your breathing. Stay in this position for at least five minutes. Ten minutes is even better. As you do, surrender yourself completely to the position. Sink into your breathing.

It is important not to come out of the Savasana pose too quickly. When you are ready to do so, bend your knees and roll slowly to one side. Pause for a moment or two, then gently push yourself up to a seated position.

For an even deeper breath prayer experience, try either of these methods while wearing earplugs. When you close out all external noise, you are left with only the sound of your breath as it enters and exits your body. If you haven't ever listened to this sound, it can be pretty amazing. We tend to take life—and breath—so much for granted. Focusing on it intensely, which is what wearing earplugs will make you do, may help you sense a greater connection to breath prayer and gain a deeper understanding of its role in your prayer practice.

Chapter 17

Divine Reading: Lectio Divina

Much of the praying we do takes the form of communications directed from us to God. We go to the Almighty in various ways, and, in so doing, look for answers from Him. Sometimes, however, those answers lie in simply keeping our ears open so that we can hear what He has to say. Lectio divina, the prayer style discussed in this chapter, turns the prayer paradigm around to put us in a better position to hear God's "still, small voice."

What Is Lectio Divina?

Literally meaning "divine reading," lectio divina is a form of prayer based on slow, meditative reading of sacred scripture, and in particular passages from the Bible. It has its roots in Christian monastic practices that were developed as early as the fourth century C.E. It was then that a number of devout Christians, both men and women, left their cities and villages behind and traveled to the desert areas of Egypt, Arabia, Syria, and Palestine, where, away from the distractions of civilization, they could focus on the presence of God in their lives. Some preferred to live completely alone, only emerging from their solitude when approached for spiritual advice, while others established small communities centered around various teachers, known as "abbas."

ESSENTIAL

Some of the monks of the desert became so revered that their authority rivaled that of the official leaders of the Christian church. While the two communities stayed separate for a while, by the fifth century C.E. men from the monastic tradition had replaced many of the church's most important bishops.

Lectio Divina in the Desert

These fathers and mothers of the desert, as they're often called, practiced the virtues that have come to define monasticism, including celibacy, fasting, asceticism, hospitality, and charity. Their entire lives revolved around God and being constantly mindful and aware of His presence.

As part of their devotion to the Almighty the desert fathers and mothers followed the scriptural precept to "pray without ceasing." They remained in constant contact with God by reading or hearing short passages from the Bible and memorizing them, choosing a phrase or a short sentence that had spoken to them in some way, and by continually meditating or ruminating on them. They didn't attach any preconceived ideas to the words that they meditated on, nor did they try to analyze them. They just listened to God's word, and reflected on it. As they did, they were led spiritually to new insights into the text, or different understandings of it, and through this to a deeper relationship with God.

> To get the full flavor of an herb, it must be pressed between the fingers, so it is the same with the Scriptures; the more familiar they become, the more they reveal their hidden treasures and yield their indescribable riches.
>
> —St. John Chrysostom, A.D. 347–407

Benedict's Rule

The great fifth-century mystic Benedict, who is often called "the father of western monks," continued the traditions of the fathers and mothers of the desert in the monastic order that he established. After living as a solitary for several years, he led a communal monastery and then founded a number of monasteries. He also developed a code of order, or rule, for the monastics who lived in them. Drawing from the teachings and writings of the desert fathers and mothers, Benedict's rule emphasized obedience to God through intellectual, spiritual, and manual labors.

Liturgy and prayer played a central role in the daily life of the monks who lived by Benedict's rule. So did what Benedict called "prayerful reading"—the same careful, repetitive poring over scripture practiced by the desert fathers and mothers. It was so important, in fact, that Benedict even specified how much time the monks should devote to reading—at least three hours a day—and at what times of the day they should read.

A twelfth-century Carthusian monk named Guigues du Chastel is credited with formalizing the practice of lectio divina. In a letter written to a fellow monk, he described a ladder to heaven, or God, that consisted of four rungs based on his method of reading the Bible:

1. **Lectio (reading or lesson)**—Or "busily looking on Holy Scripture with all one's will and wit."
2. **Meditatio (meditation)**—"A studious insearching with the mind to know what was before concealed through desiring proper skill."

3. **Oratio (prayer)**—"A devout desiring of the heart to get what is good and avoid what is evil."

4. **Contemplatio (contemplation)**—"The lifting up of the heart to God tasting somewhat of the heavenly sweetness and savour."

Du Chastel, who was also known as Guigo de Castro or Guigo II, further described the process as "prayer [rising] to God, and there one finds the treasure one so fervently desires, that is the sweetness and delight of contemplation. And then contemplation comes and yields the harvest of the labor of the other three through a sweet heavenly dew, that the soul drinks in delight and joy."

Idleness is the enemy of the soul. Therefore the brothers should have specified periods for manual labor as well as for prayerful reading (lectione divina).

—The Rule of Saint Benedict, 48:1

All four stages, or degrees, he wrote, are dependent upon each other, "so bound together," that each was impossible to experience without the other:

What use to spend your time in reading or listening to the deeds of the Holy Fathers, unless we bite and chew on them through meditation, and draw out somewhat and swallow it and send it to the heart, so that we may find, and by this understand, our own defaults, and after such knowing that we set ourselves to work that we may attain those virtues that were in them?
—Guigues du Chastel, from The Ladder of Monks

During the early years of Christianity, lectio divina was widely practiced by both lay people and monks. However, it and other contemplative prayer styles fell out of favor during the Reformation, when religious practices of a mystical nature became suspect. By the nineteenth century, it had all but disappeared except among cloistered Catholic orders like the Benedictines.

The Reformation is the term most often used to describe the religious movement that arose in Western Europe during the sixteenth century. Largely led by the German monk Martin Luther, it sought to reform the Catholic church, which had become increasingly powerful and internally corrupt. Instead, it caused a seismic shift in the religious framework of Europe, and split Christianity between Roman Catholicism and Protestantism.

The slow and prayerful reading of scripture and the writings of the church's fathers and mothers is still a cornerstone of the spiritual practices in the Benedictine order and in some other monastic orders. It is also steadily gaining in popularity among Christians and members of other faiths who are seeking ways in which to experience God more deeply and profoundly.

Reading Reverently

At its most basic level, lectio divina is simply praying over the scriptures. While this may make it seem like Bible study, the two are actually quite different. When studying the Bible, we're seekers. We're using God's word as reflected in scripture to learn, to answer questions we might have, or perhaps to encourage or uplift ourselves in some way. And we're actively engaged in the process.

Reading is obviously a part of lectio divina, but it is only a part. In lectio divina, the emphasis is less on reading to gain conscious understanding and more on allowing God's presence to be felt through the words. It is, as M. Basil Pennington, the Cistercian monk, writer, and revered teacher of contemplative prayer puts it, a way of "letting our Divine Friend speak to us through his inspired and inspiring Word." Instead of actively working at our relationship with God, we instead become receptive to allowing God's spirit to transform us from within.

Unlike most of the reading that we normally do, the emphasis in lectio divina is on quality, not quantity. The goal is to spend time with God through hearing His voice through scripture, not in making it through "x" numbers of Bible passages in "x" amount of time. Instead of racing through the words, we read them slowly—extremely slowly, in fact—and reverently, in order to give each word weight and allow them all to sink into the mind. In this manner, the words can, and often do lead into the other elements of lectio divina—meditation, prayer, and contemplation. They put us in better stead to listen—and hear—the voice of God: a soft voice that is all too often too hard to hear amidst the din of everyday life.

The emphasis on reading slowly and reverently does not mean that lectio divina takes hours to do. In fact, quite the opposite is true. Some who practice it say that instead of prolonging their daily prayer practice, it has instead streamlined it, even cut it in half.

Those who pratice lectio divina regularly also say that it enriches and nourishes their other forms of prayer by making them more aware of their spiritual rhythms, or the natural fluctuation between being spiritually active and spiritually receptive.

Reading seeks, meditation finds, prayer asks, contemplation feels. . . That is to say "Seek and you shall find: knock and the door will be opened for you." That means also, seek through reading, and you will find holy meditation in your thinking; and knock through praying, and the doors shall be opened to you to enter through heavenly contemplation to feel what you desire.
—Guigues du Chastel, in *The Ladder of Monks*

Getting Started with Lectio Divina

One of the aspects of lectio divina that many people find attractive is that it's never experienced the same way twice. It follows no set timelines or rules beyond the forms that one moves through during practice. It can take as little as ten minutes or last as long as two hours—the time spent in the contemplative forms of lectio divina is determined not by us but by God's spirit. You determine what you want to read, when, and where. Like other forms of prayer, however, it does take discipline and a willingness to set aside a certain amount of time for reverent reading during the course of the day. This reading can be done alone or in a small group setting, preferably with no more than a handful of people. Most practitioners, however, prefer to go solo and experience lectio divina on their own, in keeping with the practice's monastic traditions.

Preparing for Practice

Lectio divina can be done virtually anywhere. Just as the desert fathers and mothers remained in constant communication—unceasing prayer—with God by memorizing scripture and meditating upon it wherever they went, so too can modern practitioners take their practice with them wherever they go. However, those who are just learning lectio divina often have a hard time quieting their minds and shutting out distractions when they're praying. For these reasons, beginners often find it easiest to establish their practice in a quiet place before taking it on the road. Practicing at quiet times of the day, such as in the early morning before the rest of the household is awake, can also be helpful.

Many people who practice lectio divina prefer to block out a specific time of day for their practice, and to allow themselves time to move through all of the stages of it during this single period. Another possible way to do lectio divina is to do the sacred reading at night before going to bed, committing to memory the one sentence or word that speaks to you so you can recall it and reflect on it during the next day. If you choose this method, be sure to set aside a specific time for the other parts of lectio divina—prayer and contemplation—each day.

Some people like to enhance their time spent in lectio divina by creating something similar to a monastic environment through closing doors and drawing curtains, lighting candles and burning incense. If you've created a sacred space for your prayer practice, as discussed in Chapter 6, it may be a perfect place for doing lectio divina as well. Be creative with this; use whatever will sweeten the experience for you.

Choosing Your Reading Material

Prior to beginning lectio divina, you'll need to pick a biblical passage as the basis for your prayer. You can use anything that appeals to you;

however, it's a good idea to select passages that lend themselves to this prayer style. Popular choices include readings from:

- The Psalms
- The Gospels
- The letters of John
- The Ecclesiastes

Some people use lectio divina to read through the Bible and choose their passages in sequence. Others follow the readings from their church's daily liturgy. The specific words that you choose to read actually matter very little. It is a good idea, however, to select something that's short. Less is more in lectio divina. Remember that the emphasis is on reading reflectively with intention and purpose, not on covering certain amounts of text in prescribed amounts of time. Long-time practitioners of lectio divina have been known to devote months or years meditating on a single sentence. You may find yourself savoring a single word, over and over again, before you're led to move on to the next one. At other times you may find yourself moving through the text more rapidly.

QUESTION?

Can other spiritual writings besides the Bible be used in lectio divina?
While scripture from the Bible is the traditional basis for lectio divina, there's nothing prohibiting the prayerful reading of other sacred texts, including those from other religious traditions. Other possible choices are the works of early Christian writers, such as St. Augustine, St. Theresa of Avila, St. Jerome, and St. Ambrose, or those of modern spiritual authors, such as Thomas Merton, M. Basil Pennington, Kathleen Norris, Thich Nhat Hanh, and others.

Beginning the Reading

After you've chosen the passage you want to read, find a comfortable posture for reading and praying. Again, there is no right or wrong way to position yourself. If you're most comfortable curled up into a big easy chair, practice lectio divina there. Many practitioners use the same position that they assume for other types of prayer because it's the most comfortable and familiar. You may wish to do the same. Just make sure that the position you choose is conducive to prayer and reading, not for sleep.

Once you're settled into your prayer position, take a few moments to focus on what you're about to do. Allow your mind to become silent. You might find it helpful to use a breath exercise like the ones discussed in Chapter 16. Some people silently recite a special word or phrase, such as "peace," "Lord," "Jesus," "God," "mercy," and so on. Others center their thoughts by focusing on the light of a candle, a cross, or an icon. Do whatever works for you. If you should find your mind wandering off onto other things, simply return your thoughts to the word or object that you have chosen. Continue to focus on your breathing.

After you've enjoyed a few moments of silence, turn to the text that you've chosen and begin reading. Read very, very slowly. Allow your mind to caress the words. Savor them. Read more from the heart than from the head. Try to get a sense of what the writer of the words wished to convey. Allow God's spirit to direct you to a word or phrase for deeper contemplation.

Move forward only when you feel prompted to do so, not when you think you should. If you find yourself merely reading the words, slow down. If you feel like your mind is racing ahead to the next word, slow down. Reading slowly is the part of lectio divina that people find most difficult, but it is essential to this form of prayer.

One of the most difficult aspects of lectio divina is learning how to slow down the speed at which you read. Pacing yourself by matching your speed to your breathing—two words on an inhalation, two words on an exhalation, for example—can help you put the brakes on.

As you read, you may find a particularly meaningful part of the text that you want to mull over. It could be a sentence, a phrase, or merely a word. Whatever it is, allow it to lead you to the next stage of lectio divina.

Moving into Meditation

Defined in *The Ladder of Monks* as "studious insearching with the mind," the meditative element of lectio divina is where the words move from the mind into the heart. It is a period of reflecting and receiving, of sensing God's presence in the words that have been read. Guigues, the author of *The Ladder of Monks,* notes that this stage should come naturally, with no conscious prompting, and that it may not come right away to those who are new to lectio divina. If it hasn't come for you, don't feel like you've done something wrong, or that you've failed. Don't try to force or will it. God's voice is there; it just might take you more time to learn how to be still enough to hear it. Prayer practice is about many things, but most of all it's about patience.

A spiritual life without discipline is impossible. Discipline is the other side of discipleship. The practice of a spiritual discipline makes us more sensitive to the small, gentle voice of God.
—Henri Nouwen, in *Making All Things New*

If you have moved into the meditative stage of lectio divina, you may feel the need to return to what you have read, and to read it over again, perhaps once, maybe more. As you do, ask yourself why this particular word or phrase is resonating with you. Ponder the significance of the words and why they're reaching out to you. Let your mind touch on the various ways in which they might reflect God's presence in your life, or the message He's speaking to you through them.

The word *love,* for example, might lead to remembering a time when you felt God's presence so clearly that it made you shiver with joy. It might stir up memories of people who have touched your life. From there you might reflect on God's true love. The key here is not to try to guide where your mind goes. Let it travel unfettered. Stay open to the experience.

Prayer

The third form of lectio divina is prayer. Like all prayer, it is a dialogue with the Almighty. Here, however, prayer also takes the form of an offering of self, of what you have learned during meditation, of opening the heart to God and allowing Him to enter in. This prayer can be voiced or spoken with the heart and mind.

Contemplation

The final stage of lectio divina is one of resting in God's presence. It requires nothing more than just staying quietly and simply being in the place you came to through the other three stages, and being open to receiving the grace of God. At times His grace may infuse you, at other times it may not. Those who have experienced God's grace during the contemplative form of lectio divina have described it as "pure love" or as being the most intimate communication with God that is possible in life.

What Comes Next

If you're practicing lectio divina on your own, you can simply rest in silence in God's presence until such time that you feel you're ready to return to your normal routine. In the group practice of lectio divina, it is customary to discuss what was learned at the conclusion of a session.

Over time, as you continue to practice lectio divina, what you gain through your practice will spill over into the other parts of your life.

Chapter 18

Centering Prayer

Sometimes the quest to unite with God through prayer becomes too intellectual. We try too hard to use logic and reason to understand the mysteries of faith, and in doing so the understanding we seek becomes even more elusive. Religious mystics of long ago encouraged believers to put their minds on hold and instead use their hearts and souls to connect with the Divine. Centering prayer is an increasingly popular method that uses this approach.

What Is Centering Prayer?

Like lectio divina, which was discussed in Chapter 17, centering prayer is a prayer practice built around centuries-old contemplative traditions in the Christian church and on the teachings of Christian mystics. In some respects, it resembles meditation as it entails sitting quietly for a specified period of time. And, as is done in many forms of meditation, those who practice centering prayer invoke a specific word, similar to a mantra, at various times during a centering prayer session.

The goal of centering prayer is to put aside earthly thoughts in order to create interior silence. It is this silence, when it is accomplished, that allows us to experience God on a very different level than what we're normally accustomed to. As Thomas Keating writes in *Open Mind, Open Heart,* one of the best-known texts on centering prayer, "The root of prayer is interior silence . . . It is the opening of mind and heart, body and feelings—our whole being—to God, the Ultimate Mystery, beyond words, thoughts, and emotions."

Putting aside thoughts during centering prayer, however, doesn't mean resisting or suppressing them. Instead, they are accepted when they arise, and then gently and lovingly released. The goal is to move our awareness beyond them to the ultimate mystery of God.

Although centering prayer is actually a part of the contemplative prayer tradition, people often use the two terms interchangeably when referring to this prayer style. In this chapter, we'll describe centering prayer as centering prayer, and use the term contemplative prayer when discussing the tradition to which it belongs.

Let love alone speak: the simple desire to be one with the Presence, to forget self, and to rest in the Ultimate Mystery.
—Thomas Keating, in *Open Mind, Open Heart*

The Basis for Centering Prayer

Like lectio divina, centering prayer is very much a part of the spiritual traditions of the Christian church. It also has strong ties to the meditative practices of other major religions, especially Buddhism. However, unlike lectio divina, centering prayer is a modern practice based on these ancient spiritual traditions. It is similar to the contemplative practices of the mystics of centuries ago, and especially those described in a fourteenth-century book called *The Cloud of Unknowing,* but there are no references to a specific practice called centering prayer in any of the historic writings on Christian mysticism.

Centering prayer as a modern contemplative practice came about largely as the result of the Second Vatican Council in 1965. Among many of the reforms suggested by the council was a call for Catholics to depend less on priests and other church officials and more on themselves when it came to finding ways to enrich their spiritual lives. Learning more about other religious faiths and renewing the age-old practice of contemplative prayer were seen as two ways that would foster this enrichment.

In the years that followed, a number of younger Catholics heeded the Vatican's directive. However, since they knew little of the contemplative traditions in their own church, they generally studied Eastern religions and began to integrate meditative practices related to these religions into their own religious practices.

The writings of Thomas Merton, a Trappist monk for twenty-seven years, including the classic *The Seven Story Mountain,* introduced many people to the contemplative life that was led in monasteries.

In the early 1970s, Thomas Keating, a Trappist monk and the head of St. Joseph Abbey in Spencer, Massachusetts, noticed that young visitors to the abbey who had studied with Eastern religious leaders possessed an unusual spiritual maturity for their age. They were, as Keating writes in *Intimacy with God,* ". . . putting in twenty to thirty minutes of meditation twice a day in spite of being in college or professional life . . ." at a time when cloistered monks and nuns were finding it hard to practice one daily session of mental prayer. Intrigued by the practices and experiences of these young people, and their similarities to the ancient forms of Christian contemplation, Keating engaged his fellow monks in a revival. The goal: to bring back prayer forms based on the Christian contemplative tradition, and to come up with a way to make it more attractive—and more available—to anyone wishing to enrich their spiritual lives.

As part of their efforts, Keating and two other monks—William Meninger and M. Basil Pennington—met regularly with teachers from Eastern religions. The three monks also mined the writings of the church's mystics and saints—the fathers and mothers of the desert, St. Theresa of Avila, St. John of the Cross, Gregory of Nyssa, and St. Francis de Sales among them—to put the contemporary practice they were developing into a historical context.

Entering into The Cloud of Unknowing

One of these works—*The Cloud of Unknowing,* a fourteenth-century mystical classic by an unknown author (most likely an English monk)—was the primary inspiration for the format for practicing and teaching contemplative prayer. In it, believers are encouraged to put aside intellectual efforts to understand God, as He cannot be fully and truly known through the human intellect. Contemplation, or allowing oneself to enter into a union with God completely and without reservation, is the only way in which the "cloud of unknowing" that exists between man and God can be transcended.

FACT

The Cloud of Unknowing, which first appeared in the second half of the fourteenth century, consists of a number of short letters describing mystical prayer that were sent to a particular monk. The original Middle English text still survives and has also been translated into modern English for ease of reading.

The concept of the "sacred word," which is key to centering prayer, also came from *The Cloud of Unknowing.* The use of a word, preferably "a little word of one syllable," was "powerful enough to pierce the heavens" and was the only prayer that God needed to hear. Unlike a mantra, which is repeatedly chanted throughout a meditation, the sacred word would instead only be invoked when needed.

Centering Prayer Expands

Once the format for centering prayer was established, the monks began teaching it to others through retreats and workshops. As the format was refined, it became known as centering prayer, a phrase used by the contemporary Christian mystic Thomas Merton in his writings.

In the early 1980s, Keating gave a series of talks on prayer at a parish in Aspen, Colorado, where he had relocated after leaving St. Joseph Abbey. Based on the popularity of these talks, Keating helped found Contemplative Outreach, a network of individuals and small faith communities dedicated to practicing centering prayer and teaching others how to do it.

Today, countless individuals around the world practice centering prayer, either by themselves, in small groups, or at retreats. They do so in addition to their other forms of prayer as centering prayer isn't meant to replace them. Instead, the practice is done to enrich other aspects of one's prayer life. But the benefits of centering prayer go beyond this. Those who practice it regularly say that they are more at peace with their life on a day-to-day basis, and that they can more easily discern God's presence in the ordinary. It also makes them more aware of their own spirituality. In fact, most of what is gained during centering prayer is manifested before and after, not during the practice itself.

The movement of the contemplative must be a movement of the whole man, he must precipitate himself, free and unfettered into the bosom of Reality.

—From *The Cloud of Unknowing*

Learning Centering Prayer

Workshops and retreats are regularly held to introduce the practice of centering prayer to others. Because this prayer style does differ in approach from other forms of prayer, attending a workshop led by someone who is trained in the practice is often the best way to learn its basics. However, it's definitely possible to learn how to do centering prayer on your own. If you plan on taking the latter approach, the following information will help you get started. You will also find some additional resources on centering prayer listed in Appendix B.

Since there is a very specific method of practicing centering prayer, we've based much of the discussion that follows on a brief pamphlet that describes the process, which is also listed in Appendix B.

Practicing Centering Prayer

There are four basic steps to centering prayer:

1. Choosing a sacred word, which "is a symbol of your intention to consent to God's presence and action within."
2. Sitting down, closing your eyes, and silently speaking your sacred word to indicate your desire to enter into God's presence and action within you.
3. Returning to the sacred word to dispel thoughts when they enter your mind and return your focus to God.
4. Ending your prayer time by sitting in silence and with your eyes closed for a few moments.

Most of the time, centering prayer is done privately, or with a spouse or partner. Most people find that private practice is the easiest way to become familiar with the centering experience. If there is a centering prayer group in your area, consider praying with the group on occasion—once a month, maybe more—once you've learned the basics. Many people find these groups to be a great support, and a good way to keep their practice on track.

In keeping with the precepts in *The Cloud of Unknowing,* some who practice centering prayer preface their practice with a short period of lectio divina. Another option is to simply read a short selection of your own choosing from the Bible and go into centering prayer from there.

However, the two contemplative practices fit together extremely well. In fact, centering prayer mirrors the contemplative phase of lectio divina, and is an easy way to enter into it.

> So I want you to understand clearly that for beginners and those a little advanced in contemplation, reading or hearing the word of God must precede pondering it and without time given to serious reflection there will be no genuine prayer.
> —From *The Cloud of Unknowing*

Choosing the Sacred Word

The sacred word, according to the guidelines on centering prayer, "expresses our intention to be in God's presence and to yield to the divine action." In *The Cloud of Unknowing,* it is stressed that the most appropriate word is one that reflects the nature of prayer itself. For this reason, most people pick a word that in some way reflects God, the object of their prayers.

The sacred word can be chosen by praying to God and asking for His guidance. Some people simply ponder various words, rolling them around in their minds, and settle on the one that seems to be the best fit. Possible choices include:

- God
- Lord
- Jesus
- Father
- Mother

- Peace
- Love
- Abba
- Shalom

Whatever approach you take, let the word you choose be your choice. Don't ask for help on this from anyone else but God. Take however much time is necessary to choose it. You want the word to be one that you can stick with for a while. The guidelines for centering prayer state that the sacred word should not be changed during the prayer time, as doing so would engage the mind and require a return to thinking. The same can be said for exchanging one sacred word for another every time you pray. In general, it's better to find a word that resonates with you, one that can accompany you for a good while on your spiritual journey. There is nothing that says you can't change your sacred word to something else somewhere along the line if you feel so inclined. Changing it too often, however, might disrupt your practice.

Beginners of centering prayer often place far too much emphasis on the sacred word. While it is important, it's often not for the reasons they think it is. What the word actually means is of little importance. The intention behind it, which is to open oneself to God, is what's important.

QUESTION?

Is choosing a sacred word essential to practicing centering prayer?
While most people do prefer to use a sacred word, you can also use what is called a sacred gaze, which means turning your focus inward to God, as if you were looking at Him. Some people imagine a visual image to help them let go of their thoughts.

Other things you'll want to determine before you begin your centering prayer practice is when you'll practice and how you'll time it. The standard period of practice for centering prayer is twenty minutes every day, twice a day, preferably in the morning and before supper, although some people go longer than this. Many people start with one twenty-minute session and add the second at a later point, whereas others find they only have the time for one session and they may extend this one session as the spirit moves them. Two sessions, however, are strongly encouraged, and can be especially beneficial in establishing the practice as part of your ongoing prayer practice.

There are a variety of ways to time the minutes spent in centering prayer. Timers are the most popular, and there are also watches that can be set to indicate when prayer time is over. Cassette tapes and CDs are also available to measure the time spent in centering prayer.

If you're going to use a timer for centering prayer, choose one that doesn't tick audibly. Stay away from loud timers and those with buzzers as they are too abrupt a signal for this gentle practice. Find one with a soft chime instead.

Introducing the Sacred Word

The second step in centering prayer details the actual beginning of the practice, as you can choose your sacred word at any time before you begin centering prayer. It entails sitting comfortably, allowing your mind to settle down, and invoking the sacred word "as a symbol of your consent to God's presence and action within."

Finding a Comfortable Position

Finding a comfortable position for centering prayer is just like finding one for any other kind of prayer. The idea is to settle on a prayer posture that you can remain in for the specified time; however, it shouldn't be so comfortable that you find it difficult to stay awake while praying. The guidelines for centering prayer suggest using a chair that helps you keep your back straight and allows your feet to touch the ground. Other possible prayer supports include a meditation cushion, such as those used in Zen practice, or a meditation bench. If you're using a cushion, it's perfectly all right to sit in a lotus or half-lotus position.

Due to the quiet and contemplative nature of centering prayer, it is best not to do it when lying down, as this position makes it too easy to fall asleep. And, because the eyes are to be kept closed during centering prayer, it's definitely not a discipline you'll want to practice while walking or driving a car.

Finally, find a time and place where you can be away from noise and clutter. Don't set yourself up for failure by trying to practice at times when you are likely to be interrupted. If you decide that centering prayer is right for you, and you stick with your practice, you'll become expert at entering into your interior silence even when the world is swirling around you.

Many people like to set the stage for centering prayer by lighting a candle to signify God's presence. Incense is another popular choice. Not only does it enrich the centering experience, the smoke from the incense serves as a symbol of our prayers traveling upward to God.

FACT

Centering prayer is best practiced on an empty stomach, as eating a heavy meal can cause drowsiness. If you're hungry, and it's near mealtime, eat a light snack before practice and save your large meal for later. Some people find that centering prayer disrupts their sleep patterns if they practice it before going to bed. For this reason, practicing at other times of the day is encouraged.

Invoking the Sacred Word

Once you've settled into your prayer position, it is time to invoke the sacred word. This is done simply by closing your eyes and saying the sacred word silently and gently in your mind. The guidelines for centering prayer describe this as "laying a feather on a piece of absorbent cotton." Others describe their perception of the sacred word as being just slightly out of focus, floating on a rivulet of water, or being carried on a soft cloud.

In any case, the goal here is not to actively focus on the sacred word as the center point of your prayer, but to allow the word to enter into your subconscious where it can draw your heart and mind toward God. As such, it's not meant to be repeated constantly like a mantra as doing so would make the word, instead of God's presence, the focus of your efforts. It should instead rest lightly in your mind, there when you need it but not as the center of your attention.

Don't meditate on the sacred word, or contemplate it. Just think it silently. As you do, your mind will empty of thoughts. Over time, the sacred word might become vague or completely disappear from your consciousness. This is perfectly all right, and is, in fact, a good thing. Don't actively try to bring it back unless you need it. Let it drift down inside you to where it wants to go.

Do not use clever logic to examine or explain this word to yourself nor allow yourself to ponder its ramifications as if this sort of thing could possibly increase your love. I do not believe reasoning ever helps in the contemplative work.

—From *The Cloud of Unknowing*

Returning Gently to the Sacred Word

You will return to the sacred word if you find thoughts rumbling through your head. Thoughts—an umbrella term for the various emotions, images, and sensations that arise during centering prayer—are a normal part of centering prayer, although many people who are just learning this practice feel like they're not doing things right when they have them.

Keep in mind that the goal of centering prayer is not to be free of all thoughts, or to feel like you have to fight with them if they arise. Instead, you want to acknowledge their presence for a second, and then let them go so they can pass right by you. There will be times when you won't be able to clear your head, or when it will take you a long time to do so. At other times you won't be aware of them at all.

When you become aware of thoughts, just bring the sacred word up a little higher into your consciousness. Think it slowly and softly in your mind. Start with one invocation. If the thoughts won't pass by easily, and you need to think it again, by all means do so. But don't start repeating it in your head like a chant. Just use it as often as you need it. It might be a lot at first.

During your practice, expect to come in and out of your interior silence as thoughts arise. When they do, return to the word until you drop back into your silence.

Some people who have practiced centering prayer for a long time no longer have the need to think of the sacred word. They've reached the point where they're capable of moving into interior silence without it.

As you continue to practice centering prayer, you'll find that God's spirit inches in and takes increasingly greater control of your prayer. You can't will this, or wish or hope for it. You can only remain open and receptive to His presence.

The sacred word is only a symbol. It is an arrow pointing in the direction intended by our will. It is a gesture or sign of accepting God as He is. Exactly what that is, we don't know.

—Thomas Keating, in *Open Mind, Open Heart*

Quieting the Chatter

Quieting the mind so it quits chattering away is one of the challenges of centering prayer. It's amazing, in fact, how much centering prayer makes you aware of the stream of things that constantly runs through your head. However, this constant mental chitchat is what stands in the way of our being able to experience God more deeply. For this reason, it's essential to learn how to use the sacred word, or whatever alternative method you've decided on, to put your mental activities on hold and create inner silence. Some practitioners envision putting their thoughts into a little lockbox, to be opened after they're done praying.

What you don't want to do is actively focus on having no thoughts, or on making your mind a blank. Again, keep in mind that thoughts, whatever they might be about, are a natural part of the process.

Other Things You Might Notice While Praying

Some people notice increased awareness of body twitches, or aches and pains. You might, in fact, find it extremely hard to sit still at times, especially if you're coming into centering prayer after a stressful day. These are all signs of your body relaxing and resting in prayer. If possible, try to ignore them. They usually go away. If you absolutely have to scratch an itch, go ahead. But try to stay as still as you can while you're praying. If necessary, rest your mind on them briefly, and then return to the sacred word.

At times you might also notice that your arms and legs feel either very heavy or very light. This is also to be expected and is a sign that you've reached a deep level of spiritual attentiveness.

Sitting in Silence with Your Eyes Closed

When your prayer period has come to a close, simply rest with God for a few minutes with your eyes closed. Don't rush this time—it is important to give yourself a few moments to readjust to the world around you. When you feel ready to return to the outside world, open your eyes slowly. Continue to rest for a bit longer.

Many people like to recite "The Lord's Prayer" during this period. You could also recite a different prayer of your own choosing, or simply remain silent until such time that you're ready to speak.

The benefits of a moment of silence are immeasurable. Just take the time to breathe, eyes closed, and let your thoughts drift and gently fall into place. Once done, you will feel reinvigorated and ready to tackle life's stresses.

Challenges of Centering Prayer

One of the biggest problems that people have when practicing centering prayer, and especially when they are new to the practice, is dealing with mental intrusions. As previously noted, it is exceedingly difficult to get our mind to shut down and quit chattering at us, and it always seems like this is an even greater problem when our intention is to become extremely still.

The best way to get through this is to continue your practice. As you do, you will become much more adept at entering into and maintaining your interior silence. The other thing you'll be able to do is learn to accept your thoughts for what they are, which will also help you let them flow past you more easily. As you do, you'll be better able to seek God's inward presence, and to being open to the inflow of God's grace. Ⓔ

Chapter 19

Prayer in Motion

Most of the time we spend in prayer consists of staying in one place. We sit or kneel in our spot, often with our heads bowed. Being still is a time-honored way of praying. Even the Bible tells us to "be still, and know that I am God." But it is not the only way to pray. You can also take your prayer practice on the road.

Exercising Body and Spirit

At first blush, prayer and exercise may not seem like a match made in heaven. However, before you dismiss this combo out of hand, take a moment to consider the benefits of talking to God while you're moving your body. It can eliminate the "I don't have the time" syndrome that kicks in all too often when we try to do things that are good for us. Busy schedules can make it difficult for many people to squeeze in both prayer and exercise on a regular basis, but they also take the blame for lax habits in both arenas.

Above all, do not lose your desire to walk. Every day I walk myself into a state of well-being, and walk away from every illness. I have walked myself into my best thoughts, and I know of no thought so burdensome that one cannot walk away from it.

—Søren Kierkegaard, in a letter to Jette

The twenty minutes a day that health experts say is the minimum amount of exercise we should get also happens to be a great length of time for a prayer session. Instead of choosing between prayer and exercise, why not combine the two? Doing so can go a long way toward freeing up more time in anyone's life.

Mixing prayer and exercise can also bolster your physical and spiritual health in ways that go beyond the benefits of doing each separately. Although they are seemingly disparate activities, prayer and exercise actually share several important qualities. They both require concentration, and they both require work.

Combining the two can create a synergy where each practice enhances the other and lifts it to higher levels. People who pray and exercise on a regular basis often talk about getting so caught up in what they're doing that they don't notice things like time and distance. Because of this, they often spend more time praying and exercising when they do both together than when they do them separately.

Finding Inner Quiet Through Repetitive Motion

Exercise can add an extra dimension to all forms of prayer, including—believe it or not—contemplative prayer. The repetitive motion that is essential to many forms of exercise, such as stroking the oars on a rowing scull, cranking the pedals on a bicycle, or putting one foot in front of the other when walking, helps focus the mind and blocks out outer and inner disturbances. It can also help disperse extra energy that can sometimes interfere with prayer. The rhythm of the repetition, and the attention that we pay to it, can create the same inner stillness that is reached in more stationary forms of contemplative prayer. It elicits what cardiologist Herbert Benson calls "the relaxation response," a feeling of centeredness and calmness that allows the mind to take a break from its usual activities.

FACT

Prayer walking is also called spirited walking, or walking meditation. One form is fast; the other is slow. If you walk often enough and at a pace fast enough to raise your heart rate into the working zone, prayer walking can also make a significant contribution to your fitness level and health.

Calming the Jitters

While many people can comfortably sit still and pray, not everyone can. Some people have such high energy levels that just the thought of having to stay in one place makes them nervous. Others simply prefer being active to being still. If you tend to fidget while you pray, or you get bored when you sit still during prayer, you might find the combination of prayer and exercise to be a real boon to your prayer practice.

Prayer Walking

Just about any form of repetitive exercise—bicycling, jogging, walking, rowing, cross-country skiing, even raking the leaves up from your lawn or sweeping your sidewalk—lends itself well to prayer on the go. Of them, walking is a top pick. It is easy and simple. You don't have to wait for leaves to fall to do it. It can be done almost anytime and virtually anywhere—indoors and out, in gymnasiums and shopping centers, in parks and on bridle paths. The equipment needs are simple—a good pair of shoes and some comfortable clothing is about all that is necessary.

ESSENTIAL

As with all forms of physical exercise, it is best to take things slow as you begin the practice of prayer walking, especially if you are out of shape or you have some medical concerns. If either description fits you, it is strongly recommended that you check with a physician before starting any type of exercise program, even one that is as kind to the body as walking is. When it comes to your health, it is always best to be safe rather than sorry.

Prayer walking is exactly what the words suggest—praying while you are walking. There are various forms of prayer walking. One in particular involves choosing a specific area, walking through it, and praying for everything you see—people, animals, houses, schools, businesses, you name it.

While there is nothing wrong with this type of prayer walking, it emphasizes outwardly directed prayer. And, it has little to do with integrating walking into prayer practice—for the most part, it can be done just as easily in a car. For this reason, this type of walking and praying is not the focus of this chapter. Here, we'll talk about the forms of prayer walking that combine mindful breathing with movement and meditation.

Walking meditation is really to enjoy the walking—walking not in order to arrive, but just to walk. The purpose is to be in the present moment and, aware of our breathing and our walking, to enjoy each step.

—Thich Nhat Hanh, in *Peace Is Every Step*

The Mechanics of Prayer Walking

Prayer walking can be done fast or slow. There is no right or wrong speed, only the speed at which you want to go. If you are interested in emphasizing the benefits of exercise during your prayer walks, you'll want to walk fast. If relaxation and meditation are your goals, then walk slowly. Either way, you might find it easier to get into a state of inner stillness. Many people find that the rhythmic motion of walking soothes their minds and allows them to relax better than sitting still and praying.

If you already walk for fitness, you won't have to slow down to prayer walk unless you want to decrease your speed. In fact, praying while you walk might even cause you to pick up your pace.

Some people like to venture out on their own or with their dogs by their sides. Others enjoy the camaraderie of a group prayer walk. Walking alone, however, is usually less distracting and more conducive to praying. It also allows you to be silent, which is essential for a good prayer walk. Many people like to listen to music when they walk. Doing so when prayer walking, however, will keep you from listening to God.

FACT

Slow forms of walking prayer are very similar to the Zen practice of kinkin, a walking meditation in which attention is focused on each step, and the breath is measured and controlled. In Zen practice, walking meditation is often done in addition to sitting meditation to keep meditation practice in balance.

The prayerfulness part of prayer walking comes first from walking in silence. Being silent allows you to turn your attention toward God. It also allows you to focus on the other aspects of prayer walking, which are basically the same regardless of how fast or how slow you choose to go:

- **Breathing**—In prayer walking, breathing is deep and cleansing, and it matches the cadence of your stride. As you focus on your breathing, it will guide you into your place of inner quiet.
- **Stepping**—Zen prayer walking almost looks like slow motion, but that slow movement allows those who practice it to be mindful of every

part of every step they make: raising the foot, lifting the foot, pushing the foot, dropping the foot, and so on. It isn't necessary to go this slowly during your own prayer walks unless you want to follow the Zen way. Nor do you have to have your attention level set quite that high, but you do want to be mindful of how your feet strike the ground and lift off of it. This awareness is also part of the prayer walking experience.

- **Counting**—Prayer walkers both count the length of their breaths and the number of steps that they take. On the face of it, this sounds confusing, but it isn't when you do it.
- **Praying, or focusing on a sacred word**—Prayer walking is a perfect form for saying short prayers or sacred words. The words of the "Jesus Prayer," "Lord Jesus Christ, Son of God, have mercy upon me, a sinner," are a good match for the cadence of prayer walking. Other possibilities are mantra-like words such as om, peace, love, calm, God, father, and so on. You can use any word you'd like. According to researchers, choosing words with spiritual or personal significance will yield better results as they're more effective in focusing your efforts.

QUESTION?

What is a good length for a prayer walk?
It is a good idea to measure your time spent praying and walking in minutes, not in miles. Twenty to thirty minutes is about par for the course; walks of longer or shorter duration are perfectly fine as well.

It can be a good idea to decide where you are going to walk before you set out. If you are walking outdoors, it can be nice to be surrounded by beauty and quiet as you stroll. However, the inner focus of prayer walking means you can do it virtually anywhere, even on busy city streets teeming with cars and people. You can even prayer walk in shopping malls. Treadmills work, too.

Gearing Up to Walk

As previously mentioned, prayer walking does not require much in the way of equipment. If you don't have a good pair of walking shoes, however, it is a good idea to do your feet and the rest of your body a favor and get some before you start out. While walking is usually not the most strenuous form of exercise you might do, you also don't want achy feet or sore shins to interfere with your practice.

If you find a pair of shoes that you really like, buy two of them if you possibly can. Having two pairs of shoes will prolong the life of each as you can switch off between them. Having a spare pair is also nice if the manufacturer discontinues the style.

If you plan to go fast on your walks, you'll need to wear shoes that can take the additional wear and tear that speed can create. There are a number of manufacturers that make athletic shoes that work well for performance or speed walking. Finding the right shoes are especially important for you as ones that fit right will both help you walk fast and help you avoid injuries.

Walking Slow, Walking Fast

All forms of prayer walking begin with simply walking forward. As you walk, keep your body relaxed and calm. Stand tall, but not rigid. Think of your spine as a spring, not a stick. Keep your head aligned with your shoulders and hips—don't walk with your chin thrust forward or down as this will cause upper body fatigue. Keep it roughly perpendicular to the ground. Let your shoulders drop away from your ears. Let your arms and hands move naturally along with your feet. Hold your hands however you feel most comfortable, either at your waist or lower down by your sides. Just let them flow along with you as you walk. To avoid visual distractions, focus your gaze at a point about four feet in front of you.

If you are walking fast, you will find it more comfortable to keep your hands by your waist as you swing your arms. Doing so will keep your body fluids from collecting in your fingers. Some people like to pump their arms vigorously when fitness walking, but this isn't necessary. As your legs move faster, your arms will naturally join them.

If you are walking slowly, let your body's natural energy govern your pace. You might feel like walking faster on some days, slower on others. Don't feel like you have to cover a certain distance in a certain amount of time. Many people start out by walking very quickly, like they're in a race. You might do so as well. You might also find it hard to keep your pace steady at first. This will become easier to do over time.

In *Peace Is Every Step,* Thich Nhat Hanh suggests walking a little slower than your normal pace, which will better coordinate your breathing with your steps. In fact, using your breathing to pace yourself is a great way to find the prayer-walking pace that works best for you. Try taking the same number of steps—two, three, or four, whatever works best for you—with each inhalation and exhalation.

Each step we take will create a cool breeze, refreshing our body and mind. Every step makes a flower bloom under our feet. We can do it only if we do not think of the future or the past, if we know that life can only be found in the present moment.
                                        —Thich Nhat Hanh, in *Peace Is Every Step*

Regardless of your pace, it's important to pay attention to your breath. As you do, count their length. In—one, two, three. Out—one, two, three. Once you have this down, start counting your steps. Then start matching your prayer, or your sacred word, to your counts. This does sound a lot like patting your head and rubbing your belly. If you have a hard time keeping it all together, just focus on your breathing. The other parts will come in time.

As you walk, you may want to stop from time to time to admire the beauty of nature. When you do, keep breathing deeply and slowly. When you're ready to start walking again, just pick up where you left off.

At the end of your prayer walk, allow yourself a few minutes to shift your focus back to the world around you. If you've been walking at a pretty good clip, also use this period for a cooldown. Keep moving until your heart rate is fairly close to normal. When it is, treat yourself to about ten minutes of stretching. You should be very relaxed by the time you are done.

Walking in Circles

Walking slowly and meditatively along the coiled, circular paths of a labyrinth is a another very popular type of walking prayer. Tracing the mandala-like patterns of a labyrinth is an ancient spiritual practice dating back some four thousand years. In fact, of all the spiritual tools known to humankind, labyrinths are some of the oldest.

FACT

Labyrinths and mazes are often thought of as being similar. They are actually very different. A labyrinth is unicursal, meaning it only has one path in and out. The path never crosses itself or comes to a dead end. Mazes are more like puzzles and contain more than one path. Successfully entering and exiting a maze requires choosing the right paths. Labyrinths require no such choices.

Where and how labyrinths first developed isn't known, but it is believed that some of the earliest labyrinths were created for worshipping female gods and staging fertility rituals. Ancient turf labyrinths—some of them still in use today—have been found in England, Germany, and Scandinavia. There is evidence of labyrinth use at various times in many other countries as well, including India, France, Egypt, Iceland, Peru, and parts of North America.

We also do not know exactly when labyrinths became part of Christian spiritual practice as early records do not contain much mention of their use. However, it is known that they served as a substitute for making pilgrimages to Jerusalem, a practice that was central to early Christianity. When the Crusades made it unsafe to travel to the holy city, Catholic leaders designated seven cathedrals in Europe as pilgrimage destinations, and placed a labyrinth on the floor of each.

FACT

In Greek mythology, a labyrinth on the island of Crete was created by Daedalus for King Minos to contain the Minotaur, a monstrous man-headed bull. Archaeologist Sir Arthur Evans, when digging on Crete in the early 1900s, uncovered the ruins of a massive Bronze-age building believed to be the palace of the legendary king, along with enough traces of a labyrinth to prove that the palace was built along the lines of one.

Why a labyrinth? From ancient times, the form's combination of a circle and a spiral was considered symbolic of wholeness. Then, as now, traveling along the labyrinth's path to its center and back out again serves as a metaphor for life's journeys, and for our spiritual journeys with God.

Rather than risk losing their lives to the skirmishes of holy wars, followers of the Christian faith instead could fulfill their sacred vows by traveling to the cathedral cities and walking the cathedral labyrinths.

In the ongoing desire to connect modern spiritual practices to ancient traditions, labyrinth walking has gained new popularity among modern spiritual seekers of all types. Hundreds of labyrinths have been built in the United States since the 1990s when the practice was revitalized, largely through the efforts of Lauren Artress, an Episcopalian priest, who in 1992 installed a replica of the Chartres labyrinth in San Francisco's Grace Cathedral.

In keeping with their traditional use, most labyrinths have been established in spiritual settings—churches, retreat centers, outdoor prayer and meditation gardens and the like. They are also increasingly becoming fixtures in hospitals and rehabilitation centers, where they are used to assist healing, both physically and spiritually. Portable labyrinths are even brought into jails and prisons to help inmates develop their spiritual lives.

The Benefits of Labyrinth Walking

Following the winding path of a labyrinth requires you to focus on what is ahead of you. However, because you know where you are going—to the center of the labyrinth—there are no decisions to be made along the way. Unlike mazes, a labyrinth has only one circular path that winds its way to the center and back out again. All you do is follow the direction of the labyrinth, and allow it to lead you. Doing so puts your logical and rational self on hold, and allows your more intuitive side to come forward. In other words, you shift from right-brain thinking to left-brain thinking.

ESSENTIAL

The cathedral in Chartres (outside of Paris, France) contains the only remaining medieval labyrinth. Constructed entirely of pieces of individually carved inlaid marble, it measures 42 feet in diameter. The total length of the path is close to a quarter mile long. According to church legend, the design of the Chartres labyrinth was a part of King Solomon's temple, and was carried by the Knights Templar to France during the Middle Ages.

Because there is no right or wrong direction to take when walking a labyrinth, they are amazingly user friendly. People walk them at whatever pace they choose. Some even skip or crawl. Pausing to reflect on emotions or thoughts that arise along the way is standard practice. Many people walk the labyrinth as a centering exercise. Others enter it with a question or a concern and use the time they spend in it to pray. Still others simply focus on the path ahead of them and enjoy the walk. It can also be an alternative to sitting meditation.

Labyrinths are nondenominational and open to all. They offer the opportunity to reconnect to faith, or experience it in new ways, to everyone who walks them.

The Phases of Labyrinth Walking

The labyrinth experience consists of three phases, or stages:

1. **Traveling to the center of the labyrinth (purgation)**—The first stage of a labyrinth walk is symbolic of leaving everyday life behind. Other words used to describe it are releasing, surrendering, or letting go. Most people start this stage by pausing briefly at the entrance, taking a moment to center and focus. They may say a prayer or voice an intention to guide the spiritual walk they are about to take. Some people acknowledge the experience to come with a bow or a nod. Christians often genuflect or make the sign of the cross before entering.

2. **The time spent in the center of the labyrinth (illumination)**—The center of the labyrinth is a place for prayer and meditation. This is where labyrinth walkers open themselves to God's guidance. There are no specific guidelines governing how much time you spend in the center or what you do there. Many people like to reflect back on the journey they made. Others close their eyes to it and simply rest in God's presence.

3. **Traveling back out of the labyrinth (union)**—The "letting out" phase of labyrinth walking prepares walkers for re-entering the world, taking with them the knowledge they gained in the labyrinth. It is customary to end the experience in much the same way you began it.

The labyrinth is an archetype of wholeness that helps us rediscover the depths of our souls. We are not human beings on a spiritual path, but spiritual beings on a human path.
—Lauren Artress, in *Walking a Sacred Path*

A labyrinth walk is not meant to be a once-in-a-lifetime experience. Although the practice may seem odd or off-putting at first, most people are hooked after their first walk. Many will repeat the experience immediately. Others schedule an annual labyrinth walk as part of their spiritual renewal. Some people walk them every day.

Finding a Labyrinth to Walk

Labyrinths are steadily increasing in popularity, which means that there is a good chance that you'll find one near you to walk. Check with local churches and spiritual centers. If you have trouble finding one, there are several Internet-based locators that can help. You'll find one listed in Appendix B along with several other labyrinth resources, including one that you can use to do a virtual labyrinth walk.

Although it is not much for exercise, you can also walk a labyrinth with your fingers. These personal labyrinths are great for times when walking a full-sized labyrinth isn't possible. Many labyrinth fans use a personal labyrinth every day for prayer, centering activity, or meditation.

Chapter 20

Living a Prayerful Life

A prayer life never stands still. We are constantly called to lift our hearts up, to keep moving forward, to learn and re-learn from God, to continue seeking His voice and His counsel as we face the joys and challenges of life. On the following pages are some suggestions for continuing your prayer journey, and continuing to move toward God.

Praying with Your Family

Sharing your prayer practice with others—and especially with spouses, partners, and children—can be one of the richest and most gratifying ways you could ever wish for extending your prayer life. As Mother Teresa said, "Among yourselves you can share your own experience of your need to pray, and how you found prayer, and what the fruit of prayer has been in your own lives."

According to researchers, the majority of spouses do not pray regularly with each other. However, everything that prayer is all about can only be made better by including those you love the most.

Taking your prayer life beyond its customary boundaries—out of the box, so to speak—can feel a little strange at first. If you're used to praying by yourself, you might be self-conscious about sharing your communications with God where others can hear them. Feeling like you have to be an exemplar at your praying is pretty common when you're asking your family to join in. After all, you want to set a good example, right?

Well, the best example you can set is to expand your prayer practice so it does incorporate your family, and especially your children. In fact, the Bible instructs parents to do so.

Hear O Israel: The Lord our God, the Lord is one. Love the Lord your God with all your heart and with all your soul and with all your strength. These commandments that I give you today are to be upon your hearts. Impress them on your children. Talk about them when you sit at home and when you walk along the road, when you lie down and when you get up. Tie them as symbols on your hands and bind them on your foreheads. Write them on the doorframes of your houses and on your gates.

—Deuteronomy 6:4–9

The most important thing to remember about family prayer is that you don't need to be a prayer expert. What's more, your family won't even expect you to be. Keep the basic precepts of prayer in mind—that it's communicating with God and that we never reach expert level in doing this. There is always more to learn. (That's a lesson, by the way, that you want to make sure your kids understand as well.) When you pray with your family, they'll learn from you and you'll learn from them, too.

There's nothing to guarantee that your family will be gung ho about your plans at first. In fact, they may not be. Your children might even look at you funny. But don't let this deter you from making prayer a part of your family's routine.

Getting Started

There's really no magic formula or step-by-step manual for beginning a family prayer practice. However, you can set the stage for success by putting together a little game plan that outlines the basics and establishes your intentions, just like you did when you started your own prayer practice. It should include the following:

- **When you'll pray**—Praying before dinner and nighttime prayers before bed are pretty standard. You may want to add an additional prayer session at another time during the week. Keep things pretty loose.
- **Where you'll pray**—For nighttime prayers, bedrooms are best. Dining-room tables work great for other prayer times. Try to pick a spot where you can gather closely and intimately.
- **How you'll pray**—Choose the format for your prayer time. Remember, simpler is better, especially with small children.

Don't go it alone and assume the sole burden for determining these factors. You want your entire family to pray together, right? Make them a part of the process. Ask your spouse and your children what they would like to accomplish by praying as a family, what their concerns are, and what they would like to pray about. Don't make too big a deal out of this. It doesn't have to be a family meeting. Remember, prayer is a discipline, not regimentation. Keep things light, start simply, and allow God to direct your efforts.

Praying with Young Children

If your children are very young, keep your prayer times short and sweet. Little kids have short attention spans, and they'll get bored and fidgety if prayer time goes on for more than a few minutes or so. If they are already in the habit of reciting nighttime prayers, you might consider adding to their existing practice by gathering the whole family together for a quick prayer at this time. If they're not, one way to start nighttime prayers is with the classic child's prayer (if you've ever wondered where it came from, it first appeared in the *New England Primer,* printed in 1814):

Now I lay me down to sleep,
I pray the Lord my soul to keep.
And if I die before I wake,
I pray the Lord my soul to take.

Other aspects of praying with small children can include:

- Reading scripture from a children's Bible.
- Putting together a short prayer list to help everyone remember whom they want to pray for.
- Reviewing the events of the day, and asking everyone to recall a moment when they saw something that reminded them of God's presence in their life.
- Just talking to them about God and things they could, or would like to pray about.

Praying with Older Children

The same aspects of praying with small children work equally well with older kids. As their curiosity about faith grows, they may especially enjoy having their own Bibles to read and study. Praying at dinnertime or bedtime tends to work fairly well until the teenage years. By then, they're establishing their own lives and are spending more time away from home. They may also—hopefully they will—have prayer lives independent from yours as well. Try not to let their growing independence replace your family prayer times. Find ways to keep them a part of your family's shared experiences. Even if you only get together occasionally, and for just a few minutes or so, they'll be shared moments your children will cherish when they have families of their own.

As children grow older, don't hesitate to introduce them to other kinds of spiritual experiences, and especially the ones that mean the most to you. If you enjoy taking annual prayer retreats, for example, you may want to bring the family along (with the facility's permission, of course) on the next one.

Many teenagers are fascinated by spirituality, hungry to try new things, and not shy at all about doing it. You may find their enthusiasm a catalyst for some new experiences of your own. And, at the same time, you might find them willing partners for some of your wildest dreams. Zen meditation might be tough on the knees, but there's nothing like giving it a go when your daughter says she would love to try it with you.

Keeping a Prayer Journal

Many people who pray on a regular basis make little notes to themselves about various aspects of prayer. They may write down certain passages from the Bible they want to pray over, or reminders to pray about certain things or for certain people. Keeping a prayer journal can be a great way to organize all those scraps of paper into one handy resource. Having a written record of the time you spent in prayer can also help you reflect on your efforts. It's proof positive of how much you've grown in your prayer life, and how God has worked through your prayers.

Types of Prayer Journals

Prayer journals are traditionally handwritten, but there's nothing saying you can't make your journal computer based if you find tapping away on a keyboard easier than writing longhand. Some people keep their prayer journals on handheld devices like PDAs. While writing in a beautifully bound journal has a distinctly aesthetic edge over the others, choose the method that works best for you.

If you do decide to go the old-fashioned way, consider making your prayer journaling a spiritual and a sensual experience by picking a beautiful journal in which to write, and maybe even by treating yourself to a good pen. There are blank books specifically designed for journaling available at many bookstores, and ones designed especially for prayer journaling at Christian bookstores. If you prefer a less fancy approach, just use any style of journal or notebook that suits your needs. Some people even use index cards for this purpose. They're great for writing down your thoughts on the fly as you can take them wherever you go. If you want to keep them all in one place, you can paste them into a blank book, or stick them into a recipe box.

All Scripture is given by inspiration of God, and is profitable for doctrine, for reproof, for correction, for instruction in righteousness . . .

—Paul, 2 Timothy 3:16

What to Write About

You can use a prayer journal to:

- Write out your prayers.
- Make a prayer list of everyone you want to pray for.
- Record special prayer requests, both yours and for others.
- Remind yourself to pray for certain things on certain days.
- Record thoughts that come to mind when praying.
- Record the dates when prayers are answered.
- Keep track of key Bible verses.

Everyone who keeps a journal does it in a different way. You might want to write daily, perhaps following a prayer session, or just when the spirit moves you. Your writing could take the form of a log—just brief entries recording the day's events—or a conversation about your thoughts, your dreams, what's on your heart, you name it. Regardless of the approach you take, make the commitment to keep your journal going. Even if it's just a couple of words, make sure you record them on a regular basis. Stay away from writing in your journal for too long, and you'll feel like you have too much catching up to do.

Fasting

Restricting food and drink is a spiritual discipline common in many religions. It has been practiced from the earliest times, sometimes as penance, but more often in conjunction with prayer or an aid to discernment. Muslims, for example, fast from dawn to sunset every day during the ninth month, Ramadan, as a means of underscoring God's importance, to focus on spiritual goals and values, and to help believers identify with and respond to the less fortunate. Some Muslims also fast every Monday and Thursday. The Quran also recommends additional periods of fasting as a way of communing with the Divine.

FACT

In addition to Islam, fasting also plays a role in Hinduism and Buddhism. Hindu ascetics traditionally fasted while on pilgrimage and to prepare for certain festivals; modern adherents fast during festivals and on New Moon days. Modern-day Buddhists commonly fast and profess their sins four times a month as a method of purification.

Jews fast and pray on Yom Kippur, the Day of Atonement, and on five other holidays during the year. Two of them—Yom Kippur and Tishah B'av, which commemorates the destruction of the Temple—are major fasts, which call for refraining from such things as food, water, and sexual intercourse. Less stringent fasts are observed on the other holidays. Followers may also fast privately as a sign of mourning or at any other time when making a special request to God.

Fasting in the Christian Church

The practice of fasting varies among the Christian churches. It's been most rigorous in the Orthodox church, where followers traditionally observe four fasting seasons—the Great Lent, the Apostles' Fast, the Dormition Fast, and the Nativity Fast, as well as several single-day fasts. During these fasting periods, Orthodox parishioners eat no meat, dairy products, or eggs. Fish is also restricted at times.

Many Catholics in the United States follow the church's Lenten penance requirements that call for eating only one full meal and two smaller ones on Ash Wednesday and Good Friday. On these days, as well as all the Fridays of Lent, they also abstain from meat, but they can eat eggs, milk products, meat-flavored soups, gravies, and sauces, and condiments made from animal fat.

In Protestant churches, fasting is left to individual choice. Christians who belong to denominations without formal fasting calendars often maintain a partial fast during Lent, giving up a particular food or type of food for this period, and they might fast at other times of the year when they're seeking God's direction.

Fasting in the Bible

References to fasting abound in the Bible. Moses fasted for at least two recorded forty-day periods. Psalm 35 records David's use of fasting in conjunction with prayer when petitioning God for His intervention: "But as for me, when they were sick, My clothing was sackcloth; I humbled myself with fasting; And my prayer would return to my own heart" (Psalm 35:13).

In biblical times, abstinence from sleep, marital sex, anointing, and bathing were also considered ways in which people could fast. Other forms of fasting include eating only in moderation, eating only certain kinds of food, or cutting out treats such as junk food or candy.

Many Old Testament prophets—including Daniel, Elijah, Ezra, and Nehemiah—also humbled themselves before God by fasting. The Israelites fasted so often, in fact, that the prophet Isaiah railed about it having become too routine, and said it had lost its true meaning.

There are also numerous references to fasting in the New Testament. Jesus abstained from both food and water for forty days (obviously par for the course for biblical fasting). Early Christians did as well. But there isn't anything in the New Testament that specifically tells believers that they should fast. In fact, fasting didn't become a popular spiritual discipline among Christians until the Middle Ages.

Modern Day Fasting

Many great Christians fasted and spoke to its value. John Wesley, the founder of the Methodist church, fasted every Wednesday and Friday, and required the same of all his clergy. In fact, he wouldn't ordain anyone who didn't follow this schedule. Fasting and praying also played a key role in the spiritual walks of Jonathan Edwards, Martin Luther, and John Calvin.

Of fasting I say this: it is right to fast frequently in order to subdue and control the body. For when the stomach is full, the body does not serve for preaching, for praying, for studying, or doing anything else that is good. Under such circumstances God's Word cannot remain. But one should not fast with a view to meriting something by it as a good work.

—Martin Luther, in *What Luther Says*

More recently, however, fasting has been viewed by many as an outdated spiritual discipline that adds very little to worship and prayer. The central role that food plays in our culture today is often a strong deterrent to the practice. Going without food can be seen as something that damages one's health. But a fast, if done properly, can do good things, both spiritually and physically. Not only can it clear the body of excesses, it can help you reach deeper into prayer, and, through the process, bring you closer to God.

Benefits of Fasting

While fasting clearly has its physical side, the practice's primary purpose is to help us draw closer to God. An occasional short fast helps put physical needs and appetites into better perspective. A fast can also:

- Give us more time to spend with God in prayer.
- Help us better understand, and yield to, God's commands.
- Reveal certain things that play a bigger role in our lives than we'd like them to.

Fasting on a regular basis can also help develop a better sense of discipline in all areas of our lives. Focusing on food can be a great way to avoid dealing with issues that we'd rather avoid. Take that focus away, even for a little while, and there's not much standing between you and your little demons, whatever they may be.

If you have any concerns at all about your health, be sure to talk to your doctor before you begin your fast. If you haven't had a physical in a while, get one. It's a good idea to know if you have any physical problems that would rule out fasting for you.

How to Fast

First, a major, and very serious caveat: Do not even think about fasting—even skipping a meal—if it would in any way compromise your health. If you are pregnant or nursing, or if you have any of the following conditions, do not, repeat, DO NOT fast without professional supervision, preferably a physician's:

- Diabetes or hyperglycemia
- Auto-immune disorders such as HIV and AIDS
- Eating disorders such as anorexia or bulimia
- Anemia

- Chronic diseases, including heart, kidney, or stomach problems, and cancer

Fasts vary in type and duration. The most common are:

- Single-meal fasts, where you skip one meal in a day.
- Twenty-four-hour fasts, where you abstain from food for two meals.
- Extended fasts, which range from a week to the biblical tradition of forty days.

There are also different kinds of fasts, including:

- Water fasts, which should only be followed for several days at the most.
- Water and juice fasts, the most common.
- Partial fasts, during which certain foods are not eaten for a set period of time.
- Complete fasts, which are not recommended due to the obvious medical risks associated with abstaining from all food and liquids. (If you feel called to do a complete fast, definitely consult your physician first.)

There is no single way to do a fast, and no set formula for how long you should fast. In this area, let God lead your efforts. You don't have to follow any particular approach, but it's a good idea to start slowly if you haven't fasted before. Try a partial fast first for one day, maybe from dinner one night to dinner the next, or from lunch to lunch. This means skipping just two meals. Or, start by fasting for one meal a day, or one day a week, or one week a month. In time, you'll be able to fast for longer periods if you so choose.

FACT

The Bible records two types of food fasts. There are partial fasts, such as that described in the Book of Daniel, where he only abstained from delicacies, meat, and wine; and absolute or supernatural fasts, during which all food and liquid was off limits.

What to Expect When Fasting

If you haven't fasted before, be prepared for some negative physical experiences, especially in the beginning. More than anything else, you're going to be hungry. Sometimes unbearably so. Those hunger pangs, though, serve as a reminder as to why you're fasting. During longer fasts, hunger pangs tend to subside, but you'll definitely feel them on shorter ones. Headaches—often due to caffeine withdrawal—are also common during the beginning of a fast.

Fasts of longer than a day will leave you physically weakened. For this reason, it's a good idea to curtail strenuous physical activity while you're fasting. If you're feeling up to it, take short, easy walks. If you're not, don't push it. Remember, the goal in fasting is to gain new spiritual perspectives. Trying to keep an exercise program going during a fast can work against what you're working toward.

Many people develop a sour or metallic taste in their mouths when they're fasting. This is a natural side effect of your body cleansing itself of toxins and is nothing to be overly concerned about. Making sure you drink enough water is one of the best ways to avoid these sensations. If they bother you, try chewing on some parsley (a natural breath freshener), or adding some lemon to your water.

What to Do Instead of Eating

The time you'd usually spend eating should instead be spent in prayer or other spiritual pursuits. These may also be good times to catch up on your devotional reading or to journal your thoughts.

How to Break a Fast

If your fast is for a short duration, say you've only skipped one meal, you don't have to do anything special when you return to eating. Try not to overeat, however.

Fasts of longer duration call for easing yourself back into food:

- On the first day after a fast, restrict yourself to foods that are easily digestible, such as clear soup, gelatin, mild fruits such as bananas and melons, and vegetable juice. Keep the portions very small.
- Add solid but bland foods in your second day after fasting. Choose from potatoes, chicken, yogurt, cooked cereals, and cooked vegetables. Continue to keep the portions small.
- As you feel able, continue to move back into your regular eating pattern. Don't be surprised, however, if certain foods aren't as appealing to you as they once were. Remember, fasts redirect the body as well as the spirit.

Guiding the Spirit

Throughout history, many people seeking a better connection to the Almighty have enlisted the help of a trusted adviser to help guide them. In modern times, these learned sages often take the form of spiritual directors or guides.

The person that is alone without a spiritual guide, and has virtue, is like a glowing ember that is alone. It will become more frigid than hotter.

—John of the Cross

Spending time with a spiritual director—someone who is committed to helping you grow in your spiritual life—can be immensely rewarding, especially if you're seeking a different perspective on where you're going in your relationship with God. People often misunderstand what spiritual directors do, and feel they should only consult with one when things aren't going well in their spiritual lives. But this isn't the case at all. Spiritual direction can be sought at any time you feel you need a little extra help-in good times and in bad. Individuals wishing to work in some aspect of ministry are often encouraged-and sometimes required-to meet with a spiritual director to determine if their call to ministry is true, and to help them determine what their best area of service would be. But spiritual direction is by no means limited only to matters of discernment.

FACT

Ministers, pastors, and other church leaders, of course, are spiritual directors, as they direct the spiritual growth of the people under their charge. But the term here refers to someone other than a church leader, someone who can guide your growth, help you discern your spiritual gifts and direct you to them.

Spiritual direction is sometimes confused with therapy or pastoral counseling. The practices, however, are very different. Most spiritual directors confine their efforts to helping people sort out their spiritual lives and helping them become more aware of God's presence in their lives, and are generally not qualified as counselors. If you're seeking a more therapeutic relationship, look for someone with the credentials to provide such services.

Finding a Spiritual Director

Sometimes God puts a particular person in our lives to serve as a spiritual guide. Most often, however, you have to go find one. If there is someone you know whose spiritual life you respect, you may want to consider asking that person to work with you. If it's something you both want to do, and it feels right to both of you, you'll know it.

Many people prefer to take a more formal approach to finding a spiritual director, including:

- Asking a church leader—a pastor or minister—for recommendations.
- Asking friends if they know of one or have worked with one.
- Checking with Spiritual Directors International, an association of spiritual directors founded in 1989. You'll find more information in Appendix B.
- Contacting local religious institutions, such as churches or monasteries.

You might have to search a little longer than you'd like to for someone to work with. Spiritual directors usually take a pretty low profile, and they often don't advertise themselves as such, even when talking about what they do. Instead, they rely more on word of mouth and referrals from past and present clients.

Choose your spiritual director carefully. Consider what you're about to embark on as a long-term relationship. It may not end up being one—there is nothing that says you have to keep seeing one spiritual director forever—but you certainly want to approach it that way. You want someone who is capable, and willing, to go the distance with you, however long that distance might be.

Also consider what you want in a spiritual director. Do you want this person to be a member of the same faith as yours? Should he or she be specially trained? Would you feel comfortable working with someone who is a member of your spiritual community? Would you prefer someone outside of your usual circle of friends and acquaintances? Should this person be a member of the clergy, or will a layperson with a compassionate heart be more in keeping with your vision of what you'd like your spiritual direction to be about?

Due to the intimate nature of these relationships, most people prefer to have some distance between them and their spiritual directors. In fact, it's often best to not have any sort of a relationship with the person you choose outside of this. Another fairly standard approach to choosing a spiritual director is to pick one of the same sex—for the obvious reasons. This isn't to say that there aren't any male-female spiritual counseling relationships, as there definitely are. For the most part, though, spiritual relationships work best when there is no sexual tension between the participants.

ESSENTIAL

Listening is one of the most important qualities of a spiritual director. Make sure the person you pick is more interested in hearing you talk than in talking about himself or herself.

Once you've found a person or two who are potential candidates for the job, it's a good idea to talk to him or her a little first before making a firm commitment. Think of it as an informal job interview. Ask questions about his or her philosophies, approach, and experience, and what he or she expects of you. Some spiritual directors give their clients assignments or activities to work on between meetings. Find out how often your spiritual director wants to meet, and where you'll meet. Most important, make sure that this is a person you want to work with, someone you feel has the requisite experience and skills to function well in the job you're ready to assign.

What to Expect from Spiritual Direction

Regular meetings, about once a month or so, are about average for spiritual direction. During these meetings, you'll talk about what's been going on in your life. Your spiritual director will listen, for the most part, and will ask you questions when appropriate. He or she might suggest books for you to read, or various spiritual disciplines for you to explore. Most sessions begin and end with prayer, and sometimes a few moments of silent reflection. Unlike counseling sessions, which can sometimes leave you shaky when your time is up, you can look forward to leaving your sessions with your spiritual director feeling uplifted, calm, and peaceful, and perhaps re-energized about your spiritual journey.

QUESTION?

Is it appropriate to pay a spiritual director?
Some provide their services without a charge, others don't. You can avoid embarrassment or confusion by clarifying payment issues up front.

A Final Word

We have come to the end of this particular journey in prayer, and we'll now bid you farewell. But we're leaving you in very good hands, in fact, the best hands of all. Use prayer to continue moving toward God. He will never disappoint you. Ⓔ

Appendices

Appendix A
Glossary of Terms

Appendix B
Prayer Resources

Glossary of Terms

ACTS:
The acronym for a prayer style that includes stands for adoration, confession, thanksgiving, and supplication.

Agni:
The Aryan god of sacrificial fire.

Allah:
"The God" (from Arabic).

Anglican prayer beads:
Prayer ropes of thirty-three beads used by members of the Episcopal church.

apocrypha:
From the Greek for "things hidden away." Refers to Jewish and early Christian writings excluded from the Scriptures.

Baghavad Gita:
Meaning "The Song of the Lord," one of the basic religious scriptures for Hinduism.

Bible:
From the Greek *ta biblia,* meaning "the books."

Book of Common Prayer:
Also known as "BCP," the official prayer book of the Anglican and Episcopal churches.

Brahma:
The Hindu god of the creation.

Buddha:
The "Enlightened One," or the "Awakened One."

canon:
A set of religious writings regarded as authentic and definitive, which form a religion's body of scripture.

Celtic cross:
The cross used by Celtic Christians.

censer:
A vessel, usually suspended from chains, used for burning incense. Also called a thurible.

cherubim:
Supernatural creatures associated with the presence of God. Also thought of as angels.

chotki:
The prayer rope used by members of the Russian Orthodox church.

common prayer:
The regular cycle of services of the Anglican and Episcopal churches, including the Daily Office, the Litany, and the Eucharist.

communal prayer:

Prayer that is done by a group. Also called corporate prayer.

compline:

The last of the seven separate hours that are set aside for prayer each day.

colloquy:

A discussion or conversation.

contemplation:

Concentration of the mind on spiritual matters, such as achieving closer unity with God.

contemplative:

Somebody who practices contemplation as a spiritual exercise, especially a member of a Christian monastic order.

corpus:

The carved figure of the body of Christ attached to a crucifix.

covenant:

A solemn agreement that is binding between all parties.

crucifix:

A cross that bears a representation of the body of Christ.

Daily Office:

The order of service followed by the Anglican and Episcopal churches.

discernment prayers:

Prayers prayed for direction.

Divine Office:

Another name for the Liturgy of the Hours.

doctrine:

A body of ideas taught to people as truthful or correct.

Eastern Orthodox cross:

A cross of early Christianity. Also called the Byzantine cross, the Eastern cross, and the Russian Orthodox cross.

Eucharist:

The religious ceremony that commemorates the last meal of Jesus Christ before his death. Also called Communion, or Holy Communion.

Gospels:

The New Testament books of Matthew, Mark, Luke, and John.

Hanukkah:

The Festival of Light in Judaism, celebrating the rededication of the Temple in Jerusalem in 165 B.C.E.

Havdallah candle:

The candle that closes the Sabbath in the Jewish faith.

humility:

The quality of being modest or respectful.

icons:

Depictions of holy figures—often the Holy Trinity, the Holy Family, or Jesus and Mary—and religious events.

Indra:

The Aryan god of the air and the storm.

intercessory prayers:

Prayers said on someone else's behalf.

Jesus Prayer:

Also called the Breath Prayer or the Prayer of the Heart.

kinkin:

A Zen walking meditation in which attention is focused on each step and the breath is measured and controlled.

Knights Templar:

Members of a Christian military order founded in 1119 to protect pilgrims after the First Crusade.

komboskini:

The prayer rope used by members of the Greek Orthodox church.

Krishna:

One of two forms of Vishnu, the Hindu god of sacrifice.

labyrinth:

A single-path, unicursal tool for personal, psychological, and spiritual transformation.

lauds:

The first prayers of the day in some churches.

lectio divina:

A form of prayer based on slow, meditative reading of sacred scripture.

litany:

A series of sung or spoken liturgical prayers or requests for the blessing of God.

liturgy:

A form and arrangement of public worship determined by a church or religion.

Liturgy of the Hours:

A Catholic liturgy consisting of prayers, psalms, and meditations for every hour of the day. Also called the Divine Office.

malas:

Prayer counters used by Buddhists and Hindus.

Maltese cross:

A cross with eight points, representing the eight Beatitudes of Matthew.

mantra:

A sacred word, chant, or sound that is repeated during meditation.

Marduk:

The primary Babylonian god.

Mars:
The Roman god of agriculture and war.

meditation:
Emptying one's mind of thoughts, or concentrating on one thing.

monastics:
People who live with others in a monastery and observe religious vows.

mezuzah:
A small case holding a roll of scripture and the name of God, placed on the doorposts of Jewish homes.

mindfulness:
The state of paying attention or being careful.

mystic:
Someone who practices or believes in mysticism.

negative prayer:
Prayer that can affect someone negatively, or have a negative outcome.

officiant:
Someone who conducts a religious ceremony.

order of service:
Another term for liturgy.

Orthodox church:
A Christian church that originated in the Byzantine Empire.

pantheon:
A collection of gods.

petition:
An appeal or request to a higher authority or being.

piety:
Strong, respectful belief in God.

polytheism:
The belief in more than one god or many gods.

prayer:
From the Latin word *precari,* meaning "to entreat."

prayer walking:
Praying while you're walking. Also called spirited walking or walking meditation.

prehistory:
The time before civilization.

private prayer:
Prayer said privately, as opposed to with a group.

prostrate:
To lie flat on the face or bow very low in worship or humility.

Psalter:
A book containing psalms, or the Book of Psalms, used in worship.

Quran:
The holy scripture of the Islamic faith.

Rama:
One of two forms of the Hindu god Vishnu, the god of sacrifice.

rational prayer:
Prayers of the mind, where thoughts are expressed in words and sentences.

Reformation, The:
The religious movement that arose in Western Europe during the sixteenth century.

religion:
The outward expression of spiritual impulses, in the form of a specific religious impulse or practice.

retreat:
A period of quiet rest and contemplation in a secluded place.

rosary:
The string of prayer beads used by Catholics. The term comes from the Latin word *rosarius*, which means garland or bouquet of roses.

ruach:
The Hebrew word meaning breath or spirit.

sacred space:
A special place set aside for prayer, decorated with objects to enhance the prayer experience.

scripture:
Sacred writings, often used to refer to those from the Bible.

secular:
Not religious or spiritual in nature, not controlled by a religious body or concerned with religious or spiritual matters.

Shema:
The oldest daily prayer in Judaism.

simple prayer:
Prayer in its simplest form, a pouring out of the heart to God. Also called expository prayer, meaning that it sets forth facts.

siddur:
The prayer book used by followers of the Jewish faith. The plural of "siddur" is "siddurim."

Siva:
The Hindu god of destruction and reproduction.

Soma:
The Aryan god of intoxication.

spirit:
The vital force that characterizes a living being.

spirituality:
An inner sense of something greater than oneself.

St. Andrew's cross:

One of the most ancient crosses, it resembles the letter "X."

supernatural:

That which is not from the observable, tangible, or measurable universe.

supplication:

A humble appeal to someone who has the power to grant a request.

synagogue:

The place of worship and communal center of a Jewish congregation.

Tao-te Ching:

The sacred text that is the basis for Taoism, meaning "The Way and Its Power."

Taoism:

The Chinese religion that seeks harmony and long life.

tefilah:

The Hebrew word for prayer is *tefilah*, which, loosely translated, means "to judge oneself."

tefillin:

The symbols of faith that Jewish men wear on the head, above the eyes.

theology:

The study of religion, a religious theory, school of thought, or system of belief.

transformation:

A complete change, usually into something with an improved appearance or usefulness.

transliterated text:

Foreign words spelled out using the English language to aid in their pronunciation.

Upanishads, The:

One of two sacred texts of Hindu scripture.

vespers:

An evening church service. Also known as Evening Prayer, or Evensong.

Vishnu:

The Hindu god of sacrifice.

visualization:

Creating a clear picture of something in the mind, often done to promote a sense of well-being.

Yahweh:

The God of the Hebrews.

yartzeit candle:

In Judaism, a special candle customarily lit on the anniversary of a family member's death.

Yoga:

The Hindu disciplines that promote the unity of the individual with a supreme being through a system of postures and rituals.

Appendix B

Prayer Resources

Books

à Kempis, Thomas. *The Imitation of Christ: How Jesus Wants Us to Live.* A Contemporary Version by William Griffin. New York: HarperCollins Publishers, Inc., 2000. (There are many different translations and versions of this classic work. This is a very modern translation, which makes à Kempis's words extremely easy to read. It may not be for everyone.)

Armstrong, Karen. *A History of God: The 4,000-Year Quest of Judaism, Christianity and Islam.* New York: Ballantine Books, 1993.

Basit, Abdul. *Essence of the Quran: Commentary and Interpretation of Surah Al-Fatihah.* Chicago, IL: KAZI Publications, 1997.

Casey, Michael. *Sacred Reading: The Ancient Art of Lectio Divina.* Liguori, MO: Triumph Books, 1995.

Casey, Michael. *Toward God: The Ancient Wisdom of Western Prayer.* Liguori, MO: Triumph Books, 1996.

Chinmoy, Sri. *Commentaries on the Vedas, the Upanishads and the Bhagavad Gita: The Three Branches of India's Life-Tree.* New York: Aum Publishing, 1997.

Davis, Kenneth C. *Don't Know Much About The Bible: Everything You Need to Know About the Good Book, but Never Learned.* New York: Eagle Brook, An Imprint of William Morrow and Company, Inc., 1998.

Donin, Rabbi Hayim Halevy. *To Pray As a Jew: A Guide to the Prayer Book and the Synagogue Service.* New York: Basic Books, 1980.

Dossey, Larry, M.D. *Be Careful What You Pray For . . . You Just Might Get It: What We Can Do About the Unintentional Effects of Our Thoughts, Prayers, and Wishes.* San Francisco: HarperSanFrancisco, 1997.

Dossey, Larry, M.D. *Healing Words: The Power of Prayer and the Practice of Medicine.* San Francisco: HarperSanFrancisco, 1993.

Easwaran, Eknath (trans.). *The Bhagavad Gita.* Tomales, CA: Nilgiri Press, 1985.

Easwaran, Eknath (trans.). *The Upanishads.* Tomales, CA: Nilgiri Press, 1987.

Fischer, Norman; Goldstein, Joseph; Simmer-Brown, Judith; Yifa. *Benedict's Dharma: Buddhists Reflect on the Rule of Saint Benedict.* New York: Riverhead Books (a member of Penguin Putnam, Inc.), 2001.

Forest, Jim. *Praying with Icons.* Maryknoll, NY: Orbis Books, 1997.

Foster, Richard J. *Celebration of Discipline: The Path to Spiritual Growth.* San Francisco: HarperSanFrancisco, 1998.

Hanh, Thich Nhat. *Peace Is Every Step: The Path of Mindfulness in Everyday Life.* New York: Bantam Books, 1991.

Hall, Thelma. *Too Deep for Words: Rediscovering Lectio Divina.* Mahwah, NJ: Paulist Press, 1988.

Johnston, William. *The Cloud of Unknowing and the Book of Privy Counseling.* New York: Image Books, Doubleday (division of Random House), 1996.

Keating, Thomas. *Open Mind, Open Heart: The Contemplative Dimension of the Gospel.* Warwick, NY: Amity House, 1986.

Keen, Sam. *Hymns to an Unknown God: Awakening the Spirit in Everyday Life.* New York: Bantam Books, 1994.

Kortge, Carolyn Scott. *The Spirited Walker: Fitness Walking for Clarity, Balance, and Spiritual Connection.* San Francisco: HarperSanFrancisco, 1998.

Kushner, Harold S. *When Bad Things Happen to Good People.* New York: Schocken Books, 2001.

Mein, Patricia S. *Worship Without Words: The Signs and Symbols of Our Faith.* Brewster, MA: Paraclete Press, 2000.

Mother Teresa. *Everything Starts from Prayer: Mother Teresa's Meditations on Spiritual Life for People of All Faiths.* Ashland, OR: White Cloud Press, 2000.

Mundy, Linus. *The Complete Guide to Prayer-Walking: A Simple Path to Body-and-Soul Fitness.* New York: The Crossroad Publishing Company, 1997.

Pennington, Basil M. *Lectio Divina: Reviving the Ancient Practice of Praying the Scriptures.* New York: Crossroad, 1998.

Prager, Marcia. *The Path of Blessing: Experiencing the Energy and Abundance of the Divine.* Woodstock, VT: Jewish Lights Publishing, 2003.

Redmont, Jane. *When in Doubt, Sing: Prayer in Daily Life.* New York: HarperCollins, 1999.

Tickle, Phyllis. *The Divine Hours: Prayers for Summertime: A Manual for Prayer.* New York: Doubleday (a division of Random House, Inc.), 2000. This is the first of three prayer manuals compiled by Publishers Weekly religion editor Phyllis Tickle as a contemporary Book of Hours (Liturgy of Hours).

Web Sites

✑ *www.centeringprayer.com*—The Web site for Contemplative Outreach, based in Butler, NJ. One of the best Net-based resources for information on centering prayer. This is also the place to go to get a copy of "The Method of Centering Prayer," a short brochure that provides an excellent overview of what centering prayer is all about and how to do it.

✑ *www.faithlinks.org*—A Christian Web site sponsored by the Living Church Foundation, which promotes and supports the spiritual growth of members of the Episcopal church in the United States. Rich in content, most of it linked to various facets of the Episcopal church. Sponsors an online prayer center.

✑ *www.gracecathedral.org/labyrinth*—A content-rich site sponsored by Grace Cathedral Church in San Francisco, where the ancient practice of labyrinth walking was reintroduced to modern spiritual seekers. Among the offerings here are an online locator for earthly labyrinths and a gift shop with labyrinth-inspired items, including finger labyrinths for meditation.

✑ *www.healingscripture.com*—A site including prayer chains, discussion about healing, readings, articles, daily devotionals.

✑ *www.labyrinthonline.com*—Want to walk a labyrinth but don't have one handy? This site lets you experience two different versions—the Cretan Labyrinth, shorter; and the Chartres Labyrinth, a twenty-minute experience.

✑ *www.osb.org/lectio*—This is part of a Web site run by the Order of St. Benedict. It has links to many classic texts, including some must-reads on lectio divina, such as excerpts from *The Cloud of Unknowing* and Guigo II's epistle that defined the practice of lectio divina.

✑ *www.unification.net/ws/*—The Web site for World Scripture, a comparative anthology of sacred texts. There are scriptural passages from 268 sacred texts and 55 oral traditions, organized along 164 common religious themes.

✒ *www.universalis.com*—A resource for praying the Liturgy of the Hours.

✒ *www.catholicfirst.com*—Cyber home to many great Christian spiritual works, including the writings of St. Catherine of Siena, Thomas à Kempis, St. Ignatius of Loyola, St. Theresa of Avila, and St. Benedict.

✒ *www.beliefnet.com*—Have questions about faith? Want to network with others walking a spiritual path? This site covers all the bases, offering information on a variety of world faiths, chat rooms, discussions, meditations, and articles by some of the top spiritual thinkers writing today.

✒ *www.sacredspace.com*—This Web site, run by the Irish Jesuits, is one of the best ones offering online prayer experiences. Making a "Sacred Space" in your day, and spending ten minutes praying with the Jesuits, is a great way to rest with God.

✒ *www.fourgates.com*—An online retailer of prayer and meditation supplies, including incense, prayer cushions and benches, candles, Tibetan singing bowls, and Tingsha bells.

✒ *www.religiousmall.com*—Billed as "The Complete Christian Religious Online Mall," this site has an extensive collection of icons and other prayer supplies, including candles, crosses, incense, and incense burners.

✒ *www.solitariesofdekoven.org*—The Solitaries of DeKoven supports and encourages the solitary religious life within the Episcopal church. They also make prayer beads, which can be viewed and ordered on this Web site.

✒ *www.missionstclare.com*—An online version of the Daily Office.

✒ *www.spiritsite.com*—A Web site rich with excerpts from spiritual books, columns, and more. A great place for test-driving books about the spiritual journey before buying them.

www.sdiworld.org—The Web site for Spiritual Directors International.

Retreat Information and Locators

✎ *www.spiritsite.com*—Among the offerings on this site is a spiritual retreat center directory. Many popular retreat spots listed, representing a wide range of spiritual traditions.

Kelly, Jack and Marcia. *Sanctuaries: The Complete United States—A Guide to Lodgings in Monasteries, Abbeys, and Retreats.* New York: Bell Tower, 1996.

Jones, Timothy K. *A Place for God: A Guide to Spiritual Retreats and Retreat Centers.* New York: Doubleday, 2000.

Regalbuto, Robert J. *A Guide to Monastic Guest Houses, Fourth Edition.* Harrisburg, PA: Morehouse Publishing, 2000.

Miller, Jennifer. *Healing Centers & Retreats: Healthy Getaways for Every Body and Budget.* Emeryville, CA: Avalon Travel Publishing, 1998.

Music

Buddhist Nuns at Chuchikjall. *Tibetan Prayer Chants.* Sounds of the World, 1999.

Deuter. *Nada Himalaya.* New Earth Records, 1998.

Iobst, Benjamin. *Seven Metals Singing Bowls of Tibet.* 1999.

Surasu, Thea. *Singing Bowls of Shangri-La.* Inner Peace Music, 1998.

Various artists. *Journey into Light.* New Earth Records, 2001.

Garfein, Rebecca; Barash, Morris. *Sacred Chants of the Contemporary Synagogue.* Bari Productions, 1998.

Ni Riain, Noirin. *The Virgin's Lament (Caoineadhi Na Maighdine).* Sounds True, 1998.

von Bingen, Hildegard. *A Feather on the Breath of God.* Hyperion, 1993.

Das, Krishna. *Pilgrim Heart.* Razor & Tie, 2002.

Rumantsev, Victor; Arkhipova, Irina. *Sacred Treasures III: Choral Masterworks From Russia and Beyond.* Hearts of Space, 2000.

Cello Contemporary Music for Centering Prayer, 3-Track Meditation Timer. Available from *www.centeringprayer.com*

Bourgeault, Cynthia. *Singing the Psalms: How to Chant in the Christian Contemplative Tradition.* Three cassettes. Available from Sounds True, 1-800-333-9184.

Index

THE EVERYTHING CATHOLICISM BOOK

By Helen Keeler and Susan Grimbly

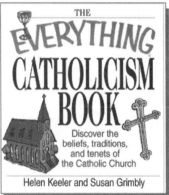

Trade paperback
$14.95 ($22.95 CAN)
1-58062-726-9, 304 pages

With over 1 billion members, Catholicism is one of the oldest—and largest—organized religions in the world. Thought-provoking and stimulating, *The Everything® Catholicism Book* helps you understand and appreciate the complexity of the traditions and tenets of the Catholic faith. From the Seven Sacraments to basic Church doctrine, this comprehensive book unravels all aspects of the Catholic Church—making it much easier for you to grasp. *The Everything® Catholicism Book* provides exhaustive information on baptism, church doctrine, confession, liturgy, and more.

OTHER *EVERYTHING®* BOOKS BY ADAMS MEDIA

BUSINESS

Everything® **Business Planning Book**
Everything® **Coaching and Mentoring Book**
Everything® **Fundraising Book**
Everything® **Home-Based Business Book**
Everything® **Leadership Book**
Everything® **Managing People Book**
Everything® **Network Marketing Book**
Everything® **Online Business Book**
Everything® **Project Management Book**
Everything® **Selling Book**
Everything® **Start Your Own Business Book**
Everything® **Time Management Book**

COMPUTERS

Everything® **Build Your Own Home Page Book**

Everything® **Computer Book**
Everything® **Internet Book**
Everything® **Microsoft® Word 2000 Book**

COOKBOOKS

Everything® **Barbecue Cookbook**
Everything® **Bartender's Book, $9.95**
Everything® **Chinese Cookbook**
Everything® **Chocolate Cookbook**
Everything® **Cookbook**
Everything® **Dessert Cookbook**
Everything® **Diabetes Cookbook**
Everything® **Low-Carb Cookbook**
Everything® **Low-Fat High-Flavor Cookbook**
Everything® **Mediterranean Cookbook**
Everything® **Mexican Cookbook**
Everything® **One-Pot Cookbook**
Everything® **Pasta Book**

Everything® **Quick Meals Cookbook**
Everything® **Slow Cooker Cookbook**
Everything® **Soup Cookbook**
Everything® **Thai Cookbook**
Everything® **Vegetarian Cookbook**
Everything® **Wine Book**

HEALTH

Everything® **Anti-Aging Book**
Everything® **Diabetes Book**
Everything® **Dieting Book**
Everything® **Herbal Remedies Book**
Everything® **Hypnosis Book**
Everything® **Menopause Book**
Everything® **Nutrition Book**
Everything® **Reflexology Book**
Everything® **Stress Management Book**
Everything® **Vitamins, Minerals, and Nutritional Supplements Book**

All Everything® books are priced at $12.95 or $14.95, unless otherwise stated. Prices subject to change without notice.
Canadian prices range from $11.95–$31.95, and are subject to change without notice.

HISTORY

Everything® **American History Book**
Everything® **Civil War Book**
Everything® **Irish History & Heritage Book**
Everything® **Mafia Book**
Everything® **World War II Book**

HOBBIES & GAMES

Everything® **Bridge Book**
Everything® **Candlemaking Book**
Everything® **Casino Gambling Book**
Everything® **Chess Basics Book**
Everything® **Collectibles Book**
Everything® **Crossword and Puzzle Book**
Everything® **Digital Photography Book**
Everything® **Family Tree Book**
Everything® **Games Book**
Everything® **Knitting Book**
Everything® **Magic Book**
Everything® **Motorcycle Book**
Everything® **Online Genealogy Book**
Everything® **Photography Book**
Everything® **Pool & Billiards Book**
Everything® **Quilting Book**
Everything® **Scrapbooking Book**
Everything® **Soapmaking Book**

HOME IMPROVEMENT

Everything® **Feng Shui Book**
Everything® **Gardening Book**
Everything® **Home Decorating Book**
Everything® **Landscaping Book**
Everything® **Lawn Care Book**
Everything® **Organize Your Home Book**

KIDS' STORY BOOKS

Everything® **Bedtime Story Book**
Everything® **Bible Stories Book**
Everything® **Fairy Tales Book**
Everything® **Mother Goose Book**

EVERYTHING® KIDS' BOOKS

All titles are $6.95
Everything® **Kids' Baseball Book, 2nd Ed.** ($10.95 CAN)
Everything® **Kids' Bugs Book** ($10.95 CAN)
Everything® **Kids' Christmas Puzzle & Activity Book** ($10.95 CAN)
Everything® **Kids' Cookbook** ($10.95 CAN)
Everything® **Kids' Halloween Puzzle & Activity Book** ($10.95 CAN)
Everything® **Kids' Joke Book** ($10.95 CAN)
Everything® **Kids' Math Puzzles Book** ($10.95 CAN)
Everything® **Kids' Mazes Book** ($10.95 CAN)
Everything® **Kids' Money Book** ($11.95 CAN)
Everything® **Kids' Monsters Book** ($10.95 CAN)
Everything® **Kids' Nature Book** ($11.95 CAN)
Everything® **Kids' Puzzle Book** ($10.95 CAN)
Everything® **Kids' Science Experiments Book** ($10.95 CAN)
Everything® **Kids' Soccer Book** ($10.95 CAN)
Everything® **Kids' Travel Activity Book** ($10.95 CAN)

LANGUAGE

Everything® **Learning French Book**
Everything® **Learning German Book**
Everything® **Learning Italian Book**
Everything® **Learning Latin Book**
Everything® **Learning Spanish Book**
Everything® **Sign Language Book**

MUSIC

Everything® **Drums Book (with CD)**, $19.95 ($31.95 CAN)
Everything® **Guitar Book**
Everything® **Playing Piano and Keyboards Book**

Everything® **Rock & Blues Guitar Book (with CD)**, $19.95 ($31.95 CAN)
Everything® **Songwriting Book**

NEW AGE

Everything® **Astrology Book**
Everything® **Divining the Future Book**
Everything® **Dreams Book**
Everything® **Ghost Book**
Everything® **Meditation Book**
Everything® **Numerology Book**
Everything® **Palmistry Book**
Everything® **Psychic Book**
Everything® **Spells & Charms Book**
Everything® **Tarot Book**
Everything® **Wicca and Witchcraft Book**

PARENTING

Everything® **Baby Names Book**
Everything® **Baby Shower Book**
Everything® **Baby's First Food Book**
Everything® **Baby's First Year Book**
Everything® **Breastfeeding Book**
Everything® **Father-to-Be Book**
Everything® **Get Ready for Baby Book**
Everything® **Homeschooling Book**
Everything® **Parent's Guide to Positive Discipline**
Everything® **Potty Training Book**, $9.95 ($15.95 CAN)
Everything® **Pregnancy Book, 2nd Ed.**
Everything® **Pregnancy Fitness Book**
Everything® **Pregnancy Organizer**, $15.00 ($22.95 CAN)
Everything® **Toddler Book**
Everything® **Tween Book**

PERSONAL FINANCE

Everything® **Budgeting Book**
Everything® **Get Out of Debt Book**
Everything® **Get Rich Book**
Everything® **Homebuying Book, 2nd Ed.**
Everything® **Homeselling Book**

All Everything® books are priced at $12.95 or $14.95, unless otherwise stated. Prices subject to change without notice.
Canadian prices range from $11.95–$31.95, and are subject to change without notice.

Everything® **Investing Book**
Everything® **Money Book**
Everything® **Mutual Funds Book**
Everything® **Online Investing Book**
Everything® **Personal Finance Book**
Everything® **Personal Finance in Your 20s & 30s Book**
Everything® **Wills & Estate Planning Book**

PETS

Everything® **Cat Book**
Everything® **Dog Book**
Everything® **Dog Training and Tricks Book**
Everything® **Horse Book**
Everything® **Puppy Book**
Everything® **Tropical Fish Book**

REFERENCE

Everything® **Astronomy Book**
Everything® **Car Care Book**
Everything® **Christmas Book, $15.00 ($21.95 CAN)**
Everything® **Classical Mythology Book**
Everything® **Einstein Book**
Everything® **Etiquette Book**
Everything® **Great Thinkers Book**
Everything® **Philosophy Book**
Everything® **Shakespeare Book**
Everything® **Tall Tales, Legends, & Other Outrageous Lies Book**
Everything® **Toasts Book**
Everything® **Trivia Book**
Everything® **Weather Book**

RELIGION

Everything® **Angels Book**
Everything® **Buddhism Book**
Everything® **Catholicism Book**
Everything® **Jewish History & Heritage Book**
Everything® **Judaism Book**

Everything® **Prayer Book**
Everything® **Saints Book**
Everything® **Understanding Islam Book**
Everything® **World's Religions Book**
Everything® **Zen Book**

SCHOOL & CAREERS

Everything® **After College Book**
Everything® **College Survival Book**
Everything® **Cover Letter Book**
Everything® **Get-a-Job Book**
Everything® **Hot Careers Book**
Everything® **Job Interview Book**
Everything® **Online Job Search Book**
Everything® **Resume Book, 2nd Ed.**
Everything® **Study Book**

SELF-HELP

Everything® **Dating Book**
Everything® **Divorce Book**
Everything® **Great Marriage Book**
Everything® **Great Sex Book**
Everything® **Romance Book**
Everything® **Self-Esteem Book**
Everything® **Success Book**

SPORTS & FITNESS

Everything® **Bicycle Book**
Everything® **Body Shaping Book**
Everything® **Fishing Book**
Everything® **Fly-Fishing Book**
Everything® **Golf Book**
Everything® **Golf Instruction Book**
Everything® **Pilates Book**
Everything® **Running Book**
Everything® **Sailing Book, 2nd Ed.**
Everything® **T'ai Chi and QiGong Book**
Everything® **Total Fitness Book**
Everything® **Weight Training Book**
Everything® **Yoga Book**

TRAVEL

Everything® **Guide to Las Vegas**

Everything® **Guide to New England**
Everything® **Guide to New York City**
Everything® **Guide to Washington D.C.**
Everything® **Travel Guide to The Disneyland Resort®, California Adventure®, Universal Studios®, and the Anaheim Area**
Everything® **Travel Guide to the Walt Disney World Resort®, Universal Studios®, and Greater Orlando, 3rd Ed.**

WEDDINGS

Everything® **Bachelorette Party Book**
Everything® **Bridesmaid Book**
Everything® **Creative Wedding Ideas Book**
Everything® **Jewish Wedding Book**
Everything® **Wedding Book, 2nd Ed.**
Everything® **Wedding Checklist, $7.95 ($11.95 CAN)**
Everything® **Wedding Etiquette Book, $7.95 ($11.95 CAN)**
Everything® **Wedding Organizer, $15.00 ($22.95 CAN)**
Everything® **Wedding Shower Book, $7.95 ($12.95 CAN)**
Everything® **Wedding Vows Book, $7.95 ($11.95 CAN)**
Everything® **Weddings on a Budget Book, $9.95 ($15.95 CAN)**

WRITING

Everything® **Creative Writing Book**
Everything® **Get Published Book**
Everything® **Grammar and Style Book**
Everything® **Grant Writing Book**
Everything® **Guide to Writing Children's Books**
Everything® **Screenwriting Book**
Everything® **Writing Well Book**

Available wherever books are sold!
To order, call 800-872-5627, or visit us at everything.com

Everything® and everything.com® are registered trademarks of Adams Media.